# Hear Today, Gone Tomorrow

## *A True Story of Love, Hearing Loss, Heartbreak, and Redemption*

# John J. Geoghegan

NEW HAVEN PUBLISHING LTD

First Edition
Published 2018
NEW HAVEN PUBLISHING LTD
www.newhavenpublishingltd.com
newhavenpublishing@gmail.com

Cover design©Pete Cunliffe
pcunliffe@blueyonder.co.uk

Front Cover author photo courtesy of Emil Petrinic ©

# Dedication

*To Lynn Murphy and Kerry Graser for taking me in.*

*And for Susan Broussard and Kieran Hannon for encouraging me.*

# Contents

**Part III
Off the Rails**

**Part IV
Redemption**

# Part I

# Hear Today

# Chapter 1
## The Empire Strikes Back

It was September 2006, another glorious California day, and I was sitting in my office at LucasArts awaiting an important phone call.

As Vice President of Global Sales and Marketing for LucasFilm's videogame division I had a spectacular office. The view from my window confirmed as much. No expense had been spared landscaping our new, $350 million, campus in San Francisco's Presidio, the former Army base turned national park. A carefully groomed lawn sloped towards Lombard Street while the Palace of Fine Arts sienna-tinted dome poked over the tree tops. San Francisco bay sparkled in the distance.

With a life-sized Admiral Akbar, the rebel trout leader, standing in a glass case outside my door, and a bronze statue of Yoda near the lobby, I had no trouble remembering I worked for George Lucas, the *Star Wars* impresario.

As I tapped my fingers impatiently waiting for the phone to ring, I mused over the conversation I'd just had with our president's assistant. He was running late, she informed me. Our weekly meeting was delayed. She'd call when he was ready. Since my boss valued punctuality in his subordinates more than himself, I sat chained to my desk waiting to be beckoned.

I'd worked at LucasArts for nearly two years. Though I didn't consider myself a huge *Star Wars* fan, I'd enjoyed the first three films like everybody else. But the much anticipated fourth film had been so disappointing I hadn't bothered seeing the fifth. Now I found myself hawking *Stars Wars* video games in the months leading up to the release of Lucas' sixth installment: *Revenge of the Sith*. At 49 years of age I was a bit long in the tooth to be chasing space aliens.

Though I'd only met him a few times, there was no doubt George Lucas was unusual. Of course, anyone worth $4 billion is allowed their eccentricities, but I suspected his had been there from the start.

In case you're one of three people on the planet who don't know what George Lucas looks like, he's short and relatively slight with a head of curly, dark hair and an unkempt beard. Every time I saw him he was dressed like a junior in High School. In the few meetings we had together, he'd always been reserved. I didn't expect him to be warm and chatty. After all, he was a world famous celebrity. But he projected such a formidable force field he didn't bother making eye contact. It took less than a minute to realize that even though you worked for him you meant nothing.

George, as everybody called him even when they didn't know him, was deep in post-production on *Revenge of the Sith* and had put on a lot of weight. He now sported a strange, bubble-shaped gullet that was hard not to stare at when he talked. I took this as an indication of how much pressure he was under and cut him some slack. It's amazing what some celebrities can get away with.

Still, people loved working for George despite his remoteness. This meant he could get away with paying below market salaries since young people would do anything for a piece of his cachet. In other words, working at Lucas was like working at Versailles with a lot of fawning courtiers.

By way of example, the first thing you noticed was how everyone professed to know what George liked, George felt, or George cared about; just saying his name seemed to make you special. But the truth was we barely saw him. Occasionally, he'd pop into the commissary with someone like Steven Spielberg in tow, but when he did, you had to pretend not to see them.

The biggest problem was that it was nearly impossible to get George to make a decision before it was too late. I'd been present at more than one hastily called meeting only to hear that George had blown up yet another storyline for one of our videogames. Since we were never invited to meet with George, we weren't privy to his reasoning, which meant it was back to the drawing board without understanding what had gone wrong in the first place. Fair enough. George owned his companies outright. He could do what he wanted. But it made for a strange work environment.

One story I loved was how George hired Lawrence Halprin, the noted landscape architect, to design the grounds of his new Presidio campus. Halprin didn't work on a budget. You paid him what he charged or he didn't take the job. He was a lot like George that way.

Neither man negotiated. While designing George's Presidio campus Halprin found a creek in Sonoma whose sound he fell in love with. George bought the creek from the farmer who owned the land lock, stock and barrel. Then, each rock was numbered, dug up, and relocated to the new campus where it was reassembled to replicate the original right down to its babbling brook-ishness. It must have cost a fortune, which made me wonder: if George would spend that kind of much money just for landscaping why didn't he pay his employees better?

Of course, George spent what he wanted safe in the knowledge that almost anything with *Star Wars* on it sold insanely well. In fact, he made way more money licensing the brand than he did from the movies. I had the opportunity to see this first hand while marketing his videogames. It never ceased to amaze me how much fans would spend on a *Star Wars* game even when it sucked.

I soon learned after arriving at LucasArts that the company had a history of selling crappy videogames. As a result, the division was in poor shape. I'd been brought in by the new president to serve on his management team and help turn things around. After being told to lay off half my staff I set about developing a marketing and sales plan for our new slate of titles. I was also responsible for convincing retailers like Target, Wal-Mart, and Gamestop to take another chance on us.

I may have been new to the videogame industry, but peddling *Star Wars* was a breeze compared to some of the other products I'd marketed. Still, turning LucasArts around was like changing a tire on a car going sixty miles an hour. We were always undermanned with limited budgets and little time for planning. I spent many long nights either at the office or traveling, despite being married with two young children.

Much of our success I attributed to our division president whose call I was awaiting. We'd started our careers at the same Madison Avenue advertising agency and had kept in touch over the years. When I'd heard Lucas' VP Marketing job was open I'd contacted him, after which he invited me for an interview.

Of course, I jumped at the opportunity. After twenty years in advertising, LucasArts seemed the right combination of prestige and stability for that stage of my career. I didn't understand just how much the place was run by kids. In fact, I was the only "adult" on the management besides my boss.

As it turned out, LucasArts was a high-profile, high stress job that looked a lot better on paper than it was in reality. Then again, that's true for a lot of companies.

The fact is I had nobody to blame but myself. There was nothing I wouldn't do to get ahead. I'd put up with grueling hours, unrealistic demands, personal abuse, and a chaotic work environment if the path led to success. I could even be an asshole when required.

But there was one significant drawback. My boss had a temper. He was not only mercurial, he was abusive. He swore and threw things. Employees called him Darth Vader much to his undisguised pleasure. That's when I realized the only people crazier than ad execs worked in Hollywood.

I had no doubt my boss was a talented executive; even brilliant. I believed in his ability unquestioningly. Physically larger than life, he was over six feet tall and bordering on obese. How much does obese weigh? I'm not sure but I know it when I see it. He was an accomplished pianist as well as having played football in college—an unusual combination. If this wasn't impressive enough he'd also held his own working with Steve Jobs and Bill Gates. After five years heading up marketing for LucasFilm there was no doubt he knew what he was doing.

I may not have been happy about my boss's behavior, but it did get results. It also made our weekly meetings stressful. At best, he made me feel like I wasn't working hard enough. More often, he yelled at me for doing something "stupid." It was a merciless way of motivating people but it worked in my case. I constantly strived to please him.

One reason I was willing to put up with all this was that LucasArts was a chance to launder my resume. After fifteen years managing advertising agency offices for Saatchi, WPP, and IPG, I figured a few years working for George and I could go anywhere I wanted.

A couple of things had me worried, though. First, the position I'd interviewed for was VP of Marketing, but since the VP of Sales job was also open my boss decided to combine the two. I didn't have the requisite sales experience, so I questioned my ability to handle both jobs and told him as much. Sure, I was game to learn, but I didn't want to get in over my head. But my boss wanted to eliminate a salary and urged me to take both jobs, so being ambitious I said yes.

That had been two years ago. Since then we'd gone from having the biggest loss in company history to earning more profit in one year than the company had earned in all of its years combined. I was proud of how much we'd accomplished and enjoyed the work though I continued struggling with the sales aspect of my job. It helped that things were heading in the right direction. Then one day everything changed.

I hadn't noticed it at first but I was having trouble hearing. It was my colleagues who pointed it out to me. I did okay in one-on-one conversations but anytime two or more people were in the room I had trouble understanding what was said. Our Tuesday morning executive meeting was especially difficult. That's when I reported on the past week's sales results. My presentations were fine, but I couldn't hear the questions people asked me. I also realized I was having trouble on the phone.

And there were other signs. Straining to listen is physically taxing. By the end of each day I was exhausted. At home, my wife complained I had the television on too loud. This was strange because even on the highest setting I couldn't hear the actors. I relied on the captions instead.

Hearing loss is a bit like Alzheimer's: you can't always tell when you're slipping. I already wore hearing aids, having been diagnosed with a slight hearing deficiency when I was 29. But my hearing had been stable for two decades. Now, things had suddenly got worse.

To compensate, I turned my hearing aids to their highest setting. But more volume doesn't mean more clarity; it just means distortion and an embarrassing amount of feedback. It didn't take long before I realized there was no point on the amplification spectrum where I could grasp human speech. Meanwhile, my twin hearing aids whistled like tea kettles.

I should have known something was wrong, but like the slowly boiling frog I found it hard telling the difference between difficult and impossible to hear. What I did notice was that departmental get-togethers, client dinners, and even lunch in the commissary were painful to navigate. I even started hearing words that hadn't been said, the most dangerous thing that can happen in a business setting.

Partial hearing won't cut it in an industry where the difference between selling "9,000" and "90,000" units could cost you your job, yet they sounded the same to me.

It wasn't until my presentation at an all-staff meeting that the severity of my problem was revealed. I was reviewing the marketing plans for the launch of our *Revenge of the Sith* videogame and the presentation was going well. The entire company was gathered in

12

LucasFilm's beautifully appointed Premier Theater. I could feel the attention of hundreds of people on me and enjoyed it. But as I introduced our new slate of television commercials I mispronounced the name of Chew-bacca, the famous Wookie pilot, calling him "Chew-y-bacca" instead.

OK, maybe I hadn't drunk the Kool-Aid, but I knew who Chewbacca was. I also knew how to pronounce his name. But my hearing had declined to the point where it was starting to impair my speech. I could no longer hear myself well enough to pronounce all my words correctly.

Mispronouncing the name of a seven foot tall Wookie, once referred to as a "walking carpet," was not the kind of mistake that went unnoticed at LucasArts. My boss, in the front row, raised his hand, stopping my presentation and demanding I pronounce Chewbacca's name correctly. The embarrassing thing was I couldn't hear him well enough to understand what he was asking. All I could divine was the stunned, silent look on hundreds of faces.

I was by far the most experienced marketing guy LucasArts had ever had, but it's hard to overcome a hearing impairment as severe as mine, particularly when I was intent on minimizing it. Oh, sure, people knew I had trouble hearing. After all, they could see my hearing aids. But hearing loss is the invisible disability; people have no way of knowing just how much you can't hear. I'd been able to mask the full extent of what felt like an infirmity for over a year. Now the whole company knew.

If my behavior sounds strange, it's not unusual for someone with a hearing loss. Often we hide it, too embarrassed to admit we have a problem. We'll even pretend to understand what you say when we clearly don't. This allows for any number of embarrassing situations, including the one I'd just suffered.

In case you don't know, the medical community groups hearing into four categories: mild, moderate, severe, and profound. My loss had started out as mild, become mild to moderate, and was now in the moderate to severe range. But something had recently changed. Instead of a gradual diminishment, my hearing felt like it had dropped off a cliff.

Though I didn't realize it at the time I'd suffered what is called a "precipitous hearing loss." In my case, speech comprehension had gone from a high of 92% in my right ear to a low of 40%; and from a high of

60% in my left ear to an abysmal 28%. In other words, my ability to understand speech had suddenly been cut in half.

What people don't realize is that measuring hearing loss is like measuring an earthquake—a change may appear numerically small but it's a magnitude of difference. LucasArts was a fast paced environment with lots of conference calls, high-level meetings, and international travel. To be VP of Global Sales and Marketing while not being able to hear was a game changer. My usual strategies of arrive early, work late, and manage upwards didn't help. Every time I walked into a meeting, took a phone call, or met with my boss, I didn't know whether I'd be able to understand what was said.

Finally, my phone rang.

When I picked it up, I guessed at as much as heard what the assistant said.

"He's ready for you now."

After that I headed for the door. A minute later I was sitting on my boss's couch.

As I've said, my boss was a big man. Bent over his computer studying an email his body appeared mountainous, his head its summit. I killed time taking in the movie poster of George C. Scott playing General Patton that hung on his wall. Then, without warning, he swiveled in his chair to face me, his countenance drained of expression.

"So, what's on the agenda?"

"Well," I replied, "I'd like to talk about increasing the salary for the secretarial position we're trying to fill. As you know, we let the last person go because you didn't like her, but we're having trouble filling the position at that salary."

My boss blinked impassively.

"We're not here to discuss salary," he said. "Salary for the position remains the same. We're here to talk about your performance."

"Oh?" I said. "What about?"

"I'm firing you."

And you know what, dear reader? My hearing was so bad I asked him to repeat himself. Twice.

# Chapter 2
# Getting the Message

That night I parked the car on a street near my house afraid to go inside.

I had good reason to be concerned. I faced a significant financial commitment with no idea how to meet it. Not only did I carry a $1 million mortgage, I had two young children, one in private school, with many years of expenses ahead of me. I also owned two luxury cars, only one of which was paid for, a part time nanny, gardener, and cleaning lady, and $20,000 in property tax coming due. How was I going to pay for it all?

I'd always gone for the high risk, high reward jobs, so this wasn't the first time I'd been fired. But the financial comfort of my family was in jeopardy. Finding another job at my salary level would not be easy. I had no idea what to tell my wife.

It took me an hour to work up enough courage to go inside. When I did, my family was the picture of domesticity. My wife was busy in the kitchen making dinner, and my two daughters were lining up their animal figures in a nightly ritual they called the parade.

I motioned to my wife to step into the den so we could talk in private. When she did, I closed the door, trying to find the words to tell her what happened.

"You're home early," she said.

"I got fired."

My wife paused a moment then screwed up her face.

"How could you!" she hissed. It was more an accusation than a question.

I wasn't surprised my wife was upset. Most people marry their spouse for richer not poorer. She'd grown accustomed to a certain lifestyle; adjusting would be difficult.

My wife was Japanese and Japanese wives have a saying: the best husbands are healthy, working, and far away. I'd been the perfect

Japanese husband up until now. Still, her reaction made me feel fired twice in one day.

There's nothing like the stomach-clenching, freefall sensation of losing your job. I'd be less than honest though, if I didn't admit to struggling with corporate life for a while. I'd done my best to conform. Whoever I really was, I'd made sure to tamp down during my 20 year career. Conformity was the rule. But I was kidding myself to think I could ever be anything other than who I was. Yes, I'd been super focused, super driven, and super ambitious, but my nonconformist self kept getting in the way. Now corporate life was sending me a message; a message I ignored at my peril.

My situation was further complicated by the fact that the further up the food chain I got the more I realized I didn't have what it takes. You don't get to the top of an organization without a killer's instinct. I lacked that gift and though I'd done my best to imitate it, I didn't have the heart.

Importantly, it seemed the longer I stayed in corporate life, the less I got out of it. I don't mean salary, there was plenty of that. I mean a sense of purpose and satisfaction. But with a wife and two daughters, I didn't have a choice. I was in it for the duration.

Sometimes we do things because we believe we should rather than we want to. In my case, it wasn't just my hearing that hindered success, it was realizing I was no longer succeeding as I once had.

When your career turns bumpy it's important to ask why. As long as I believed there was room to climb the corporate ladder, I'd shimmy up that pyramid no matter how steep. But I soon realized there was little chance of reaching the top. Not only was I never going to be the boss, I was always going to work for one. There was nothing more discouraging.

After years of striving, I was unemployed approaching 50 with little heart for the corporate life I had chosen. It was time for a change.

The first thing I did was look into a cochlear implant.

Surgeons have been implanting a device to improve hearing with varying results since 1972. The procedure's now so routine they have you in an out in a couple of hours. But there's a catch. You have to "qualify." Test results confirmed I'd lost the ability to distinguish most speech, but I was still "borderline" for an implant. I was advised to wait.

16

Wait? I was already missing most of what people said! Did I have to become telepathic before I qualified? Meanwhile, my bank account imploded.

After months of looking for a job, a friend invited me to join his Executive Recruiting firm. It was April 2007 and I thought headhunting might be a good fit since it required many of the same skills I'd developed in advertising. Best of all, you were your own boss. There was also a strong correlation between how hard you worked and how much you succeeded. For once, I'd be the captain of my destiny.

Unfortunately, the telephone turned out to be mission-critical for a headhunter. At least 50% of the job was spent qualifying candidates by phone. Given I couldn't hear, I had to find other ways. At first I used email to contact people, but that didn't work because email was easy to ignore. My next solution was to meet candidates in person, but since I might have to qualify a hundred people during the early stage of a search I found myself driving all over the Bay Area just to meet applicants. It was not only inefficient, but doubled the time of a search. On any given day I might rack up 200 miles driving in heavy traffic. It wasn't a sustainable strategy.

At first I invited candidates to Starbucks. This proved untenable because their latte machines drown everything out. Eventually, I shifted to hotel lobbies which were quieter, but there wasn't always a posh enough hotel nearby. Nevertheless, I operated this way for more than a year.

As time passed, one-on-one conversations grew increasingly difficult. Once, when I accompanied a partner on a credentials presentation, I found myself answering a question different from the one the prospect had asked. I only realized this from the mystified expression on my partner's face. I can backpedal with the best of them, but it made me look dumb not deaf.

It's fair to ask why I didn't tell my partners about the extent of my hearing loss. The answer is simple. Though my partners were good people, nobody wants a deaf headhunter on their team. It's like asking a blind person to referee a football game. It's a non-starter. And just as my partners wouldn't have knowingly taken on a deaf recruiter most companies wouldn't hire a headhunter with a hearing deficit. I knew. I'd worked both sides of the aisle. No one said it to your face, they always find a non-discriminatory reason to pass on you, but you never get the job. And how could I complain? Not even I would recommend a candidate with my severe hearing loss. My clients wouldn't have stood for it.

Sadly, most of my clients preferred talking by phone rather than in person. I remember one hotshot CEO calling me from his car to talk about a search. I'd already suggested we meet in his office since sales pitches are best done in person. But CEOs of Silicon Valley start-ups are too busy to meet with "vendors."

In my Maslow Hierarchy of Things I Don't Need phone conversations were near the top, cell phone conversations were worse, but nothing beat someone calling from their car. One thing I knew for sure, I needed this search. I had a big payment due to my partners and funds were required at home. It was crucial I win the business.

The conversation started out fine since it was a simple exchange of rote pleasantries, which of course lulled the CEO into thinking I could hear perfectly. It wasn't long though before I found myself straining to understand what he said. Fortunately, the CEO was a talker, which provided much needed cover, but the moment he asked a question I was dead.

At best, I was getting twenty-five percent of what he said one moment and 5% the next. And since he was talking about the search, I was missing important information. I tried thinking of ways to turn the situation to my advantage, but the phone wasn't helping. In fact, it was my mortal enemy.

Unable to divine more than a few words of what was said I began to panic. My breathing turned shallow as my heart raced. It wasn't long before I started blinking back tears. Finally, the CEO paused, meaning he'd asked me a question. Unfortunately, I had no idea what it was.

"You're breaking up!" I improvised.

"Really, I can hear you fine."

"I'm losing you!"

"Problem's not at this end."

"Let's meet in person…"

"Haven't got time. We need to do this now."

"Hello? Hello?"

Then, I did the unthinkable. I hung up on him.

I was hoping my prospect would think we'd been cut off, but when he called a few seconds later I let him go to voicemail. Needless to say, I didn't get the search.

After that, when a client called I put them on speakerphone and asked our office manager to sit in. As the call progressed, she'd pass me notes so I could follow what was said. When I missed something, she jumped in to cover.

It's a terrible feeling knowing you've run out of options. Sure, I asked for a captioned telephone but our phone network couldn't accommodate the technology. Besides, for all of its high mindedness the Americans with Disabilities Act (ADA) is a joke. Yes, there were instances where a deaf or hearing impaired person can do a job better than a hearing person but that wasn't my case, at least not as an executive recruiter. Besides, what the law considers a reasonable accommodation for deaf people and what deaf people need are often two different things. And even if it weren't, getting a corporation to take a chance on me when there were so many excellent recruiters to choose from made the question academic.

I hung on as long as I could, but my days were numbered. The strain of hiding what felt like a disability took its toll. By the end of most days I was so debilitated I went home, had dinner, and went to bed. I was not only exhausted from trying to hear all day, I was on the brink of despair.

I tried making my situation work, but I needed a job that didn't require hearing. Unfortunately, few jobs fit this description. And who should know better than me, an executive recruiter paid an exorbitant sum to place people? Like it or not, my time had run out.

# Chapter 3
# The *Tokyu* Express

My mood soon took a nose dive, but since depression bears a stigma in the hearing world worse than deafness I did my best to hide it.

I can't say it was the first time I'd been depressed. When I was young, I didn't have a name for it. Later, when I was older, I bulled my way through. In fact, I had such a high tolerance for being depressed I considered it one of my finest qualities. But once my hearing made it impossible to work I began to founder. Being deaf was a problem I couldn't ignore.*

Knowing I was in trouble, I confided my feelings to a primary care physician who wrote a prescription for Wellbutrin. I'd never taken Wellbutrin before but since it was an anti-depressant I was keen to give it a try.

I waited a month for the drug to take effect. When November 2007 rolled around and I wasn't feeling better, I called my GP. She explained the drug took a while to work, so I should keep taking it. Wanting to be good patient, I complied. Meanwhile, I'd never felt worse.

My wife had plans to take our kids to visit her mother in Tokyo during the Thanksgiving vacation. I'd been looking forward to the trip, but once I got to Tokyo things fell apart.

The only way to describe it is that a hole had been punched into my subconscious and only the darkest, most hideous thoughts were leaking out. I did my best to hide them. I took my kids to the neighborhood playground every morning and watched them go down the slide. But I had to keep my head turned away so they wouldn't see the tears streaming down my face.

*It's important to note that being connected to the Deaf Community would have significantly helped me with my depression, but it would take me many years before I discovered them as a resource

Years of depression had toughened me, so I kept taking the Wellbutrin and hoped for the best. Mornings I spent reading on the tatami-mat floor of my mother-in-law's house. Afternoons, I traveled around the city interviewing people for a magazine article I was writing in my spare time. More than that, I couldn't handle.

The point of medicine is that you take it to feel better. When you don't, you keep on taking it hoping it will kick in. But sometimes the reason you're not getting better is because it's the medicine that's making you sick in the first place. The moral of the story? Be careful when messing with brain chemistry.

I knew I'd reached the end of my rope when, standing on the platform of the Setagaya station, I felt an overwhelming desire to jump in front of the train. Since Japanese trains are timed to the minute, I knew precisely when the express would arrive. As the station clock ticked down I thought how best to make my jump. Then, edging past the yellow line marking the platform's edge, I waited until the twin headlights of the Shibuya Express came into view. It was just a matter of timing.

As I watched a silver and red-striped train round the curve and head into the final straightaway I picked the section of track I planned to land on. I could feel the platform vibrate as I steeled myself to jump.

My intention must have been clear because as I stepped forward a station attendant in blue shirt and navy pants gently placed his white-gloved hand upon my shoulder and said in the most extreme form of Japanese politeness:

"Please step back from the edge of the platform, sir."

Suicide is a national epidemic in Japan. Most people do it at home to minimize inconveniencing others, but a dismaying number of salarymen end their lives by jumping in front of a train. It's because of this Japanese station attendants are schooled to spot suicides before they happen. I'd been made as one of them.

A lot was communicated by that stationmaster's touch. We both knew what I was thinking. Nevertheless, he wasn't going to embarrass me by saying as much. Instead, he saved my life, bowed slightly, and moved on.

Embarrassed I'd been caught, I stumbled back to my mother-in-law's house where I wrote a long, rambling email to my brother-in-law explaining my life was one long series of failures and I was better off dead. After hitting the send button I curled up in the safest place I could imagine, the bottom of the guest closet where the futons were stored, and went to sleep.

A few hours later the telephone rang. It was my brother-in-law calling. I remember being impressed that he'd managed to obtain my mother-in-law's number despite the fact he lived in California and didn't speak Japanese, but that's how crazy my email sounded.

My brother-in-law was calling to say he'd talked to a psychiatrist who said I should stop taking the Wellbutrin immediately, and get on the next plane home. When I arrived in San Francisco the next day my brother-in-law was waiting. He drove me straight from the airport to the psychiatrist's office where I was diagnosed with Wellbutrin-induced psychosis. Shortly thereafter, I was admitted to the psychiatric ward at Stanford University Hospital for a ten day stay. I was relieved to be under a doctor's care, but even then I couldn't stop thinking:

*Jesus Christ, it's bad enough I'm deaf! Am I crazy, too?*

# Chapter 4
# Greed is Good

I was first diagnosed with hearing loss in November 1986. I was working in advertising at the time, a business where listening skills are considered essential. My supervisor had been encouraging me to have my hearing tested for a while. Like most people my natural inclination was to wave it off. After all, you don't know what you can't hear. But I couldn't ignore my boss, so I finally made an appointment to have my hearing tested.

The first time I didn't like the results, so I looked for a second opinion. The second time my results came back the same as the first. I had what was called a "bi-lateral sensorineural hearing loss." This means the nerve running from my inner ear to my brain was damaged in both ears. Even so, my hearing was pretty good; my left ear was slightly worse than my right but both were close to normal. Unfortunately, the loss was smack in the middle of the decibel range of human speech. Any further deterioration and I'd be in trouble.

My audiogram indicated I had a "mild" loss in both ears, but the diagnosis was surprising. No one in my family suffered from hearing loss, and when I was screened for the gene associated with deafness, I didn't have it. But the smoking gun wasn't hard to find. Like vision, hearing loss varies from ear to ear. My impairment was atypical in that I had virtually the same level of loss in both ears. Perfectly matched hearing loss suggests a drug-related cause, so when my doctor took my medical history I told him about the antibiotic I'd taken every day from the age of twelve until I graduated from college. Nobody knew Tetracycline damaged your hearing back then; they just thought it prevented acne. In other words, I'd sacrificed my hearing in the name of vanity. It wasn't a tradeoff I'd have made given a choice.

Not every doctor was confident Tetracycline had caused my hearing loss. This was typical of my experience with Otolaryngologists, or hearing doctors. Not only couldn't they tell me the reason I'd lost my hearing, they didn't know how quickly it might progress, or even whether I'd eventually go deaf. This shouldn't have surprised me given it was the medical profession that caused my hearing loss in the first place. Still, the lack of certainty was annoying.

One thing the doctors could tell me was that my cochlea nerve had a number of tiny hairs called stereocilia that were either dying, or already dead. Since these hairs transmitted the signals necessary for my brain to convert electrical impulses into sound losing them was non-trivial. Without them my hearing was screwed. It was about the only thing the doctors could tell me for sure.

It's bad enough losing your hearing at a young age, but when a doctor recommends you wear hearing aids it's horrifying.

"Hearing aids? At 29? Are you kidding me?" I demanded.

The truth is I felt insecure. There may be something sexy about a woman taking her earrings off at night, but there's nothing sexy when a man removes his hearing aids. It's just plain gross. As far as I was concerned, hearing aids were for the old and disabled. I wasn't even 30. Just the thought made me cringe.

The good news was my hearing loss was mild enough I could get by with a discreet, in-the-ear type of hearing aid. And so I spent several thousand dollars to purchase two, one for each ear.

My hearing aids were small, putty-colored plastic that you tucked inside your ear where they were out of sight. They may have been invisible, but I knew what people thought. I'd had the same thoughts whenever I'd seen someone with a hearing aid and it wasn't kind.

Aesthetic considerations aside, it took a while to get used to my hearing aids; sometimes your brain needs to adjust. And though I felt self-conscious, I wore them every day until it was second nature. I have to admit, it was nice getting part of my hearing back even if sounds were sometimes so loud they hurt. My problem wasn't solved, though. I still had difficulty hearing.

\*\*\*

The 1980s were a go-go time in America. Ronald Reagan was President and "greed was good." It seemed like all you had to do to make money was live in New York and work hard. I fit right in.

Advertising was still glamorous before industry consolidation, and the Internet, robbed it of fun. My first agency was Doyle Dane

Bernbach, which true to form was on Madison Avenue. To be smart, young, and ambitious in a business priding superficiality over depth was like a shot of adrenalin. My days were spent working on national ad campaigns for the Hershey Chocolate Company while nights were spent chasing all the young lovelies advertising had to offer. At 26, it doesn't get better than that.

But by age 30, I was sleeping on a fold out couch in a studio apartment I could barely afford. Meanwhile, my college friends who'd gone into finance were buying second homes in posh resorts. I needed a way to turbo-charge my career.

Believe it or not there are limitations to how fast you can ascend in advertising. What I needed was a competitive advantage, an accelerated learning curve to vault me past my peers. And I wasn't going to let a minor hearing loss hold me back.

So, I left Doyle Dane to go to work for Saatchi & Saatchi Advertising on their Tide account. Tide was Procter & Gamble's billion dollar laundry detergent, and one of Saatchi's biggest accounts. It had a reputation for brutal hours, but working on Tide was the equivalent of getting an MBA. It wasn't just a competitive advantage, it was the accelerated learning curve I was looking for too.

After three years, I got my big break when Saatchi won their first P&G assignment in Japan: the introduction of Head & Shoulders shampoo. It was news to me the Japanese suffered from dandruff, but when Saatchi asked me to move to Tokyo to set up the business, I jumped at the chance.

The only thing I knew about Japan came from *Godzilla* movies. Not exactly promising. Still, it was the kind of fast-track career move, not to mention salary boost, I was hungry for. And so I moved half way around the world to a country whose language I didn't speak and whose culture I had little interest in simply because it moved me up the corporate ladder. As it turned out, dandruff, or *fuke* in Japanese, is a major problem in Japan, and P&G was prepared to spend serious money treating it.

The biggest surprise came when I realized how much I loved living in Japan. If the 80s were capitalism's go-go years, Japan was a gold rush. Tokyo not only had all the wealth, power, and culture of New York City, it had terrific art, food, and literature. I grew so attached to Japanese language, history, and culture I couldn't imagine returning to New York.

My hearing was stable during this period. It made learning a new language difficult, but I did a passable job. Importantly, buying custom-made suits, jetting around Asia, and staying at five star hotels proved immensely gratifying.

I was 33 now, a time when many men want to settle down. I'd justified my bachelorhood by telling people I'd skipped the first wife and was waiting for the second, but that was a lie. The truth was I didn't want to get married. My parents had had a terrible marriage, so I hoped to avoid the problem by never getting married. There was one problem, however. I was lonely.

My co-workers encouraged me to date a girl in our office, and though I refused at first I eventually gave in. She was a nice girl: pretty, slim, and five feet tall. Since her father worked for a major Japanese trading company, she'd grown up around the world. Her English was fluent and she seemed interested in many of the same things I was. Best of all, she worshipped me, which was as seductive a mindset as I'd ever encountered.

It was the fall of 1990 and we were having dinner at a Tokyo restaurant on a Saturday night. I must have known something was up because I got way more hammered than usual. I don't remember much about the evening other than my date was wearing a rope of freshwater pearls I'd bought in Hong Kong.

For some reason there was a photograph of Jimmy Carter on the wall behind her, which stared at me throughout the meal. Why the President of the United States had eaten at a fish restaurant in Roppongi was beyond me, but his toothsome grin was unnerving.

I hadn't planned on popping the question, but at the end of the meal, overcome by liquor and poor impulse control, I found myself proposing. Nobody was more surprised than me. But my future wife accepted, claiming she was "the luckiest girl in the world." She was wrong, of course, but it would take a few more years for her to realize it.

I awoke the next morning with a massive case of regret and a hangover to match. A few weeks after I was transferred to Bangkok and I sent her a letter calling the whole thing off. Her response was to fly to Thailand and move in with me. Coward that I was, I folded.

A lot of arranged marriages turn out happy, so to justify my cowardice I decided to think of my marriage as arranged. I was kidding myself. Getting married because you're lonely rather than in love is never a good idea. All marriages have their problems, but that one is a non-starter.

# Chapter 5
## Sharp Objects

I was admitted to Stanford's psych unit seventeen years to the day I'd proposed to my wife. Just in time, too. On my lone drive to the hospital I kept thinking how easy it would be to stop on the Golden Gate Bridge and jump off. That's a good indication of what a mind hijacked by Wellbutrin is like.

I'd never been hospitalized before. It was November 2007, the week after my trip to Japan, and I felt so ashamed I didn't tell anyone I was committing myself. After filling out the necessary paperwork, a nurse led me into a small, windowless room where my bag was searched for anything I could use to hurt myself. Now, in addition to feeling ashamed, I felt embarrassed.

Stanford was not some Malibu rehab facility but it wasn't *Cuckoo's Nest* either. The hallways were wide enough for two beds to pass each other, and the wallpaper was wipeable for when someone hurled dinner across the room. There was also a 24 hour nurses' station and an atrium where patients congregated to watch TV, work a puzzle, or stare into space.

After confiscating my razor and toothbrush, the nurse issued me a powerful anti-psychotic called Zyprexa. I was depressed not agitated, but took it thinking if I cooperated they might let me out sooner. Instead, I was transformed into a zombie who barely who knew his name.

The first thing you realize once you've admitted yourself to a psych ward is how much you want to leave. This is not unusual, but the clinicians persuaded me it was in my best interest to remain. Since I wanted to get better, I complied, but I still wanted to flee.

I didn't speak to anyone my first two days because I wanted nothing to do with them. They were crazy. By the end of the week, however, I learned my roommate was a well read ophthalmologist who suffered from depression. His bedside tower of books was so impressive they easily passed my scrutiny. I also met a handsome black kid who turned out to be a second year medical resident coming apart at the seams. There was also a woman who never relinquished the stationary bike that was friendly and talkative. After a few days she confided it was her third stay.

A Wellbutrin-induced psychotic break may have been the reason I was in the hospital, but hearing loss had as much to do with it as my problematic marriage. Admitting they were problems helped, but I was a long way from being cured.

I wasn't allowed visitors at first, which was fine. I didn't want anyone knowing I was there, especially my kids. As for work, I told them I was in the hospital and wasn't sure when I'd get out.

There were any number of activities designed to restore our sanity. These included group therapy, individual counseling, and the much dreaded art and craft session. But the thing that helped me the most was writing.

Writing has always been my greatest love. My first job out of college was working for a regional magazine. I'd also freelanced for the *New York Times* and edited a weekly newspaper.

But after five years of being poor the siren call of money lured me into advertising. I'd never stopped writing, though, and once I was a headhunter I used my spare time to revive my freelance career.

It didn't take long before I was contributing to the *New York Times*, *Smithsonian Air & Space*, *Popular Science* and *WIRED*. None of my editors knew about my hearing loss. Since we communicated by email there was no reason they should. If one of my stories required an interview I conducted it in person, or did it by email. As strange as it may sound, I soon realized writing was the one job I could do that didn't require hearing.

We'd gone to Japan to take my kids to visit their grandmother, but another reason was so I could interview a former Imperial Japanese Navy officer for a story assignment I'd pitched to *Aviation History*. I wanted to write about a fleet of giant World War II submarines purpose-built by the Japanese to launch a surprise aerial attack against New York City and Washington, DC as a follow up to Pearl Harbor. Virtually no one knew about these subs, which had been envisioned by Admiral Yamamoto, the brains behind Pearl Harbor. They seemed so marvelously counterintuitive I couldn't resist their story.

In between my crying jags and desire to jump in front of a train, I'd managed to interview the captain of the flagship sub. I gave thanks for my high pain threshold because the more research I did the better the story got.

Once the Wellbutrin wore off I wrote my article. Each day, while my ward mates watched TV, I worked on my laptop. Ten days after admittance I was ready to be discharged. When I sent my article in, it was not only accepted, it was made the cover story.

Since the bills were mounting I went back to work as a headhunter, but an interesting thing happened. My writing career took off. The article I'd written about the Japanese submarine led to a PBS documentary. In the meantime, I sold more articles. When I realized there was more to the Japanese submarine story than my article or the documentary had uncovered I decided to write a book.

It was November 2008, a year after my hospitalization, when I took a week off from work, wrote a book proposal, and sent it to a list of literary agents. Within six hours I had my first yes. Before the end of the week, five agents wanted to represent me. The agent I chose was an experienced pro who sent my proposal to a dozen publishing houses. Ten expressed interest. A week later I was meeting them in New York to talk pitch my story.

A strange thing happened before my first meeting, though. I was sitting in my agent's office when I asked how I should handle my hearing impairment. He looked surprised.

"Don't mention it!"

"Why?" I asked.

"You don't want a publisher thinking you can't do promotion. It could kill your deal."

"Oh," I said, not wanting to kill anything.

My meetings went well because I did the talking, meaning I didn't let anyone ask a question I might mishear. Within a week I had a six figure deal to write my book. What had once seemed impossible now seemed likely.

Needless to say, once I had a book contract I quit my headhunting job. It had always been my dream to write a book. It may have been foolish to roll the dice, but the way I saw it hearing loss didn't give me a choice. There was one important obstacle, however. My wife hated the idea.

# Chapter 6
## On the Rocks

Statistically, you stand a better chance of contracting Ebola than earning a living as a writer. According to one recent study only one in ten authors earn a living by writing. That's not surprising given approximately 80% of all trade books fail to turn a profit.

But my decision to become a writer was not as rash as it sounds. Since I'd revived my freelance career I'd begun making a name for myself writing about unusual inventions that fail in the market despite their innovative nature. I called these inventions "white elephant technology," and since most were from the past I spent my time researching in libraries. In other words, I rarely had to interview anyone, which was ideal for someone losing his hearing.

Though I made more money from headhunting, my articles on white elephant technology began appearing regularly. Plus, I had a six figure book contract. If that didn't make me a writer what did?

Still, writing was chancy. At the very least it necessitated a drastic lifestyle change; something my wife did not relish. I thought it was doable. If we radically downsized we could stretch the publisher's advance the three years it would take to write my book. It would involve selling our house and dropping out of the upper class, but it was an investment in our future. If we deferred gratification, payout would come. As far as I could tell, we didn't even have to leave town. We could rent a nearby apartment and keep the kids in school. I'd seen a hundred start-ups operate on the same principle, why not us? Besides, what choice did I have? I was at the age where it's difficult to find a decent job, and my hearing wouldn't make things easier.

My wife had a point, however. In many respects, it was late to be starting over. I wasn't a fresh faced college graduate; I was 51, a time when my peers were at their peak earning capacity. Pursuing an alternate route was risky. Nevertheless, I was determined to make it work.

Still, my wife thought it a foolish idea. We had two daughters both under ten, and many years to go before we were free of a sizeable financial commitment. As an alternative, she suggested I keep my job and write on the side. But this was my chance to realize a dream. If not now, when, especially since my hearing might worsen?

Rolling the dice never seemed easier.

\*\*\*

My marriage, like my hearing, was stable in its early years. After settling in Bangkok, where I managed the Saatchi office, we enjoyed all the benefits of expat life including a house, a cook, a car, and a driver.

But after three years my life began to grate. There's little glory selling disposable diapers in third world countries to people who neither need nor can afford them. The fact that we successfully introduced yogurt to the Thais, who are lactose intolerant, was nothing to be proud of.

So in 1994, after eight years with Saatchi, I returned to the States where I took a management job in the San Francisco office of J. Walter Thompson. Meanwhile, my hearing continued to decline.

I was tested annually, and upgraded to better hearing aids as technology improved, but the number of times when speech sounded garbled was on the rise. In fact, my hearing loss progressed to the point where I was beginning to lose vowel sounds. Aspirates like "p's" and "t's" also sounded the same. And there were other problems. My marriage was falling apart.

The dissolution of a marriage is never pretty and mine had been coming unglued for a while. It didn't help that its underpinnings were shaky. It came out in other ways, though. My wife, who lacked confidence, always felt bad about only having an Associate Bachelor's degree, so I encouraged her to go back to college. When she did, she dropped out after a year. When she said she wanted to work, I helped get her an interview with a company that paid handsomely for Japanese language skills. When she got the offer she turned them down flat.

I also resented the fact she didn't have the social skills necessary to entertain my clients. It wasn't her fault she couldn't hold her own with men and women older and more accomplished than her, but I worried it held my career back. As time passed, I realized an inequity had crept into our relationship. It hadn't been obvious in Bangkok, but now that she was a stay at home wife in the U.S. I felt the pinch.

Part of our understanding had been that we wouldn't have kids. But after a decade of marriage my wife wanted a child. I resisted for as long as I could, but eventually gave in. After our first daughter, my wife told me she wanted a second. Like Hitler in Czechoslovakia she now wanted Poland. It turned out to be the best decision we ever made but I fought her like the Allies.

It's unfair to blame my wife as the problem. I was hardly a model husband. The farther I climbed up the corporate ladder the more pressure I felt. I worked all the time, was never home, and barely there when I was.

Furthermore, instead of addressing the problem I repressed my resentment which led to expressing it in other ways. I began getting curt and condescending with my wife. I started calling her idiot, stupid, and cunt. As my frustration grew I pinched and pushed her. I even slapped her once or twice. This was reprehensible behavior. There can be no excuse. And yet I couldn't stop.

We tried marital therapy. I even took an anger management course. When I didn't get enough out of it, I repeated the class. Unfortunately, marriage counselors are incentivized to keep you together even when it no longer makes sense. After a few years of this behavior, we moved into separate bedrooms and communicated only by email. Things were so bad I worried about the kids.

What really surprised me was when my wife accused me of faking my hearing loss. For one thing, her soft, high-pitched voice was difficult for me to hear. I constantly asked her to repeat herself. Since she often complained about this I didn't understand how she thought I was faking.

I may not have loved my wife, but I didn't wish her harm. Nor did I want our children to suffer. Once I realized all my anger came from being married I had to take action. But it wasn't until my wife told me not to write the book that I filed for divorce. As far as I was concerned, I had no choice.

# Chapter 7
## Madge

Since we'd gotten married on my wife's birthday (March 1993) I thought it appropriate that we separate on mine (November 2009). But leaving turned out to be the easiest part. Telling the kids was much harder.

I knew in my heart I wasn't meant to be a husband, but once we had kids I never regretted being a father. But how can you love your children and blow up their family? It was a horrible contradiction.

As the four of sat us on the living room sofa my nine-year-old daughter, Dana, and her little sister sat wedged between my wife and me. Since we rarely held family meetings Dana knew something was up. Her sister, too young to comprehend, was the heartbreaking picture of happy innocence.

My wife and I agreed to tell the children together. We even outlined what to say. But once I began telling the kids we were getting a divorce my wife refused to participate. It's not unusual for a husband and wife to love their children more than each other. Though my wife's reticence forbade her from saying what she felt, I already knew. She hated me. I also knew I was shattering their world, but as I delivered the news, I had no idea of the repercussions.

My daughters accepted the news with equanimity. Though they claimed not to have any questions I knew once they grew up they'd have plenty. In the meantime, I felt relief it was over.

A week or so later I was driving them to school when Dana from the backseat asked out of the blue, "Dad, are you going to D-A-T-E?"

I could only assume she spelled the word out because she didn't want her little sister sitting next to her to know what she was asking. When I told her no, she let out a sigh of relief.

At first everything was fine. My new apartment may have been in a building catering to retirees, divorcees, and Section 8ers, but it was close enough to home that I walked the kids to school in the morning.

My deck overlooked a river where a local club rowed every day. At night, the neon lights of an art deco theater glowed across the valley. My world may have been modest, but it was mine.

The most important thing after my kids was my writing. Just the thrill of an unexpected insight, of finding the right sentence or a novel approach to shaping a chapter, was among my great pleasures. Inspiration frequently came when I least expected it: in the shower, during long walks, or before I fell asleep. My notebook swelled with ideas.

Few divorces go smoothly; mine was no exception. The big issue according to the lawyers was earning capacity. Could I still earn a living as a big, corporate, muckety-muck? If so, alimony would be set at a high monthly figure. On the other hand, if my hearing so disabled me I could no longer work the same kind of jobs I once had, my monthly payment would be lower.

The answer seemed obvious, especially since I had every audiogram showing my hearing decline going back to 1988, but my wife's lawyer had other ideas. Chief among these was that I should return to headhunting, or better yet, Lucas. And so he requested I undergo an occupational assessment to determine my fitness.

I asked my lawyer, a short, personable guy who talked so much I worried about his billing hours, whether I could be forced to return to the corporate world.

"Oh, definitely," he replied. "If the court decides you're able they can set alimony so high you have to go back to your old type of job. Either that or go to jail."

I wanted to make the divorce as easy as possible on my wife, including giving her the majority of our assets, but my wife's lawyer had a card up his sleeve. He wanted my occupational assessment to be conducted by someone who was deaf. It was a brilliant strategy. Who better to evaluate me than someone with profound hearing loss? Of course that person would consider me fit for the corporate world. After all, my Grand Inquisitor held a conventional job, why not me?

When I was told my occupational assessment would be conducted by a woman named Madge I wanted to learn more about her. I was interested to see there was no mention of Madge's hearing impairment on her website. Nor did her photo show signs of a hearing aid since hair covered both her ears. The first thing I thought was that she was hiding it - something I could relate to. Nevertheless, my lawyer kept reminding me this woman was my enemy. I should be careful what I said.

I'm not a duplicitous person. It's my nature to tell the truth. Still, I was nervous as I drove to San Mateo for the interview. My future as a writer was at stake.

Madge's office was on a side street in a part of town I'd never been before. I parked next to a one-story house that had been converted into offices. Both it and the neighborhood had seen better days. A nondescript sign by the front door told me I was in the right place. When I went in, I wandered down a dark hallway until I found Madge's one-room office.

The low-ceilinged space was cramped and disorganized. Papers were piled on every conceivable surface and the walls were old and dingy. Overhead, water-stained ceiling tiles buckled and flaked. Not even the California sunshine streaming in through the window could brighten the place.

After a few minutes a short, shapeless woman walked in and introduced herself as Madge. She wore a navy blue pants suit of synthetic material from a place like Ross or Mervyn's, and her hair was shaped into an upward blaze of radical red. It was then I realized Madge might not just be deaf, but blind, too.

My Occupational Evaluator hardly projected the image of a successful business executive. On the contrary, I found her lamentable. Neither the clothes she wore, nor the office she kept, were designed to impress.

If I'm being unduly harsh it's because I could tell Madge had never set foot inside the lobby of a Fortune 500 company. How then could she assess me? Madge didn't know what it was like to be a C-suite executive. She'd never raised $25 million in venture funding, or launched a national ad campaign. I'd not only held many of the senior positions she was evaluating me for, I'd been paid handsomely to fill those positions. In other words, I was better qualified to evaluate Madge than she was to evaluate me.

Obviously, I knew Madge didn't have my best interest at heart, which is probably why I'm being cruel. And yet circumstances forced me to make a choice: a choice between the hearing world and the deaf. It wasn't a choice I relished. And yet as my hearing continued to decline I wondered if I'd ever have a choice. Maybe Madge's world was the best I could hope for. As it turned out, Madge wasn't a good representative of the Deaf community.

"Make yourself comfortable," Madge said, waving to a misshapen chair opposite her desk.

Next, she turned on a tape recorder. I assumed she intended to have our conversation transcribed so she didn't miss anything that I said. I recognized this as one of the tricks hearing impaired people use to compensate for their deafness. I'd used it myself.

Since Madge was born deaf, she'd never heard the words she spoke pronounced correctly. On one level, it was amazing she could speak at all. But as Madge explained the assessment process, her voice sounded like she'd swallowed someone who was struggling to get out. Given my prejudice and ignorance, I felt her voice undermined her credibility, but mostly I felt sorry for her. Worse, I knew my own pronunciation was starting to slip. Did that mean I'd eventually sound like Madge?

"Don't be nervous," Madge said. "Do you know why you're here?"

"I'm here for an assessment."

"That's right. I've been retained to evaluate your suitability for work."

"But I have a job."

"What job is that?" Madge asked, watching my lips.

"I have a six figure contract to write a book. That's my job."

"Well," she said, unimpressed. "We're going to assess your suitability for other work, too."

"But I have a job," I repeated. "I don't need another one."

Madge ignored my comment and continued.

"The purpose of our meetings is to learn everything there is to know about your education, health, work history, and any issues you have related to employment."

"You mean like hearing loss?"

"Your what?"

"My hearing loss."

"I'm sorry. Can you repeat that?"

"My hearing, Madge. Will you take into account that I can't hear anymore?"

Madge grimaced. "Of course! After that, I'll write a detailed report about the job opportunities you're best suited for."

"But I already have a job, Madge."

And so it went.

Madge's surroundings shocked me. If this was the best a deaf person could achieve, I wanted nothing to do with it. I'm not saying Madge was a bad person. I'm sure she was wonderful in her own right. But stories about disabilities lean toward the inspirational. They're the exception not the rule. The truth is there was little glamour in my being handicapped. Life was mostly an endless grind of misunderstanding and accommodation. Every time I went to the bank, supermarket, or post office I experienced a daily round of humiliation. Now, she was telling me nothing was wrong.

I had three meetings with Madge. All went about the same. Though I eventually grew to like her I knew the fix I was in. She'd been hired to prove I could work in the corporate world and that would be her finding.

A year passed and along with it what little money I had left. Predictably, Madge's report concluded I could return to corporate life though she said it might take me eighteen months to land a job.

Finally, against my lawyer's advice, I gave my wife the majority of our assets. Since she'd be starting over I wanted her to have as much cushion as I could provide. Besides, she was the mother of our children; I didn't want her to suffer. When I was finished, I walked out of family court with $10,000 left. But it was worth it. Now I could follow my bliss.

# Chapter 8
# Listening Skills

The good thing about being deaf is it's not being blind. It's also better than being paralyzed, brain damaged, or dead. In other words, deafness isn't the worst thing that can happen, or so I told myself. Of course, if it were up to me I'd rather have all my faculties, but that wasn't something I controlled.

It's important to remember that hearing loss isn't terminal. Nobody ever dies from deafness. It's a nuisance disability like losing your sense of taste or smell, or maybe a thumb. It slows you down, it sets you back, but it doesn't finish you off.

The confusing thing is outwardly you look fine. No one sees deafness, nobody knows it's there. This creates a problem. If you're blind, no one asks you to go to the movies. If you're in a wheelchair, nobody expects you to run a 10k race. But when you're deaf no one knows how much you can't hear. That's because hearing loss is the invisible disability. Even when you say you're deaf people have a hard time understanding what that means. Blindness, yes; paralyzed, yes - people can imagine these things. But deafness, no.

What made my impairment so insidious is that I could tell someone was speaking, I just couldn't make out most of the words. It was like listening to a trumpet—I heard its sound not its individual notes. The difference between uh-huh (yes) and unh-unh (no) is vast in meaning if not pronunciation, but for me the difference was unfathomable.

The best way to experience a hearing impairment is to look at a document that's been redacted. All you see are the words that don't matter. That's hearing loss. Or, if you want to experience deafness first hand press the mute button on your TV remote and watch a program without sound. Now try and figure out what's happening.

People don't do these things so it's impossible for them to gauge what it's like being deaf. They have no idea what decibel range I'm weak in, or which ear is stronger. My impairment is a mystery even when I explain it.

If someone sees I wear hearing aids they often make the mistake of thinking I hear everything. Unfortunately, it's not that simple. Somebody in a wheelchair may be mobile but they remain paralyzed. Climbing up stairs is impossible. In other words, hearing aids don't solve a hearing problem, they just make it less pronounced.

Admittedly, hearing is a difficult concept to grasp. If I say I have only 30% hearing in my right ear it means I can only distinguish 30% of spoken words without a hearing aid. With a hearing aid I might understand up to 50%. But that means half the words in a sentence don't have enough sharpness or clarity for me to understand. Add to that feeling tired, background noise, or someone speaking with a beard or accent and comprehension is further diminished. Now try and have a conversation where you hear less than half of what's said.

We take our five senses for granted. You don't realize how important they are until one is gone. After my precipitous hearing loss there were a number of things I could no longer enjoy. There were no more TED talks, podcasts, or Terry Gross interviews. No YouTube, Rhapsody, or Spotify. No radio of any kind, which included traffic reports because the announcers spoke so fast they were unintelligible.

Author talks, professor lectures, books on tape, and live theater were out as were voicemail, cell phones, audio guides, and ear buds. There wasn't enough room in my ears for ear buds anyway. Hearing aids took up all the space.

I could no longer watch movies in theaters (before captioning systems), TV without subtitles, or listen to a comedian. Impressionists were a non-starter for similar reasons as was anyone with a foreign accent, speech impediment, or a beard. I had special difficulty with names. Since I could no longer process sound correctly, I often had to ask someone to either spell out or write down their name. As it was, I hadn't heard a name correctly in five years.

Not only could I no longer hear a waiter describe the specials, I couldn't hear in a restaurant, period. Cocktail and dinner parties were a no-go for the same reason.

Drive-thrus were problematic whether fast food, bank or pharmacy because I couldn't understand the intercom - a problem even for those with acute hearing. AI's like Siri or Alexa were also out as was the Sat-nav voice in my car. As for airport announcements like flight cancellations or gate changes, they may as well have been in Farsi. Train, bus, and subway announcements suffered the same problem.

My impairment may have put me at a disadvantage, but there were strategies I used to close the gap. Picking the right environment helped. Ambient noise is a killer for the hearing impaired. Running water, whether from a fountain, fish tank, or dishwasher, rendered conversation unintelligible. Air conditioners were especially heinous, but a weed whacker, washing machine or ceiling fan had similar effect.

The best rooms for conversation had a low ceiling and wall to wall carpeting because these made for ideal acoustics. Rooms to be avoided had stone, tile, or bare wood floors, high ceilings, or an absence of sound absorbent material.

Another useful strategy was repeating back what I thought a person had said. This was a form of double checking that saved me from misunderstanding. More often than not it saved me from making embarrassing mistakes.

Asking people questions was also a good tactic. Rather than enduring the jump ball of an unstructured conversation questions allowed me to steer it in a direction I felt comfortable. For example, if I asked someone how their wife was I could anticipate their response. Done artfully, the other person never realized what I was doing. It also had the benefit of flattering them since I appeared keenly interested in what they had to say. I became so adept at this technique people complimented me on being a good listener, which is funny considering I was functionally deaf.

The most successful strategy was asking a person to repeat themselves. Sometimes I had to ask five or six times before getting their sentence straight. Usually, you only get one or two chances to ask a person to say something twice. After that they say "never mind."

For those who don't know it, "never mind" is the worst thing you can tell a hearing impaired person. It's our version of the "N" word. It means you don't care enough to communicate with us. The fact most people don't know this goes to show that the hearing impaired regularly face discrimination. In the meantime "never mind" was something I heard almost daily.

When someone refused to cooperate with my hearing loss they could come in for some pretty rough treatment. My favorite thing was to see how many times I could get them to repeat themselves even though I heard them the first time. This tactic was usually reserved for family members who complained about my hearing, but I'd also use it on people who talked too fast, covered their mouth when speaking, or refused to follow my directions on how to communicate. I thought of it as revenge of the hearing impaired. It didn't solve my problem but it was a relief to fight back.

Later, I learned that some deaf people won't use their voice even when they can speak clearly. The reason for this is that if a hearing person knows you can talk, they assume you can hear. This leads to all sorts of miscommunication. By not talking, however, the deaf deprive the hearing of speech which helps level the playing field. In other words, when the deaf render the hearing mute both sides are equal—one is deprived of language, the other of hearing. It also forces the hearing to use pantomime, a visual form of communication which a deaf person readily understands.

This may sound perverse but the strategy makes sense. It not only improves what is usually a one-sided communication, it teaches the hearing (to some small degree) what it's like to be deaf. I never used this tactic but I can appreciate why some people like it. It wasn't so much revenge of the deaf as a means of promoting understanding. I'm certain that if hearing people realized how poorly they treat the deaf many would change their ways… many, but not all. For the truth is, the hearing world dominates. They make the rules. But the hearing world is oppressive and discriminatory where the deaf are concerned just as much as white bigotry is discriminatory against blacks. Sadly, the hearing world has little idea of this.

Fortunately, there were tricks I could use to compensate for deafness. I'm not technologically savvy but I could walk into anybody's house and, regardless of what TV or cable company they had, use their remote to navigate to the closed caption setting. The Internet was another blessing. There was so much you could get done on it without speaking to another person it was a godsend. Every once in a while, though, a road block appeared. Neither the *New York Times* not Comcast will let you cancel your account online; you have to call a customer service representative. Since they work off a script most service reps don't know how to communicate with the hearing impaired. They bombard you with a lot of non-germane questions you can't hear well enough to answer. All I wanted was to cancel my subscription, but they wouldn't deviate from their script. It's enough to bring you to tears, especially stranded in the middle of nowhere with a flat tire and two kids in the back who needed to pee. In that case, I talked my nine year old through a call to AAA. The operator thought we were pranking her.

Even face to face interactions could be frustrating. My worst fear was a chatty cashier since you never knew what they might say. But even fast food workers trying to upsell you were a nightmare.

"Medium or large?"

"Want fries with that?"

"For here or to go?"

Most of the time I had to guess at what they were saying.

A hearing impaired person has to be an active listener, which requires concentration and laser focus. Sometimes I found closing my eyes helped. By reducing outside stimuli I could hear better. Even then it might take my brain up to 10 seconds to get enough traction before I understood what someone was saying. Plenty of time, I wasn't even sure it was English. At the end of the day I was exhausted.

\*\*\*

Little things are the first to go when you lose your hearing. I could no longer hear rain drumming on the roof, crickets chirping in a field, or the warning sound of a mosquito before it bit. Wind chimes vanished as did church bells and a cat's purr.

By the time I went into headhunting I could no longer hear an oven timer, water boiling, a sink left running, or the phone ring. Nor could I hear an elevator, ding; the microwave, beep; or an alarm clock, buzz. I might wander around the house for the better part of a day wondering where a particular noise came from before discovering I'd left the fan on over the stove. I even had to pay attention when peeing because I couldn't hear if I hit the bowl.

Music was a particular challenge. With hearing aids I could grasp some semblance of human speech, but music was damn near impossible. If I knew the song I might be able to reassemble it from memory, but if it was something I'd never heard before, forget it.

The problem with music was certain threads were stripped out. I might detect percussion, or bass, but miss the melody because I couldn't hear that decibel range. My brain tried filling in the gaps, but it never came out sounding right. Having the memory of a song you once knew and listening to the tinny, distorted version that remained was too sad to endure. If that's hard to understand, imagine ordering a club sandwich and receiving two slices of bread with nothing in between. That's the culinary version of music for a person with hearing loss. Most of what matters is missing.

As a result, I no longer listened to pop songs or went to musicals. Movie soundtracks and TV themes might as well never have been composed. Though I could no longer hear Christmas carols I could make out 'Happy Birthday'—that's how ingrained in our brain it is; you just wouldn't want me to sing it.

I still went to my children's concerts even though I couldn't hear them play—the point was to show my support. But on a field trip to hear the San Francisco Symphony with my youngest daughter and her classmates I had to content myself with the orchestra's visual appeal. Having once been a classical music lover who played the violin I found the experience disheartening.

But these are just gripes. The truth is a person can survive these losses. None of this will kill you. What can kill you is not being able to hear the smoke alarm when a fire breaks out. Given I slept without hearing aids, I worried about this happening at night.

In addition to having trouble identifying certain sounds I couldn't tell the direction they came from. I'd beaten one smoke detector to death with a hammer only to discover the alarm was coming from a different one. I had a particularly hard time hearing sirens. Not knowing whether a driver is honking at you is one thing, but failing to pull over for an ambulance can be dangerous. In fact, I was amazed the state of California let me drive. Obviously, you can't drive if you're blind, but you'd think there were limitations to being hearing impaired that affect road safety. As it turns out, statistics reveal that the deaf and hearing impaired are safer drivers than hearing people.

Since I couldn't judge sound direction my startle response became my quickest reflex. A person walking unexpectedly into a room scared the pants off me. Bicyclists passing me on the sidewalk also made me jump. It was like living in a horror movie where the killer constantly leaps out at you. You never knew when he might strike.

Other situations were more irritating than dangerous. Unlocking my car in a crowded parking lot was a crapshoot. Since I couldn't hear the beep, if I didn't see the headlights flash I couldn't find my car. Stranger still was my brain's propensity for making up sounds. Often I found myself reacting to something that wasn't there. Other times I didn't react when I should, like when someone called my name. The result

44

was a Mr. Magoo-like existence floating cluelessly from one near catastrophe to the next.

Phantom sounds are common for people with hearing loss. The brain expects auditory input but when sound is absent it fills in the blanks. Once, my brain turned jazz music (which I love) into the sound of a barking dog. Another time, honking geese flying overhead sounded like people conversing.

Many hearing impaired experience a ringing in their ears called tinnitus. More often I heard imaginary music. The most common music I heard was Gregorian chants, but I also heard bagpipes, ethereal choirs, and a woman practicing an unknown scale. One night I fell asleep to surf music. That didn't happen often enough as far as I was concerned.

None of it was real, however. My brain was making it up. This was especially devastating when it came to conversation. Sometimes your brain hears a different word than the one spoken. This gives the hearing impaired a false sense of security about what's been said. It took me a while to catch on to this, and when I did the realization was far from comforting. If you can't trust your brain to tell you the right word, what can you trust? That's when I started questioning everything I heard. It also moved me a few inches closer to despair.

# Chapter 9
## Paradise

After two years of lawyer's fees, child support, and daily expenses, I ran out of money. With my book still a year away from being finished the situation looked grim.

Fortunately, I caught a break. It was July 2011 and my sister, who lived in Woodside, California, offered me a place to live rent free. It was a 1950s ranch house on the property next to hers. She and her spectacularly successful husband had bought the place to keep potential neighbors at bay. She said I could live there until my book was published. In the meantime, she'd cover the cost of my gas, electric, water and garbage. It was too good a deal to turn down.

You've probably never heard of Woodside but it's a paradise. That's why it's so expensive to live there. Located in Silicon Valley at the base of the Santa Cruz Mountains, Woodside is a town for rich people, but not just any rich people, only super-rich people.

A number of tech elite call Woodside home. Larry Ellison, founder of Oracle, and Scott Cook, founder of Intuit, live there, as does John Doerr, the venture capitalist. Each has a net worth well in excess of $2 billion, which is why the actress, Michelle Pffeifer, wasn't exactly slumming when she built her second home there.

One reason the tech elite love Woodside is that it's a fast commute to Stanford University and the nearby start ups. It's also within striking distance of Google, Apple, and Sand Hill Road where the tier one VCs reside. San Francisco is only thirty-two miles away; San Jose, twenty-six.

But convenience isn't the only reason rich people live in Woodside. It's also beautiful. Houses sit on a minimum of two acres, usually many more, and strict zoning limits the kind of structures that are built. Even fences are regulated. Live oak forests alternate with golden meadows to give the town a rural feel. In other words, Woodside would have been God's country if God could afford it.

Of course, Woodside was the wrong place to be given my economic circumstances. I wasn't rich. In fact, by the time I moved there I had less than $500 in the bank. My car wasn't just ten years old. I'd recently given up health insurance because I couldn't afford it. I didn't belong in any capacity other than as groundskeeper.

But Woodside turned out to be ideal for a writer. The house was empty when I moved in. Still, I'd managed to salvage enough furniture, pictures and rugs from my divorce to create the perfect writing environment. Sitting at my desk overlooking a three acre meadow, I gazed with satisfaction upon my well-oiled dining room table (custom-made in Bangkok); my antique Turkoman rugs (purchased in Singapore); and my toy soldier cabinet (modeled after Churchill's at Blenheim). I even got a dog to keep me company, a golden retriever my eldest daughter named Austin.

Surrounded by hundreds of books and photos of my heroes, I quickly fell into a routine. Each morning, I woke early to watch the sun creep over the meadow. As I stirred, Austin's tail thumped a drumbeat on the bedspread. Following a quick shower, I'd fetch the morning paper, then Austin and I would inventory the property to see what had changed during the night. By 8:30, I was at my desk where the pages mounted quickly.

My caretaker duties were limited, so I had plenty of time to write. All I had to do was mow the lawn and keep the house clean. It didn't bother me I was the only person in Woodside who cut their own grass - the lawn wasn't mine to begin with. Given my domesticity I was happy to comply.

It didn't take long for me to realize that being given a chance to write was a gift, its many satisfactions a luxury for which I was grateful. I'd finally achieved what I'd set out to do, I was finishing my book, and nothing, not George Lucas, Madge, my ex-wife or my hearing loss, could stop me.

*** 

Once every two weeks my writing was interrupted when my daughters came for a visit.

They loved spending weekends in Woodside. They romped in the meadows, played with the dog, swam in their aunt's pool, and skateboarded down the driveway. Since Woodside is horse country there was a treasure trove of horseshoes and rusty carriage parts to discover in the meadow. One day they brought home a snake skin, another day a paper wasps' nest. We even found a little green army man whose parachute had long since disintegrated. I lined up their finds on the kitchen windowsill where they joined the pine cones and snail shells that Austin had unearthed.

Broken harness parts, rusty horseshoes, and plastic paratroopers appealed to me. There was also a small farm next door with goats, chickens, and geese. My kids loved feeding the goats, bouncing on the trampoline I'd bought but couldn't afford, and roasting marshmallows in the fire pit at night. It was in every way a paradise.

Though I assumed the divorce had been hard on them there was no shortage of joking - usually at my expense. My youngest liked sneaking up and scaring me, which was easy since I couldn't hear her approach. There was also laughter whenever I misheard something, which was often. My youngest once said, "I'm feeling clever." When I looked at her questioningly and said, "You smell leather?" she broke out in hysterics. Another time, my oldest asked whether I was "enjoying the meal" to which I responded, "The Jewish man stole my veal?" It soon became our catchphrase anytime I got something wrong.

It didn't help that I'd pipe up enthusiastically about something only to learn that one of my daughters had said the exact same thing minutes before. They got embarrassed when I spoke too loudly in public, and annoyed when I didn't hear them. But these are small matters. Most of the time we had a blast. Whether it was singing 'Here Comes the Sun' in the kitchen, or floating boats in the creek, I felt great when my daughters were around. If only it could last.

# Chapter 10
# Trouble in Paradise

Woodside's lack of distractions meant it didn't take long to finish my book. After I turned it in, however, I entered a weird period of purgatory.

The publishing process is glacially slow. I was told it would take a year to eighteen months before my book reached stores. It was bad enough I had to wait for the final installment of my advance, but I couldn't sell my second book until publishers had seen how the first one had sold. I didn't expect my maiden effort to be a bestseller, few books are, but I did hope it would do well enough to earn me a second book deal. Given I wanted a writing career everything depended on it.

Fortunately, I already had an idea for a second book. In fact, most of the research was done. So rather than wait a year to see if a publisher was interested, I decided to start writing.

Writing could only fill so much of my time, however. Since my daughters' visits were limited to twice a month, I had plenty of time to spare. At first, I tried meeting people, but the rich aren't friendly. Houses in Woodside are not only set far apart, they're surrounded by fences. I might go days without seeing anyone.

True, my sister lived just across the meadow with her husband, but they were so busy with their own lives they rarely visited. I could go months without seeing them. It soon reached the point where the only time I encountered another person was when I got the mail. Even these sightings were confined to people passing by in cars, or riding on horseback. It was hard not to feel alone.

At first I wasn't worried; I was used to being on my own. My parents were in their 40s when they had me. My three older siblings were already grown and out of the house. Since my parents were pretty burned out on child rearing I was sent to a sleep away camp in Maine every summer beginning at age nine, followed by four years of boarding school, and a college far from home. I had lots of practice being alone.

Still, strange things happen when you're isolated. Once, I went several days before realizing daylight savings had turned the clock back an hour. Nor did I always know what day of the week it was, or even when a major sporting event like the Super Bowl was happening. At one point, I stopped wearing hearing aids altogether because there was no one to listen to.

Meanwhile, my hearing continued to decline. To give you an idea of just how deaf I'd become, when I took my hearing aids out to mow the lawn I couldn't tell if the mower was running until I touched the handle.

The main reason I'd ended up in Woodside was financial, but my hearing had a lot to do with it, too. Unfortunately, hearing loss limits your social activity. Friends suggested I date, but I felt so radioactive after my divorce I didn't want to contaminate another person. Instead, I focused on my daughters and worked on my second book. This may sound extreme, but when you can no longer make sense of the simplest verbal communication, and you've yet to discover the Deaf community, you're thrust into a social Stone Age. It felt like I had no other choice.

The one time I did find myself socializing with an age appropriate female it was by accident. My sister and I were having dinner at a Woodside restaurant when one of her girlfriends joined us. It was a fun meal with lots of wine and laughter, but afterwards, when my sister's friend tried kissing me in the parking lot I got out of there so fast I nearly ran her over. After that, I wore my wedding ring as a deterrent.

But loneliness was only one of my problems. I was also broke.

It helped that I didn't have to pay rent, but the divorce had cleaned me out. For starters, I had support payments in excess of my monthly income. I was happy to pay them since it was for my children, but I soon find myself living below the poverty line in one of the wealthiest zip codes in America.

To address the problem, I increased my freelance writing. But many of the magazines I wrote for took so long to pay I sometimes didn't get a check until a year after a piece had been accepted for publication.

No one is poor in Woodside. They might economize by foregoing their annual Hawaii vacation, but everyone has enough to eat. For me, being poor in Woodside meant no savings, $25,000 in debt, and little income.

It helped that my needs were modest. All I required was the *New York Times*, six hours of solid writing, and a book before bed. This is how I learned to enjoy the small things in life. But pretty soon, I couldn't afford those.

Instead of lamenting my financial situation, I chose to celebrate nature. I loved the way sunlight flooded the kitchen when I made coffee in the morning, or the sound of the screen door slamming in the summer. Since there were two creeks on the property, a towering oak, and a prodigious amount of wildlife, I focused on them. I learned to appreciate the tribe of black squirrels that bickered over my walnut tree, or the way a great blue heron occasionally breakfasted on gophers in the meadow. I also looked forward to the visit of a three-legged coyote who wandered through at dusk in search of a deer family that lived nearby. You couldn't ask for better company.

It's been said that the only people who don't want things are dead. You could almost believe it living in America. But once I cured myself of wanting, life was a lot easier. I learned to walk a grocery aisle looking straight ahead so as not to see the products beckoning me. When I did want to buy something I developed the trick of waiting twenty-four hours to see whether it was a "want" or a "need." Only the "needs" were purchased. Suddenly, I knew what everything cost. I learned to buy on deal, clip coupons, and knew what BOGO meant. After robbing the piggy bank I'd kept as a child I became intimate with Coinstar.

Still, it wasn't long before I ran out of money. Since food was my biggest expense, I began eating smaller portions, making the weekend meals I made for the kids last the week. Soon I was down to two meals a day, some days only one. When I broke a molar I didn't go to the dentist because I couldn't afford to fix it. When I got a flat tire I traveled on the spare and borrowed time.

I already had the cheapest cell phone plan since all I did was text, but I needed to cut costs further. When my car's headlights burned out, I stopped driving at night. I reduced gasoline purchases so much I ran out more than once. When I could, I rode my bike instead.

The worst thing was not knowing if I had enough money to buy Christmas gifts for my children. But small things also bothered me. As my economic footprint shrank everything became a calculation. I didn't rent videos because I could get them for free from the library. I cancelled my *New York Times* subscription even though it was my only form of entertainment other than books. Even my dog came in for economizing. I stopped taking Austin to the vet, eliminated his heart worm medicine, and bought the cheapest brand of dog food.

By now my credit cards had been cancelled, my cell phone turned off, and the plug on my Internet pulled. I had so little money I couldn't afford $6 for the bridge toll to pick up my kids. And then one day my bank account reached zero.

There had never been a time in my life when I wasn't on an upward trajectory. I may have lived in Woodside, but I was broke, deaf, and alone. It seemed a high price to pay for chasing one's dream. Still, I had nobody to blame but myself. I guess that's what you get for following your bliss.

# Chapter 11
## Crazy in Woodside

Thanks to Lexapro, the anti-depressant I'd been prescribed by the doctors at Stanford Hospital in 2007, my mood was stable. But once I dropped my health insurance Lexapro tripled in cost, so I dropped that, too. That's when things got interesting.

There are benefits to quitting your meds—besides saving money their side effects disappear. In my case, Lexapro caused lethargy, weight gain, and reduced my libido to a pilot light. Months went by when I couldn't work up enough enthusiasm to masturbate; when I did I had to concentrate like it was a sobriety test.

The first few months I felt great. My tiredness vanished, my creativity soared, and I needed to sleep only a few hours. Importantly, I started having feelings again. Just the thought of the chipped spout on my mother's iced tea pitcher was enough to make me tear up. Even my golden retriever's love felt like a solid, tangible thing. Life was terrific.

But as months passed I noticed a change. I started listening to music again. This may surprise you given my level of hearing, but I only listened to songs I already knew. For example, when I caught a bit of melody my brain filled in the blanks by recreating the song from memory. It was like recognizing a familiar object in the dark from its shape alone. It didn't work for music I'd never heard before, but for music I'd grown up with it worked just fine.

Once I quit Lexapro, old songs began amplifying my feelings in ways I'd never experienced. The right song could jack me into emotions so powerful it was like traveling on a time machine. Suddenly, I was back in a period of my life when I was happy, unencumbered, and strong.

By May 2012, Joe Cocker's 'You Are So Beautiful', Ringo Starr's 'You're Sixteen', and Crosby Stills Nash's 'Love the One You're With' hijacked my brain on a daily basis. The only way to satisfy the addiction was to listen to these songs morning, noon and night, so that's what I did. Each airing felt like a jab of heroin; a fantastic warmth flooding my brain followed by a swooning, emotional oblivion that decreased over time. No problem, I soon found another song to take its place.

Everybody has songs they love. What they don't all have is my reaction. One morning, while listening to Herb Alpert's 'This Guy's in Love with You', I was so overcome I collapsed on the kitchen floor. Suddenly, I'd been transported thirty-eight years back in time. I was seventeen again during a period of my life that was filled with promise. Anything seemed possible. My life today was a void by comparison and that realization, courtesy of Mr. Alpert, was too much to handle. I lay on the floor and wept.

At first I didn't notice what was happening. I made my bed every morning, mowed the lawn each week, and washed the dishes after every meal. The problem with depression is that it can grow so gradually you don't know you have it until it's too late. For example, I found myself getting angry at trivial things. Anything that slowed me down: poor drivers, retail clerks and customer service reps were subject to my withering verbal abuse. Meanwhile, my problem-solving skills began to falter. If I tried to fix something I grew so befuddled I had to stop. Eventually, I gave up altogether. Things reached a point where nothing in my house worked.

I even gave up on my finances. Since I didn't have money to pay my bills I threw them into a box unopened. When debt collectors called I let them go straight to voicemail. I couldn't hear them anyway.

Broke, with only my dog for companionship, I slowly went crazy. What had once been procrastination became the inability to get things done. Failure to complete a task became an endless cycle of recrimination, self-loathing, and disgust. Even taking Austin out filled me with dread. Every time I left the house it felt like a space walk without a tether.

It was about this time I developed a rash. It started as a red, scaly, patch on my ankle but quickly grew into a shiny exoskeleton encompassing every part of my body. The itchiness was so absurd all I could do was scratch. Within a month I had more scabs than a leopard has spots. It got so bad I had to wear a long sleeved shirt and pants whenever I went out.

The technical term for what I was suffering was clinical depression, but I didn't know that then. I thought I was fine. That's the thing about going crazy. You're the last one to recognize it.

# Chapter 12
## No Problemo

The saving grace during this period was that my book was finally published. When author copies of *Operation Storm* arrived on my doorstep I couldn't believe it. My dream had culminated in an attractive 478 page book. It almost didn't seem real.

My publisher set up a series of events to promote its publication. The first was a talk at a Palo Alto bookstore that C-Span intended to film for *Book Talk*. I was worried about the Q&A session since I didn't want my inability to hear embarrassing me on TV. My solution was to place a pencil and index card on every audience member's seat. That way they could write down their questions, which I would read during the Q&A session. Hearing never came into play.

The second event was a radio interview at KQED in San Francisco. Since it was held in a recording studio I couldn't have been happier. Not only was the room soundproof, which helped me to hear, I wore a pair of hi-fidelity headphones that pumped the interviewer's voice directly into my ear. Better yet, we sat so close together I could easily read her lips. I swelled with newfound confidence.

The rest of my parade did not go as smoothly.

My publicist had agreed that I would only do live radio interviews if they were in person. What I didn't count on were radio interviews being conducted by phone. When I learned about these, I insisted they had to be taped since I wanted the radio station to have the option of editing out any mistakes I made from not being able to hear properly.

Since the majority of stations were outside California the most expedient way to do interviews was by phone. But I hadn't heard on a phone since 2007. What made them think I could do it now?

At first, this was a show-stopper. But then I got a captioned telephone for the hearing-impaired. This enables an operator listening in on your conversation to type what they hear in real time with the text appearing on an LED screen.

It took a while to get the phone since I needed to qualify for a state program first. When it did arrive I only had two days to practice with it before my phone interview. I tried it out by calling a few friends. It wasn't perfect. Sometimes there was a delay between what the person said and when it appeared on my screen, but it worked well enough I thought I'd get by.

Finally, the day came for my first out of state interview. It was a highbrow program syndicated out of Chicago—an excellent platform for promoting my book. The radio host, whose name was Steve, called me a few minutes before the interview to break the ice. I took the opportunity to explain my impairment. Thankfully, Steve seemed unperturbed; but that was because he wasn't listening.

"No problemo!" he said with the blithe manner so many radio hosts adopt. "Since we're doing this live let's go to the countdown!"

"What? We're live? I thought we're taping?"

Steve's voice abruptly disappeared followed by a series of beeps I recognized as a countdown signal. Then, after a brief pause, he returned.

"So, John, tell me about your book, *Operation Storm*? Did the Japanese really plan on bombing New York City and Washington, DC?"

The fact we were live threw me for a loop. I understood the first couple of words of Steve's sentence, but as he gathered steam I lost the thread. No problemo! I had my captioned telephone to turn to for translation. I soon learned, however, the speed of the readout was wholly dependent on the operator's typing skill. After an uncomfortably long delay, during which my blood pressure skyrocketed, the operator's version of Steve's first question appeared on my screen.

**- - So, Jon, dngng ~ ga amd g 130 ;090 { ..tol…mbnoueln dmnsod [ abd \ book 3#59))+,,,,dd [oofsd bok ^dond .knd ???**

There was so little coherent information I didn't know how to respond. Was it possible I'd gotten the only operator with their own hearing impairment? I was doomed.

I asked Steve to repeat his question, but when I failed to understand a second time, I knew I couldn't ask a third. My only choice was to launch into an enthusiastic description of my book and hope it somehow related to Steve's question.

The first rule of interviewing is never talk more than a minute. But I needed to postpone Steve's next question, so I rambled on. Meanwhile, sweat dripped down the underside of my arms while my heart tapped out a beat like a military snare drum. When I finally finished, I awaited the next question with dread.

Again, after a lengthy delay, the operator typed out what Steve had asked:

**& ] ^ xlkhnd  kpnn *lidll* and   ln o 3\*0 ther in~ fo =+dfz ll';4-|| '
n3x???**

The only time I can remember suffering like that was speaking to that Silicon Valley CEO on his cell phone. For all I knew I sounded like an idiot.

When the interview was finally over, Steve thanked me and hung up. I had no idea whether I'd gotten away with my deception, but after the single longest hour of my life, my hands were trembling. If this was book promotion for a deaf guy, I was in trouble.

# Chapter 13
## All I Need Is the Air That I Breathe

Then in May 2014, I got some bad news.

My agent emailed to say the editor who had acquired my first book was leaving his publishing house. In other words, he wouldn't be buying my second book. Worse, after sending my proposal to a dozen publishers, no one else wanted to buy it either.

I was shocked by the news. Writing was my only way to make money. If no one wanted my second book how was I going to make a living?

Deep in my heart I knew I could write, but the commercial market was telling me otherwise. Even though I knew they were mistaken I was being rejected in the same way the business world had rejected me. Short of my daughters dying I couldn't think of worse news.

I was well acquainted with depression. But nothing triggers depression like stress, and now that I'd stopped taking Lexapro my world fell apart.

A few weeks later I was home one night watching *Finding a Friend for the End of the World*. The only reason I'd chosen the film was that I had a thing for Keira Knightly, which occasionally led to poor Netflix decisions. The plot was simple. Scientists, having identified an asteroid was on a collision path with earth, announce mankind only has weeks to live. Subsequently, two sad sacks played by Knightly and Steve Carroll are abandoned by their mates, meet cute, and resolve to see the end through together.

The movie is a black comedy, but nothing was funny about the reaction I had watching Steve Carroll carry a sleeping Keira Knightly to a plane so she can see her family one last time. It wasn't the selfless act of love that moved me, though, it was the song playing over the scene.

The Hollies' 'The Air That I Breathe' barely registered on my radar when it debuted in 1969. I was 11 years old and paying attention to other things. But that night it triggered the worst psychological meltdown I'd had since Tokyo. Consumed by hopelessness, wracked by despair, I sat in my chair a sobbing mass of irrational thought.

If it's a fact that people suffering from depression are poor judges of their condition, I was no exception. Whether my depression was biological, situational, or hearing induced it was clear my brain chemistry was out of whack.

Shortly after the episode, I reached out to the psychiatrist who'd helped get me admitted to Stanford, the same psychiatrist my sister used and highly recommended. Though relations with my sibling had deteriorated (after all, who wants a deaf, surly, and withdrawn brother living next door?), our mutual shrink had patched things up enough that my sister agreed to pay for my Lexapro. This was hugely important in getting me back on my feet, and the first thing I realized once I felt better was that I needed a job.

*** 

Once I started taking Lexapro again everything changed for the better. My mood improved along with my ability to function and what once seemed impossible now seemed likely. The most important thing was finding work.

I knew my hearing loss would not permit me to do what I once had, so I focused on jobs I thought I could do. I'd always been passionate about books, so I began applying to local bookstores for work. I also liked the clothes at Brook Brothers, so went online to apply for a sales position.

I knew these jobs paid minimum wage, but at least it was a start. I also thought they'd allow me to work on my book even if only on nights or weekends. What I couldn't do was continue down the path I'd been following.

I'd given an author's talk at the first bookstore I interviewed with. I'd not only shopped there, I was familiar with their customer base and inventory. I thought for sure they would hire me.

The second bookstore I interviewed with was part of a West Coast chain. Since I didn't know anyone there, I sent a letter to its President explaining I'd be the most accomplished bookseller he had. Not only was I a published author, I'd worked in bookstores during college, and at Doubleday Publishing in New York.

The President forwarded my letter to the manager of his Palo Alto store, after which I received an email inviting me for an interview. I approached the meeting with enthusiasm but after ten minutes I could tell I wouldn't get the job. I realized I'd made a rookie mistake in going over the manager's head. But when she told me she'd never hire someone who couldn't answer the phone I felt insulted.

An outraged friend later insisted it was discriminatory. Perhaps, but my work experience didn't mean much if I couldn't answer the phone. Still, they weren't the only bookstore in town. I kept looking.

When I didn't hear back from Brooks Brothers I stopped by my local branch to drop off my resume. I prepared for the visit by dressing the part. I wore Brooks Brothers khakis, a Brooks Brothers shirt, and a pair of Brooks Brothers boxers though nobody would know it.

When I arrived at the store I was greeted by a patrician-looking gentleman. We were the only two people in the place, so I didn't think I was imposing. Still, when I explained I was looking for a job and handed him my resume he took it between pinched fingers. After scanning it briefly he wrinkled his nose and said, "You're overqualified."

"Yes, but I can do this job," I said firmly. "I not only love Brooks Brothers, I've worn it all my life! Plus, I have sales experience and am good with people."

"There's an online application, but…" and here he cocked his head to take in my hearing aids, "you might make our customers feel uncomfortable."

I never let pride get in the way of my job search. I didn't care if the jobs I was applying for were a "step down" from where I'd been. Given the feedback I knew I'd be lucky to get hired. But when the bookstore where I'd given my C-Span talk didn't hire me it was time for a new approach. By that point I was willing try anything.

# Chapter 14
## A Second Chance

I can't remember how I learned about the California Department of Rehabilitation (DOR) as a resource for the hearing impaired but I was leery given it was a state agency. I may have been invited to speak at the Smithsonian and given interviews to NPR, but I still needed a job. That's when I decided to check out the DOR since they offered advice to deaf people seeking employment.

Their website was dismayingly bureaucratic. First, I had to complete the DR-222 form also known as the Vocational Rehabilitation Services Intake Application. This determined my eligibility to receive counseling as well as the urgency with which said counseling would be provided. After my application was approved I would then (and only then) be allowed to schedule an interview with a job counselor or "Employment Coordinator" as DOR termed it. What interested me most was the mention of a job bank for people with disabilities. This suggested there were companies that hired someone like me. I wanted to learn more.

The DOR's "One-Stop Center" was located in a suburban office park on the northern edge of Silicon Valley. After I checked in, I was escorted to an interior conference room done in varying shades of cost-saving blue. As I waited, I wondered if it was meant to put me at ease.

The first thing I noticed was how young my Employment Coordinator was. No older than her twenties, she had long dark hair and a tight smile. She also had the brusque, impersonal manner of a much-abused state employee. Nevertheless, I gave her an ingratiating smile before launching into what by now had become a well rehearsed explanation of my situation.

After a few perfunctory questions, she asked to see my resume. When she finished reading it, she placed it on the table and looked at me with hooded eyes.

"What kind of job do you want?"

"I'm a writer, so something writing-related would be nice."

Picking up my resume she read aloud: "Managing Director, Saatchi-Bangkok. General Manager, J. Walter Thompson. V.P. Global Sales and Marketing, LucasArts. What does any of this have to do with writing?"

"It doesn't. It just shows I've held senior-level positions and can be trusted."

"Get rid of it. It will only confuse people. Do you have any actual writing experience?"

"You'll see at the bottom I've written for the *New York Times, The Wall Street Journal* and a bunch of other publications."

"Fine. But right now you're all over the place. Redo your resume focusing on your writing experience and email it to me. Here..." She slid a piece of paper across the table. "This is a ten point list of how to write a resume. What else?"

"One problem I've had is that when I tell a prospective employer I'm hearing impaired they lose interest."

"Don't disclose it then."

"You mean lie?"

"Not lie, but timing is important. You're under no obligation to disclose you're hearing impaired."

"Won't that be misleading?"

"The idea is to get your foot in the door. When the time is right, you can explain your situation."

"But won't I create an expectation I can't fulfill?"

"Look, do you want a job or not?"

The rest of the meeting went like that. I left dispirited but determined to do what was necessary to access their job bank. If this meant erasing twenty years of experience, so be it.

I may not have been employed but I was making progress. Now I had to work on my social life. Which is why it came as both a surprise and a delight when out of the blue I received an email from my old college girlfriend, Allison Katz.

I didn't realize it at the time but my life needed some shaking up. Given our past experience, Allie was an expert.

# Part II

# Allie

# Chapter 15
## First Contact

Allie's email was short and to the point.

*I've often thought about you over the years. I'm planning a trip to visit my stepson in San Francisco and wondered if we might get together. Interested?*

You could read a lot into an email like that. It all depends on your frame of mind. I may not have talked to Allie in 35 years, but I remembered her well enough. Still, someone doesn't contact you after three decades unless they have an agenda.

The first time I'd met Allie was in college. Her aunt, who lived in my hometown, had been bugging me to ask her out. I knew Allie's aunt fairly well since we played doubles tennis on my mother's court every weekend.

Allie's aunt had always struck me as a bit off. It was the early 70s and she was a swinger. She'd slept with some of the married men in our tennis group while maintaining a long running lesbian affair with her best friend. It was hard to know how much Allie knew about her aunt's affairs, but if the gossip had filtered down to my level she probably knew something.

Allie's aunt may have been odd but the only time she made me uncomfortable was during a dinner party she was hosting when she'd drunkenly leaned over and told me in the middle of the meal she'd like to sleep with every man at the table. I was only 18 at the time and didn't know what to do with this information other than worry I was on the list. I managed to escape that night unharmed but it was one of the reasons why I didn't take her suggestion and contact her niece. By fall of my senior year, however, I found myself in between girlfriends, so decided to give Allie a call. I didn't know it at the time but that call changed everything.

***

It was a beautiful fall day in October. The maple leaves were alight and a brisk wind made them shiver. I'd agreed to meet Allie at her dorm. Since she attended one of the all girl colleges nearby I took the bus to get there.

I felt a certain amount of trepidation about meeting Allie. I'd never seen a picture of her, so had no idea what she looked like. Being a typically shallow college boy I planned to cut the visit short if she was ugly. If she was pretty, smart, or both, I'd extend my visit. Either way, I was nervous.

I bounded up the steps to her Gothic-looking dorm, pushed open the door and entered a cavernous lobby.

"May I help you?" a petite redhead with a Peter Pan haircut asked from behind the bell desk.

Men weren't allowed past the lobby of her dorm unless they were signed in and only then if they were escorted. That's because in 1979 a faint whiff of animosity towards men lay just beneath the surface at many all-girl schools courtesy of second wave feminism. It could be intimidating, especially if you were alone, male, and meeting your date for the first time.

As I hovered over the bell desk, I launched what I hoped was a nonthreatening smile.

"I'm here to see Allison Katz."

"Hmm, let's see," she said running her finger down a ledger. "Name?"

"John Geoghegan."

She looked puzzled. "Why are you here?"

"To see Allison Katz."

"Is she expecting you?"

"Yes. We made a date for 3:00."

"Well, you found her," the girl replied, her eyes flashing a challenging look.

"Pardon me?"

"I'm Allie, John. I've been waiting for you."

"Aren't you the bell girl?"

"No," she said laughing. "She's on break. I filled in temporarily to see what you looked like."

"Do I pass?"

65

"You pass," she said grabbing my hand. "Let's get a beer."

I wasn't used to drinking at 3:00 in the afternoon but it seemed a good way to get over my nervousness. Allie took me to a campus bar reserved for alumni, but that didn't stop her. It was the kind of effrontery that appealed to me.

We hit it off immediately. In fact, we had so much in common we couldn't talk fast enough. Born and raised in Pennsylvania, her family had all the trappings of wealth. She'd attended Hotchkiss, summered in Maine, and could swim, sail, and snow ski with the best of them.

Scottish on her mother's side and Dutch on her father's Allie had inherited her mother's coloring. She was tiny with pale skin, strawberry freckles, and bright green eyes. It was the same kind of understated freshness that reminded me of Caroline Kennedy.

I also noticed the hacking jacket she wore - a beautiful piece of tailoring made from a handsome checked material. Most girls on campus wore jeans and a button-down shirt. But Allie's jacket fit so well it had to be custom made. She looked fabulous in it.

What I found most captivating about her, though, was her mischievousness. Allie loved to push boundaries. Small in stature but full of energy, she was as fearless as a giant. And boy, could she drink. I tried matching her, but after half a dozen beers my eyes were floating.

Time flew by that afternoon. Before I knew it, I'd missed the last bus home. When Allie invited me back to her dorm, I accepted her invitation.

Obviously, I was hopeful about where this was going, but I hardly expected her to rip my clothes off once inside her room. I wasn't used to such passion from a "five college" co-ed. For some reason, I found myself dating girls who required an unreasonable amount of effort to convince into bed. Allie, on the other hand, needed no persuading.

That night remains the single greatest moment of unexpected passion in my life, which is a shame given it was 37 years ago. Still, I cherish it.

When I woke up the next morning she was gone.

I wasn't sure what to do. I didn't want to wander the halls looking for her since I was deep in enemy territory. Besides, I had a hangover and no idea where she might be. I didn't even have the courage to use the bathroom.

I was lying in bed thinking of what to do when a knock came at the door. Without waiting for a reply, a girl Allie's age walked in. She was

66

dark haired and pudgy with cupid bow lips. She failed to identify herself but mumbled she was looking for something. Then she began rummaging through Allie's bureau.

In addition to being hungover I now felt self-conscious. I was naked in a strange girl's bed with only a sheet wrapped around me. Nevertheless, the pudgy girl seemed not to mind. In fact, she seemed to be enjoying herself. Finally, after finding a round plastic case that looked like it held a retainer, she left without saying goodbye. An hour later, Allie returned.

"Where did you go?" I asked.

"Downstairs to breakfast."

"A friend of yours stopped by."

"Oh? Who?"

I described the person.

"Oh, that's Lydia. She's always borrowing my diaphragm. She probably wanted to spy on you."

For once, I didn't know what to say.

*** 

Allie and I started seeing each other after that though it was only on weekends and always at her school. Our favorite place to go was a 19th century inn where the bar was filled on Saturday nights with college girls and their dates. So many people jammed in on the weekends it was always loud and hot.

Allie had a habit of disappearing to visit her friends during our dates. I could see she needed freedom, so gave her plenty of it. While she flitted about the bar I developed a friendship with the inn's piano player, a janitor named Artie, who played jazz, rag, and boogie woogie. I got to know Artie well since Allie could be missing for an hour. We'd drink in between sets and talk about our favorite musicians like Noble Sissle and Eubie Blake. I thought Artie a terrific guy.

Allie always kissed me enthusiastically when she returned tasting of Miller Lite and Marlboro cigarettes. She was also a liberal consumer of coffee and once opened her mouth to show me how stained the back of her teeth were. It was an accomplishment of which she was proud and which I found equal parts fascinating and appalling.

As I've said, Allie drank a lot. She not only drank more than I did, she drank more than any girl I'd ever known. I was surprised at first, but since we always ended up in bed, I didn't complain. What I remember most though was not her drinking, but how fantastic sex with her was. Two things were clear: Allie liked to fuck, and she was good at it. She was not only up for anything, she made most of the suggestions. I also appreciated that she could come at the drop of a hat.

Once, after our love making, Allie apologized for blowing me in an awkward position. As a college boy I was happy to get blown at all, but no one had ever apologized about it before. Another thing Allie was fond of was blurting out what people thought but never said. Allie made these confessions with glee. One of her more harmless stories had to do with Lydia, her pudgy friend. She'd told Lydia not to fuck her boyfriend right after anal sex, but Lydia had ignored her advice and now had an infection. OK, that was more than I wanted to know, but once again I found Allie's honesty equal parts fascinating and appalling.

Not long after, Allie told me about the time she and Lydia traveled to Manhattan to visit one of their boyfriends. They'd waited in his duplex, greeting him nude when he returned from work. After that, they all had sex.

Now, mind you, I came from a town where a bisexual mother of three was sleeping with my tennis partners, so I wasn't exactly sheltered. But this was extreme behavior even for me. When Allie let slip that she and the girl down the hall had had an affair without once speaking to one another, I knew something was wrong.

Clearly, Allie was damaged. What else could account for all those crazy stories? Though I found them exciting, they deviated enough from the norm that they concerned me. It also explained why her friends called her "Kat" (short for Katz) when they were being affectionate, and "Alley Kat" or "Kat-tastrophe," when they weren't.

Were all of Allie's stories true? It's possible she was pulling my leg. But the guilelessness of her declarations led me to believe that most were. Besides, I'd be lying if I didn't admit to enjoying her unpredictable-ness. She was fun to hang with, great in bed, and smart as smart could be. But one afternoon, while we were drinking beers on the inn's patio, she said something that shocked me.

It was another beautiful day, this one in November, and the two of us were alone for a change. I was reading a text book while Allie chewed on a plastic coffee stirrer, her green eyes luminous in the afternoon light. I was absolutely crazy about the girl. A pang of emotion ran through me each time I looked at her. Then, halfway through the chapter I was reading, Allie said out of nowhere: "I had sex with my father."

This admission was a magnitude greater than anything I'd heard before. I didn't say anything at first, trying to determine her seriousness. Was she telling the truth? Asking for sympathy? Or just trying to shock me? I watched her chew on the stirrer for a few seconds before responding:

"What do you mean by 'sex'?"

Allie plucked the stirrer from her mouth.

"Oral only," she replied.

"Is it still going on?"

"No." She shrugged then left for the bathroom.

At first I thought she might be making it up. After all, it was an incredible admission even for her. But the offhanded way in which she said it convinced me it was true.

Allie's story would have repelled most people, but I wanted to protect her. If this crazy, exciting, beautiful girl was broken I was sure I could fix her.

As I soon learned, that was the least of my challenges.

# Chapter 16
# Father Knows Best

Allie talked very little about her family, but after that bombshell I needed to know more. That afternoon, I asked about her father.

Harrison Katz was a Republican state operative and small time entrepreneur who always had something going, just never enough money to fund it. An engineer by training, Katz (nee Katzendorf) was a tinkerer at heart. He once built a hovercraft to get across a frozen river in the middle of winter so he could visit their house in Maine. Another time he built an amphibious boat out of a used RV to sail his family down the Mississippi river.

Brash and loud-mouthed, Harry Katz had the hard-used look of a statehouse pol. He was tall and red-faced with a bulbous nose and a personality people found charismatic. From Allie's description he was larger than life in every way except those that mattered: honesty, integrity, and restraint.

Harry Katz had as many deals in the works as he did mechanical projects. Depending on whom you talked to he engaged in real estate deals based on insider information. Was he a crook? It was hard to tell. Allie was vague when she wanted to be. Either she didn't know the details, or wasn't saying. Mostly, I was struck by her admiration.

One of the few photographs Allie ever showed me was taken in the 1960s of her father. It revealed a young married man wearing a white short-sleeved shirt, a bowtie, and a flat-top crew cut that was less than flattering. He appears squinting into the sunlight surrounded by his wife and five children, his teeth clenched in what looks more like a threat than a smile. You couldn't call him handsome. His nose was too big, his size too ungainly. But his bull-like personality made him a force to be reckoned with.

Allie had fond memories of her childhood especially summers spent at the family house in Maine. It was a charming if underfunded life. She'd learned to swim and sail with her siblings, played a mean game

70

of tennis, and burned her Scottish complexion a rosy red. But unpleasant memories mixed in with the good.

The Katz family home, which lacked for upkeep, was one missed payment from foreclosure. In other words, Harry's prosperous business image was a figment of his imagination. If, as Harry liked to boast, a Katzendorf came over on the Mayflower, it was probably as crew. As for modern day Katz's, they lived in genteel poverty. For all I knew, Allie was on a scholarship. As for the hacking jacket (the nicest thing she owned), she swiped it from a roommate.

Harry Katz could be crass. Like LBJ, he enjoyed using the bathroom with the door open, conversing with whoever was nearby. Allie's father also walked around the house naked not caring which of his three daughters saw him. Allie remembered more than once occasion being woken up for school with her father's big, hairy dick dangling in her face. Additionally, Harry Katz didn't tolerate dissent. He was always right. As a result, Allie knocked heads with her father because she was as strong willed as he was.

The other thing Allie said was that her father had a voracious sexual appetite. It was an interesting attribute for a conservative Republican frequently in the public eye, but based on Allie's stories, her father was a satyr. For one, Allie's parents made noisy, unrestrained love every week, usually with the bedroom door open. But this wasn't enough for Harry Katz. He also liked sleeping with his neighbors. At one point, he used a house from one of his real estate deals for assignations. When he wasn't otherwise engaged, Allie said he lent the place to his wife for her own affairs.

I found this news shocking, of course. When I said as much, Allie misunderstood me, saying she wasn't the only family member to witness such behavior. Her oldest brother once peered in the window of their father's love nest only to find an orgy in progress with both their parents in attendance.

Sadly, Harry Katz's sexual appetite extended towards his daughter. One summer when she was nine, Allie was swimming in the ocean when Harry chased her underwater to slip his finger under the elastic of her bathing suit. Allie was reluctant to talk about these events in detail, and I didn't press her. When she did volunteer a story, one thing was clear: her father was a monster.

I couldn't understand why Allie didn't leave home given everything that had happened. My family sentenced relatives to exile for far less crimes. But every time I said something against Harry Katz, she rallied to his defense. For Allie, he was her father first, and her molester second. She found it difficult to condemn him.

Still, I felt protective and pushed her to cut ties. I even talked about her spending Thanksgiving at my home. But you couldn't persuade Allie to do something she didn't want to; she made up her own mind. And so, I let it go.

***

Allie and I continued to see each other, the sex continued being great while her drinking continued to be excessive. Though she wasn't devoted to her studies, Allie could talk intelligently about art, music, and culture. In addition, she was a talented artist and I ended up using her drawings as interstitials for the college magazine I edited. Every weekend spent together filled me with joy.

Then late one night when we were lying in bed, she began telling me a long, convoluted story about her father's lawyer. As I held her in my arms studying the shadows on the ceiling, I tried to understand the point of her tale. It was elliptical at best, which was unusual for her. Eventually, I realized Allie was trying to tell me she was having an affair with her father's lawyer. Suddenly, I had a rival.

Allie had first met Max Hirschfield when he'd come to the house to see her father about a business transaction. Hirsch, as he was known, was involved in one of Harry's real estate schemes, which he was doing his best to keep just-this-side of legal. He was a skinny guy who wore the same kind of oversized glasses Hollywood producers favored in the 70s. With an unruly head of grey hair and an equally unruly beard, he looked like a Tootsie Pop someone had dropped on the floor.

Hirsch was a successful lawyer known for his expertise in contract law. He'd been married twice and was wealthy, which spoke well for his ability to screw his ex-wives out of their equal share. This made him the perfect legal adviser to Harry Katz.

The first time Allie met Hirsch was at home where he was counseling her father. Harry Katz encouraged them to go out to lunch together and though she claimed she didn't like Hirsch at first things moved quickly. That afternoon they became lovers.

I was upset to hear I had a rival. I was even more upset to learn he was still in the picture. Everything Allie had indicated up till then was that she "adored" me. I'd never felt "adored" and returned the feeling. Why then had she taken me to bed when she was involved with somebody else?

I'd accepted Allie's unconventional behavior because I found it titillating, but there were so many things wrong about Allie being sexually involved with her dad and his lawyer I didn't know where to begin. For starters, Max Hirschfield was old enough to be her father. In fact, he was older. How old was he? Well, to put things in perspective, he'd served in World War II.

It didn't take long to figure out Hirsch was the "boyfriend" with the Manhattan apartment where Allie and her girlfriend had their threesome. When I told Allie she shouldn't keep seeing both of us, she refused to pick a winner.

I should have given her up then and there, but I was too far gone. Instead, I defended my turf. I wasn't some old, wrinkly guy who'd dropped bombs on Germany. Sure, he'd been with her first, but I was a peer not an oldster. I was sure Allie would choose me.

It helped that I had reason on my side. I told Allie it was ridiculous for her to date a guy thirty years older. Didn't she worry what people would think? Didn't she know he'd be mistaken for her father, or worse, her grandfather? What kind of life could they make together? It didn't make sense.

Since my college was just a few miles up the road I had the home field advantage. But Allie refused to make a decision. In fact, she stopped talking about Hirsch altogether.

We'd been planning a weekend trip to Connecticut. I viewed it as a coming out party for our relationship. Since I wanted to introduce her to my family, and she wanted to visit her aunt, everything was set.

The morning of our departure I walked to the Greyhound bus station where Allie and I were to meet. An hour after she was due to appear, I found a pay phone and called her dorm room. Allie picked up right away and said in the most casual manner possible that she couldn't go to Connecticut.

"I like you," she said, "I really do. But it isn't fair to Hirsch. I have to stop seeing you."

I was devastated.

Most people would blame me for what happened. I knew Allie was trouble. The stories she'd told would have scared off the most ardent admirer. But I was in love with the girl, not in lieu of her stories but because of them. She wasn't like anyone I'd ever known. She was outrageous, provocative, and insanely exciting. My fault wasn't in loving her it was in not understanding I'd inevitably get burned by the conflagration that was Allison Katz.

I found it impossible to do school work after that. I stopped socializing and spent hours in my dorm room alone. When my twenty-first birthday came, I ignored my friends' invitation and went to dinner alone where I drank an entire bottle of Mouton-Cadet, a red so mediocre even I could tell. For a brief time, I considered dropping out of school.

It was touch and go for a while, but I eventually recovered. By spring I'd met another girl and Allie was securely in my rear view mirror. There's no denying I wore a scar, but I did my best to ignore it.

After that, I avoided anything to do with Allison Katz. It wasn't always easy given her aunt lived nearby. Still, I did my best to inoculate myself against the girl who broke my heart. One thing was clear. I never wanted to see her again.

# Chapter 17
# Reunion

The firewall I erected between Allie and myself lasted thirty years. Despite the information blackout, however, news still slipped through. For example, both her nieces emailed me when Allie's parents died. I soon read about it in the *Washington Post*, but the news only unearthed the feelings I'd kept buried inside, so I didn't contact her.

I'm not sure why I said yes to Allie's email after all those years given the rancor I'd felt. I'd been terribly hurt, but time has a way of rounding off memory's rough edges. What I recalled now was not how much I'd suffered, but how attractive she'd been, how bright, how unconventional, and most of all, how exciting in bed.

How long does heartbreak last anyway? I had no idea, but her email seemed an invitation to find out.

The truth is I was tired of being lonely, I was tired of being poor, and I was tired of being deaf. Worse, the latter seemed my destiny. After all, deafness isn't a head cold that goes away. I was ready to take a chance on reversing at least one of these things.

And now Allie was coming to Woodside!

She offered to stay in a hotel when she visited, but I insisted she stay with me. I told her she could have the kids' bedroom which had its own bath insuring some privacy. It also provided a buffer allowing me to maintain some control over the situation.

\*\*\*

Three days before she arrived, I started cleaning. I vacuumed every room and dusted every surface. I mopped the kitchen floor and removed all the smudge marks from my cabinets and door jambs. Things I'd been meaning to fix for two years suddenly got repaired. I glued back peeling wallpaper, replaced missing light bulbs, and fully stocked the fridge. I also bought a charcoal grill and a string of Japanese lanterns to hang over the patio. I washed the car, had the interior cleaned, and bathed the dog. I mowed the lawn, de-cobwebbed the house, and filled the bird feeders. I even rented a hedge trimmer to tame the bushes.

After three days of hard work I was so exhausted my legs shook. As it turned out, Allie wasn't much of a housekeeper, but it still felt good to get things in order. It was how I'd want to be greeted if I'd visited.

As the day of arrival drew near I started having concerns. One thing I worried about was how Allie would respond to my hearing loss. I'd told her about it, but it's one thing to tell someone you're deaf and quite another for them to experience it firsthand. I knew it could be exhausting for people, so I hoped to limit our activities to places I could hear.

There was also the matter of sex. The last time I'd had it was when my youngest daughter was conceived and that had been at gun point. A Selective Serotonin Reuptake Inhibitor, or SSRI, had something to do with my lack of interest. Still, why should I be concerned about sex when Allie's was a friendly visit? There was no point worrying about romance. I was old, gray, broke, fat, and deaf. Nobody would find me sexy.

The triumph of hope over common sense is never a good strategy. We are optimists at our peril. Still, I planned on taking precautions. I would be guarded at first, and take things slowly. But there are times we want something even when it's not good for us. As proof, I felt anticipation cloud my judgment before Allie even arrived. If I wasn't careful, I might get into trouble.

\*\*\*

Allie's flight was due at 9:00pm and since it was a Sunday night the airport was deserted. When I arrived, the outbound counters were closed and the concourse darkened. I'd traveled SFO so many times I knew exactly where Allie would have to pass. My only company was a girl in her 20s and a bored limo driver holding a sign. Otherwise, I was alone.

Plopping down on a black-ribbed bench I looked at my watch. I was 45 minutes early and nervous. I tried tamping down my excitement but could feel jumpiness taking over. With nothing to distract me, I needed to talk. When I made eye contact with the girl opposite I began spilling my guts.

"I'm meeting an old girlfriend tonight I haven't seen in 35 years."

"Oh?" she said, barely interested.

"I'm incredibly nervous."

She smiled weakly. "I'm meeting my husband."

I'd have liked to talk more but the woman wasn't interested. A few minutes later, people began trickling down the escalator. Shortly thereafter my phone lit up. It was Allie texting to say she'd landed and was walking towards baggage claim.

People tend to blend together in airports. I wondered whether I'd recognize her. But once she came into view I had no trouble spotting her.

I was unimpressed at first. Her manner seemed stilted, her clothes unattractive. When I took a closer look I could see she was wearing shapeless cargo pants, a black shirt with a bright pattern, and a pair of ugly sandals.

*God, are those Birkenstocks?* I wondered.

I knew people dressed for comfort when traveling, but I preferred dressing up. Nothing less than a Joseph Abboud blazer and a pair of Gucci loafers would do.

The expression on Allie's face also seemed off. Though she denied it, I could tell she was nervous. Her eyes were buggy and her smile uncertain. We hugged briefly at the foot of the escalator before I guided her to the baggage carousel. As we made uncomfortable small talk, I judged her ruthlessly.

Allie was never one for make up. She wore a little eyeliner and some lipstick, but that was it. Her Scottish complexion was lovely though. She still had her marvelous freckles and bright green eyes. She was a bit heavier but not grossly so. Since I'd also put on weight, I wasn't complaining. Overall, I had no trouble recognizing the girl I'd once fallen in love with, but how else had she changed?

We didn't get home until well past ten, which was one in the morning her time. I gave Allie a brief tour of the house and introduced her to my dog. When we finally reached the kids' room I poked my head inside. It was a comfortable enough room with twin beds, a large window, and a big closet. Since I'd removed all the kids' stuff it was ideal for a guest. Allie took one look at the twin beds though, and made a demurring sound.

"Can't I sleep with you?"

I was taken aback.

We'd already agreed on the sleeping arrangements. Additionally, I'd invoked the "no sex rule" suggesting we forego sex in the interest of getting to know each other. I wasn't hiding anything. I'd told Allie I hadn't had sex in a decade. In addition to providing context, it seemed a good way to control the situation. But I'm a people pleaser; it's hard to say no, so when she made her request I caved on the spot - so much for maintaining my distance.

Allie gave me a relieved smile and excused herself to change in the guest bedroom. And so I fell asleep spooning my college girlfriend whom I hadn't slept next to for 35 years. As my eyes grew heavy, I kept thinking how life, after being so difficult for so long, could change so quickly.

I was nothing but grateful.

# Chapter 18
# The Morning After

When I awoke the next morning Allie was up, dressed, and drinking coffee on the patio. She'd stuck three slender incense sticks in one of my potted succulents. Their calming scent permeated the morning air. Looking up from her iPad she smiled and said:

"Sleep well?"

"Very. You?"

"Oh, yes," she nodded.

"It's the first time in years I've slept next to a creature that didn't have four legs."

She laughed.

It was a lovely California day. An azure sky stretched overhead, and the light was so clear it seemed to magnify the pink naked lady flowers that dotted the meadow. I had no idea whether Allie and I had anything in common, but I noted with pleasure she was reading the *New York Times* on her iPad. This instantly made me feel close to her. It wasn't just the newspaper though, Allie was intellectually curious in ways I easily warmed to. I soon learned we were both collectors, whether it was cigar boxes, aviation-themed postage stamps, or Russian party badges. Allie had not only read Benvenuto Cellini's autobiography, one of my favorites, we'd read the same silly book about canine cognition. The coincidence seemed propitious.

I'd spent my entire life wondering whether I'd ever meet someone who loved books as much as I did. We didn't just love the same books, however, we were united by a love of art, movies, African masks and too many other interests to include here. For example, we both loved Andrew Goldsworthy, but even when there was something one of us knew that the other didn't, we soon fell in love with it, too.

Allie had taken up textiles after college before settling on painting. She was serious about her work and practiced it regularly. When she spent too much time away from her easel she complained it made her crabby.

I knew that first day Allie was my equal in many things, and probably my superior. She not only matched my enthusiasms, but had quite a few of her own. She was articulate, clever, funny, and learned; the best combination of brain-swelling opiates.

It helped that we were from the same tribe: east coast WASPs who'd attended prep-school and a small, liberal arts, college. But there was more to it than that. Time and again I felt our connection solidify despite thirty years of separation. Clearly, we were alike. Put another way, conversation never felt so good.

***

I knew the two biggest impediments to a successful visit were my hearing and lack of money. Miraculously, payment for an article I'd written arrived from a magazine just before Allie came. This provided enough cash to make her visit successful. My hearing was another story.

When Allie arrived, I'd "Mirandized" her about my hearing loss. Like most people, she didn't get it at first. She was sympathetic, but continued speaking quickly, turned her head away when talking, and favored conversation in noisy places. Our enthusiasm for each other bridged the gap, but I found myself "fake" understanding her more than I liked.

Since Allie was new to the bay area I drew up a list of activities. This list soon fell by the wayside, however, as we preferred spending our first two days doing nothing but talking. Since Allie fought jet lag we got into the habit (at her suggestion) of napping together in the heat of the afternoon. When we woke up we'd talk some more.

At night, I lovingly prepared meals which we ate outside under the Japanese lanterns. Afterwards we'd stay up late watching movies one of us insisted the other had to see. We didn't leave the house once.

Though I enjoyed time with Allie, I was still on the fence about romance. She lived in Pennsylvania, I in California. That alone made a relationship impractical. Plus, I had two small children who weren't receptive to sharing their father.

I sensed Allie was interested in sex, but I did nothing more than hold her in bed. In fact, I reveled in our uncomplicated intimacy that sleeping next to one another provided. "Go slow" was my watchword. I was pleased when we got through the first few days without anything happening.

On the third day I decided we'd spent enough time at home and took Allie to Santa Cruz. Santa Cruz was a moderately-sized, hippy town with a lovely beach, a seedy boardwalk, and enough vegetarian restaurants to keep her happy. And since it was only an hour's drive from Woodside, it was no big deal if she didn't like it.

We drove the length of Silicon Valley then over the Santa Cruz mountains down towards the Pacific Ocean. After lunch at an Indian restaurant I suggested a walk along the beach. It was a warm day; the tide was high and the ocean calm. We'd taken our shoes off to walk along the water's edge and were engaged in conversation when two black-skinned dolphins surfaced a few feet away. As they swam along the shoreline, their dorsal fins rising in unison, it seemed as if they were following us. Overcome by the magic of the moment I reached for Allie's hand. That afternoon we made love for the first time.

Middle-aged sex is potentially embarrassing. After all, our bodies aren't what they were in college. We had wrinkles, age spots, and sags in the all wrong places. I was hardly an Adonis, but my biggest concern was whether I could perform after so many years of abstinence. Twelve years without intimacy, without kissing or touching another human, is solitary confinement for emotions. I had no idea what would happen once I emerged from my cell.

Making love to a woman 35 years after you first consummated the relationship is not an everyday occurrence. Nor had I ever encountered a middle-aged woman's body. I wasn't sure what to expect. Would it be sexy, or a turn off?

As it turned out, I had nothing to fear. Yes, Allie's shoulders were more rounded, and there was a thickening to her waist and heaviness to her bottom that hadn't been there in college. But that made no difference. I found myself as aroused by her as I had been in school.

There are few things more exhilarating in life than a freshly waxed pussy. Allie's bare-naked vulva enchanted me so I felt like thanking God. When I asked why she shaved, her reply was to pick an imaginary hair from the tip of her tongue. Once again, her brazenness was enthralling.

After we made love, Allie announced she wanted to take a shower before dinner. She'd never been self-conscious about her nakedness, a trait I found attractive. As she walked nude down the hallway she was clearly no longer the college girl I'd once pursued. Hers was the body of a woman who'd borne three sons and hadn't run a marathon in longer than she claimed. I asked myself, watching her, whether I could love a body like this? The answer was yes. Undeniably, yes.

That night after dinner we made love again. When we finished, we lay quietly for a time then Allie bolted upright and looked at me.

"You're everything I hoped you would be."

I smiled.

"No, you're not hearing me, John. I love you and want us to spend the rest of our life together."

Then, leaning down and speaking into my good ear, she added, "I'm going to move to California to live with you. Let's get married."

It's the only time I can remember wishing I was deaf.

# Chapter 19
## Allie's Confession

I have to admit I found this development alarming. As much as I appreciated Allie (and enjoyed our sex), I was not ready for her to move across country, share my living quarters, and get married. And yet her visit was so invigorating I couldn't blow the whistle. If anything, I was seduced by this woman. Still, someone other than me was dictating my future - the same set of circumstances that led to my disastrous marriage. Alarm bells were sounding.

Love is an altered state, the DUI on the highway of life, the one trip you never get ticketed for but probably should. Allie had that effect on me. She was bewitching. But what I was getting into?

There's no doubt I was attracted to Allison Katz; her intellect and sex appeal were overwhelming. But our shared history was also attractive. She first appeared at a time in my life when I was brimming with confidence. I hadn't felt that way in years. Now, just having her in Woodside goosed my optimism. And if I was being honest, I saw Allie as the means to rescue myself from a harrowing life.

Her visit had its share of warning signs. The day after she proposed, we took a drive up the California coast. Something about the day made me giddy. Maybe it was the previous night's lovemaking, or the two lane road on which I was driving too fast as it snaked along the cliff tops. The setting, both beautiful and dangerous, overlooked the Pacific. It was the perfect place for truth telling.

Normally, people's stories come slowly, but Allie's tumbled out all at once. It was as if she were under a deadline to confess. She began with her marriage to Hirsch.

"You were right, you know."

"Right about what?" I asked.

"I should never have married Hirsch. He was much too old."

As I navigated the windy road, Allie reached into her purse to produce a picture of her wedding day. The photo was candid: creased, unfocused, and bleached of color. Everything about it from the couple's age disparity to the space between them appeared awkward. Bereft of wedding finery Hirsch wore a solid color business suit, Allie, a salmon-colored linen jacket. They didn't even look dressed for the occasion.

"It's the only picture taken of the reception," Allie said, showing the photo as if it were proof no one blessed the match.

If true, it was sad, but I understood why. There was something perverse about this geriatric-ally thin, World War II vet marrying a fresh-faced young woman days after her college graduation.

That first year of marriage, Hirsch took his bride to Plato's Retreat, the notorious sex club in the basement of Manhattan's Ansonia Hotel. I could just imagine Hirsch encouraging Allie to join the writhing, overweight bodies of the "bridge and tunnel" crowd. The thought sickened me.

It also turned out Hirsch rented his duplex for porn shoots, something he'd failed to tell Allie before they were married. While Hirsch went to work some adult starlet was getting nailed on camera in his kitchen. The thing Hirsch loved most about it, according to Allie, was how his duplex made money for him. Of course, he wasn't the one who had to navigate the power cords and arc lights when making lunch, as Allie did. He ate at his office.

The situation wasn't all bad. The happiest time was after they had children and spent summers on the family island in Maine. From Memorial to Labor Day Allie supervised her two young sons as they spent lazy, sun-drenched mornings swimming in the Atlantic. In the afternoon, she'd tootle them to town in her 1938, triple cockpit Chris Craft. Evenings were spent eating ice cream with her boys and watching the stars before tucking them into bed.

One thing I couldn't understand was why Allie chose to live on the same island as her father. Why live next door to Harry Katz, the man who molested her, the man with whom she continued to have dust ups? It didn't make sense. But that was Allie. Things didn't always make sense.

As their sons approached adolescence, Hirsch stopped going to Maine, electing to spend summers in the city saying he needed to work. Allie knew she'd married a sexually voracious man. On more than one occasion she'd found evidence of a girlfriend. She even suspected Hirsch visited prostitutes. But she always turned a blind eye. Trapped on an island with her father in the summer, Allie spent winters in

84

Manhattan with her emotionally neglectful husband. That's when she began to drink.

As we sped along the Pacific coast Allie talked a mile a minute. I couldn't hear everything she said. To do that I'd have to take my eyes off the road to read her lips. Given the drive was treacherous that wasn't a good idea.

I may not have caught all the details but I heard enough to know Allie's life had been one disaster after another. After marrying Hirsch, she had both her boys in quick succession. Not long after, Hirsch was diagnosed with late stage esophageal cancer. After a series of horrific operations from which he was not expected to recover, Hirsh surprised everyone by living. The surgeons had not only removed the tumor, however, they took most of his vocal chords with it. In their place, they implanted a trache which was an ugly piece of plastic that had to be cleaned after every meal. On top it, Hirsch was rendered mute.

Wiping some old guy's trache while raising two boys under 10 seemed a high price to pay for youthful misjudgment. Of course, no one regrets being told he was right, but I felt sorry for her.

After Hirsch's miraculously recovery, they sold his duplex and moved to Pennsylvania. Once again, they moved to the same town Allie's parents lived in. I'd have expected her to steer clear. Instead, she seemed trapped in her father's orbit.

Obviously, Hirsch was no prize, but he was a successful attorney who earned big money. And Allie could be difficult, too. Every weekday she woke at 6:00am to drive her boys to a Quaker school while nursing a hangover from the previous night's binge. The rest of the day she spent working on her loom until cocktail hour, which lasted until bed. Within a year, she was a raging alcoholic.

Hirsch's law practice continued to grow despite his disability. He carried a small whiteboard around with him to write down what he wanted to say. As his absences grew longer, their marriage began to crumble. By then, Allie was angry: angry because Hirsch never came home, angry because he ignored her when he did, and angry for his undermining her with the children.

Allie was never one to let anger go. Once, she got so mad she pried the lock off Hirsch's wine cabinet and smashed every bottle of his prized collection save the two she drank immediately afterwards. And Allie had her own affairs as well. Once, she fucked the father of a boy she carpooled to school with, telling me they'd pulled off the road one winter's morning to do it in his car.

"It only happened once," she said by way of defense. Then giggling, "Well, maybe twice."

A lot of things were "maybe twice" with Allie. For example, it was clear even in college she had a drinking problem. As her marriage worsened, her reliance on booze and benzos grew worse. Allie was fuzzy how long this period lasted, but she eventually became so erratic she checked herself into rehab.

When Hirsch found out, he was furious. A drunk wife is easier to control than a sober one, so when her insurance ran out he refused to pay for further treatment.

Finally, after fifteen years of marriage, Allie told Hirsch she wanted a divorce. She was so desperate to exit the relationship she waived all claim to his assets. This turned out to be a mistake because over the years Hirsch had accumulated tens of millions of dollars without her knowing.

"How did you manage to leave with nothing?" I asked.

"All I wanted was my freedom," she replied.

Other than a brief internship at Conde Nast, Allie had never worked a day in her life. If it was true she'd left the marriage with nothing, she was honorable if misguided. Still, you had to wonder where her money came from. She clearly wasn't poor. Her kids were not so lucky.

Her two eldest sons had been easy to handle when young, but their wheels came off as teenagers. Herb, her oldest, was drinking and doping by 14, eventually graduating to harder drugs. Allie, who was deep in her own addiction, didn't realize what was going on. When she finally woke up, she kicked him out of the house.

If Herb graduated High School it was by the skin of his teeth, and he never went to college. Instead, he spent the next fifteen years on the streets of Philadelphia shooting heroin. Five times Allie took him to rehab and each time he relapsed. He was currently in jail for a parole violation. It was his third time in the clink.

Unfortunately, her middle son, Saul, wasn't faring much better. Saul was a chef as well as a binge drinker who had trouble holding a job. Nor did it help that he gambled all the time. Allie helped him more than once, but it was unclear whether Saul would ever get better.

The one thing you could be sure of with Allie is that whatever story she told she had a better one to top it. In this case, she saved the best for last, directing me to pull into a scenic overlook so I could listen.

After Hirsch's recovery from throat cancer he insisted on having another child. It probably wasn't a good idea given how the first two turned out, but that never stopped anyone. Against all odds, their third son, Oscar, was a superstar. Despite being on the spectrum he'd done well enough in college to earn a Fulbright.

I could tell Oscar was Allie's favorite. She'd spent so much time helping her son with his autism they were extraordinarily tight. As for her other boys, well, no mother gives up on their children, but she was close.

Allie paused while looking out the windshield at the glittering Pacific below. Meanwhile, the ocean breeze wreaked havoc with my hearing aids. I didn't realize she'd spoken until I saw her expectant look.

"Did I miss something?"

"Oscar is George's."

"What?"

"That's what I'm trying to tell you. Oscar isn't Hirsch's son, he's George's."

"Who's George?"

As it turned out, Oscar was the product of a ten year affair Allie had been having with the caretaker of her Maine house. George lived on the mainland with his mother and did odd jobs for families in the area. Though Allie said she'd never loved him, she'd slept with him for nearly a decade while still being married to Hirsch.

"Are you sure about this?"

"Yes, I'm sure."

"Have you done a DNA test?"

"I don't need to. Oscar looks exactly like George."

The incredible thing was Allie had never told her husband that Oscar wasn't his son. Nor did Oscar know who his real father was.

"What are you waiting for?" I asked. "Oscar's 26!"

"But Hirsch is Oscar's dad," Allie insisted. "He may not be his biological father, but he was the one present all of Oscar's life."

Since it was Allie's secret to keep I let it drop. Nevertheless, it was a shocking revelation.

Allie's insistence on telling me every awful thing that had ever happened to her surprised me. Was she bragging, making a clean slate, or giving me fair warning? I couldn't tell. Her stories often contained alarm bells, though that's not how I viewed them at the time. If anything, I felt protective. Any time she talked about someone hurting her, whether it was her husband, her father, her family, or a friend, I became infuriated. If that's not love, I don't know what it is; foolishness perhaps. Sometimes they're the same.

Most people would have been put off by Allie's confession, but me? I was fascinated. Her outlandishness may not have been healthy, but it was impossible to resist. When most people would have run for the hills, I dove straight in. I don't know what that says about me; probably nothing good.

# Chapter 20
# Twin Rivers

After a five day visit, Allie returned to Pennsylvania, but not before insisting I make an airline reservation to visit her - something I wasn't sure I wanted to do. Hoping to avoid any awkwardness, I booked the flight for October thinking it would buy me enough time to figure out what I wanted.

Allie had stirred up such a snow globe of emotions I was afraid to make a decision. On the one hand, she offered a way out of my dilemma. Partnering with her would blast me out of my rut and put me on a path toward love and companionship. But these things hadn't worked for me in the past. Why did I think it would be any better with Allie? There was also the matter of her history. The very thing that made her exciting also made her trouble. It wasn't a question of whether I'd enjoy the ride; it was more like: could I survive it?

By the time October rolled around I had talked myself into going. It wasn't a hard decision. Distance not only promotes desire it mutes apprehension. If I'm being honest, I couldn't believe my luck. Allie was the kind of third-act-save that only happens in the movies. I'd spent too many days alone to pass up this chance. Together we could turn things around for the both of us.

*** 

Twin Rivers, PA, as you might expect, is located at the confluence of two rivers one of which borders New Jersey. An industrial force during the 19th century, the town had since fallen on hard times. But Twin Rivers was not without charm. Many of its red brick factories remained intact, and the blast furnace of a now defunct steel mill had been turned into the centerpiece of a beautiful park. Still, Twin Rivers was like many mill towns that once depended on water for commerce but now only drank it. It had seen better times.

89

It was unseasonably warm when I arrived. The leaves remained stubbornly glued to the trees and the air was humid and sticky. Allie had lived in Twin Rivers for almost two decades; she'd raised three boys there. Her parents' house was only a few miles away; Hirsch, one town over.

Allie's house was on a bluff overlooking the river. Only a few blocks from a small liberal arts college, her neighborhood had cachet. She owned the building she lived in. It had been a single family home in the 1920s, but had since been converted into apartments. Allie's apartment on the south side of the building took up two floors. Custom made to her specifications it had a comfortable, artsy feel.

The big social event in Twin Rivers was the Saturday farmers market. The town center was closed to traffic so vendors could set up their tents around the civil war monument. People came from all over to buy hand-stitched pillows and homemade jelly. But mainly, they came to socialize. Allie gave me a tour of the market and even showed me a few of the local sights. Most of the time, however, we spent having sex.

Sex was important to Allie. As she told me on more than one occasion, she liked it "with all the trimmings." I saw sex as an expression of love more than a daily requirement. A partner was nice, but an intellectual equal was what I craved, especially since I was back on Lexapro. I underestimated the importance of sex to Allie, though. She needed someone to accommodate her needs, which were substantial.

For example, we fucked nine times within one twenty-four hour period: three in the morning, three in the afternoon, and three before bed. I'd never had so much sex in my life. Since I was taking Lexapro I could screw all day because the drug stopped me from coming. Later, I'd wonder whether sex was the primary reason Allie entered into a relationship, but that didn't concern me then. Twelve years of pent up desire had left me with my own needs. I enjoyed the banquet.

The amazing thing about Allie was she truly loved sex. She knew what she liked and wasn't afraid to ask for it. According to her, the best part was looking, but there were plenty of other things she enjoyed that didn't require eyesight. I'd been too shy to look much in the past, but Allie's lack of self-consciousness soon had me staring.

Allie had a wonderful way of disinhibiting you. My obsession with her rump illustrates this. Allie's ass was so plush, the curvature of its muscles so divine, it drove me wild with desire. I might have ignored this feature in the past, but one day for no good reason other than I felt like it I flipped her on her stomach and began licking from the top of her neck to the dimples below her spine. Upon reaching her bottom, I found myself so overcome I gently parted her blushing cheeks and plunged my tongue deep into her anus. This was not a part of the female anatomy I'd previously explored but her moans reassured me I was on the right track.

If I'd only done it once it would have been an anomaly, but there was something about Allie's ass that attracted me. She also liked to experiment. In fact, she encouraged it. I resisted at first, but gradually lowered my guard. Finally, I surrendered to the siren call and happily lapped her downy crevice whenever I felt. I might have found it shameful had I not been under her spell.

Allie didn't just like sex, though, she appreciated men. She loved their smell, the taste of their sweat, and the way she could make their cocks bloom. She was in fact one of the few women I knew who truly enjoyed fellatio. I had no difficulty telling the difference between someone going through the motions and an enthusiast. In Allie's case, she relished the task.

What made Allie's blowjobs so great was that there was no faking her interest. It was the first thing she gave when she climbed into bed and truly seemed to enjoy it. Just watching her eyelids flutter when between my legs and her cheeks hollowed out was enough to make me come. In terms of tradecraft, she knew how to apply just the right amount of moisture versus suction. But it wasn't technique that made her extraordinary, it was conviction. Taking me into her mouth seemed to satisfy a hunger I didn't know a woman could have. It required every ounce of willpower not to release the very thing she was trying to coax out of me.

One afternoon after strenuous love making I asked Allie about it. She said she'd always liked going down on a man and couldn't understand why some women didn't. By way of explanation, she mentioned her book club where, fueled by high capacity wine consumption, the topic of blowjobs came up. The consensus, according to Allie, was that most women in the group felt they were a necessary evil. One woman denied giving any at all. Allie couldn't believe it.

The truth is Allie was all boy. She wasn't afraid to scratch a back, pop a pimple, pull a splinter, or dig a squamous cell out of your shoulder. She'd even flash her gold tooth at the least provocation. Raising three sons had something to do with it. Neither blood nor bugs bothered her. As a result, she could apply hemorrhoid cream to her dog's butthole without batting an eyelash.

The first time Allie changed clothes in front of me I was surprised. She did it with no more modesty than a football player in a locker room. I found it thrilling. Still, I admired her boy-like qualities, especially after a wife who practically threw up when she saw a spider.

There are bound to be awkward moments when two people get to know each other. Every time Allie and I made love she had a habit of cradling my head in a way that made my hearing aids squeal. I assumed she'd figure things out and stop doing it, but she never did. And so every time we made love I accommodated myself to the sound of feedback. There were worse tradeoffs.

One thing Allie enjoyed was being tied up, but I grew uncomfortable when she asked if there was anything I'd like to do.

"I'll do anything," she said. "I even tolerate pain pretty well."

Since I was still orienting myself to her body, I wasn't ready to graduate to the advanced course. Still, Allie insisted. Twice she asked what kind of pornography I liked. Porn tends to gross me out, so I wasn't keen on her suggestion. But when it comes to sex, if somebody asks more than once whether you like something it means they do even if you don't. Still, we had no trouble finding common ground. That is until I learned about the Pocket Rocket.

One of the things I liked about Allie was she knew what got her off. But one afternoon during rigorous intercourse she was having trouble achieving an orgasm. Finally, too exasperated to continue, she sat up in bed, shook her head, and said:

"I need the Pocket Rocket."

"What's that?" I asked.

"My vibrator."

"Well, get it."

"I can't," she replied. "It's broken."

I know many women have to work harder than men to achieve orgasm. It hardly seems fair. But I didn't bank on us having to get dressed, hop into her car, and hot-foot it to the nearest adult store.

The adult store in Twin Rivers is, according to its billboard, "conveniently located with plenty of free parking." Housed in a single story brick building, its vast open space looked like a party store. I could tell it wasn't Allie's first time there because she made a bee-line straight to the vibrators. It wouldn't have surprised me if she had a discount card, too.

As it turns out, the Pocket Rocket is a modest looking device despite its name. Four inches tall and made of plastic, it looks more like an inhaler than a you-know-what. After a purchase that included batteries we returned home.

I'm no expert on post-menopausal women but Allie explained she sometimes required supplemental lubrication. Her favorite type was a brand of sesame oil that not only smelled good but made things delightfully slick. After a few days of her deft ministrations just seeing her approach with that distinctively shaped bottle made my dick unfurl like a noise maker on New Year's Eve.

The first thing I noticed about the Pocket Rocket was it sounded like an electric razor. Its tinny buzzing was more annoying than sexy. What was more bizarre was watching Allie work the thing. Looking may be half the fun, but this intimacy seemed best left under the sheets. Still, I tried getting with the program.

What I didn't count on was Allie having trouble keeping her Pocket Rocket steady. Though she insisted there was room enough for both of us down there, she became so disabled by pleasure her hand would slip, shocking my dick with the Pocket Rocket like it was a joy buzzer.

They say crazy girls fuck best. This may be unkind, but experience suggests there's more than a bit of truth to that old chestnut. Needless to say I got shocked all week.

\*\*\*

It was hard sometimes to know where the boundaries lay with Allie. You could even be forgiven for thinking there weren't any, but that wasn't the case.

One night, while sitting naked in her dining room Allie told me a story from her adolescence. She was thirteen, her sister two years older. They were both home from school making peanut butter sandwiches when they began speculating what cunnilingus felt like. It's unclear whose idea it was, but when Boomer, their black lab, bounded into the kitchen, the sisters conducted an experiment. After arguing over who would go first, they took turns slathering their nether parts with peanut butter and lying on the floor where they laughingly narrated what it felt to have Boomer lick them clean.

Now if that's not a boundary-less story what is? Allie laughed when she told it, whether at its outrageousness or my reaction I'm not sure. Still, I didn't have a story close to matching it. If I did, I'd never have shared it. That wasn't Allie, though. She shared everything even when she shouldn't.

And yet, two weeks previously, I'd run smack into a boundary so firm it felt like a brick wall. It began with my wanting to send her a photo showing how I felt. Admittedly, I was taking a chance. It wasn't the type of photo I'd normally send, and no, it wasn't a dick pic, or at least it wasn't a picture of my dick.

I'd spent a lot of time searching for just the right photo on the Internet. It had to be tasteful not smutty or crass. I eventually found what I was looking for: a picture of a chiseled Adonis, sitting tan and naked by a swimming pool. The photo was taken from behind so his face was obscured, but there was no mistaking what was happening. His back was arched in ecstasy while a single, luminous strand of semen shot into the void. It wasn't only sexy, it was artful. It was also in keeping with Allie's desire to loosen my inhibitions. Besides, this was a girl who watched pornography. I thought she'd be flattered.

I texted the picture along with a caption which said: *This is how you make me feel.* But her response was disappointing.

"Sorry. I don't go for homo-erotic photos."

It felt like a slap in the face. Besides, I had no idea it was homosexual.

Obviously, Allie had boundaries. I just didn't know where they were.

\*\*\*

When it comes to love the willing suspension of disbelief is sometimes necessary. What really tested me though was Allie's anchor tattoo. I don't care for tattoos in general even if they're meant to be ironic. Hers wasn't even professionally done. It was so blurry and poorly drawn it looked amateurish. She offered to have it removed, but I had no right making such a demand. It was her body to do with as she pleased, so I declined the offer. At the very least, I hoped it made me a better boyfriend.

Later that week I discovered Allie's second tattoo. Yet again we were engaged in rigorous sex. This time I was on top, Allie on the bottom. We were practicing holding each other's stare when I sensed I was about to have one of my rare, eye-rolling orgasms. As I approached the point of no return, Allie began tugging on her bottom lip. I didn't understand what she was doing until I saw the name "John" stenciled on the inside of her lip. I was so close to coming I didn't want to stop but I did slow down enough to ask:

"Is that MY name on your lip?"

"No," she said laughing. "John was my second husband."

*SECOND husband?*

As usual, Allie was full of surprises.

*** 

Sex with Allie was an experience I found both novel and exciting. I didn't stop to consider these might be well rehearsed routines refined on a variety of men. I thought they were just for me. Perhaps I was naïve but I happily submitted, unaware how worn the groove might be. This is what they mean by love is blind.

To be clear, Allie showed her affection in more ways than sucking my tonsils out through my urethra. She not only bought my favorite coffee, she purchased the same French press I used at home. She also made the kind of breakfast I liked: scrambled eggs and bacon even though she was a vegetarian. The first time I realized how much she wanted to please me was when I found a volume on Andrew Goldsworthy in her library. This was the same Andrew Goldsworthy I'd brought to her attention when she visited Woodside. I didn't know at the time she knew exactly who Andrew Goldsworthy was; she just

95

didn't want to spoil my fun in explaining him to her. I was touched by her discretion.

Still, Allie had her foibles.

As I've suggested, she was the worst dressed woman I'd ever met. I'd never seen anyone handicapped in quite this way. To her credit, she knew she had a problem and invited me to fix it. Once again, I was not willing to admit a flaw this early in the relationship. Besides, it was who she was. I thought it best to leave her alone.

Allie's decorating instincts were also dubious. A person's home says a lot about them, and Allie's looked like Pee Wee's Playhouse. She may have loved textiles but she had no sense of color, pattern, or design. This was explained by some weird eye condition that made her see colors differently than most people - not unheard of in an artist. But nothing could explain her shag rug that looked like a dog's breakfast. It was memorably ugly.

My biggest challenge turned out to be Allie's paintings. I might have been able to overlook her taste in decor, but there was no way I could ignore her oil paintings. They were an essential part of her.

The truth was Allie needed to paint. It helped keep her sane. If she missed a day, she felt uneasy. I admired her discipline and appreciated her productivity. The problem was her paintings weren't very good. She favored life-sized portraitures in a blocky style reminiscent of cubism. Her colors were muted, her drawing skills weak, the expression of her sitters vacant. I also noticed several male nudes in her portfolio, but chose to ignore them.

I didn't tell Allie how I felt about her work. In fact, I did the opposite. I paid close attention. I pointed out what I liked, and made suggestions where I thought something could be enhanced. But mostly I asked about the choices she made when painting. In other words, I let her do the talking. The last thing I wanted was to hurt her feelings in any way.

Though they were devoid of talent Allie's paintings made me realize I'd fallen in love with her. Her ridiculous clothes, lamentable decorating, and peanut butter memories were trivial things. They could be accommodated. What mattered was loving Allie in spite of her flaws. What difference did it make that she couldn't paint if it gave her joy? What mattered was loving her unconditionally.

Still, unconditional love can be dangerous. For Allie to want to marry me after two days would strike most people as intemperate. It wasn't Allie's impulsiveness that scared me, though. On the contrary, it made me love her all the more. I'd made the mistake of thinking I could fix her in college. Now, I knew better. All I wanted was to care for her. That was what she needed, so that was my plan.

The only time I saw her falter during my visit was one afternoon after she received a package in the mail. It was a picture book her older sister had put together celebrating their parents' life. Allie looked at the cover for a moment then turned the book over to the picture on the back. It showed her mother and father toasting each other with glasses of champagne as they motored into the sunset in a beautiful wooden boat. Allie quietly looked at this image for a moment before walking outside and depositing the book in the bin at the end of her driveway. It was the closest I'd seen her come to admitting the damage her father had done.

The next day, lying in bed, my dick still twitching, Allie lifted her head from my chest and whispered in my good ear:

"There are four things I love about you, John: your nose, your eyelashes, your brain, and your cock."

I breathed a sigh of contentment. Were there four sweeter compliments in the world? I doubt it.

# Chapter 21
## Scene of the Crime

How we managed any day trips with all that fucking I'll never know but we did squeeze in a few.

One morning, we drove to N.C. Wyeth's house in Chadds Ford, Pennsylvania. Wyeth was a popular children's book illustrator in the 20s and 30s. Many of his images were indelibly stuck in my head. His house was colonial in style, similar to the one I'd grown up in, with low ceilings and a dark wood interior that made me feel right at home. We also visited his artist's studio. His antique collection of sabers, cutlasses and muskets made it easy to imagine him painting the pirates in *Treasure Island*.

The thing I'd forgotten about the east coast is how crowded with history it is. On the way home we drove past the place where General George Washington almost lost the Revolutionary War. The Battle of Brandywine is yet another thing they don't teach you in school, or if they do, I don't remember it. Other than a rough winter at Valley Forge, the father of our nation seemed invincible. Who knew he'd almost blown it all at Brandywine?

On the nights when we weren't otherwise engaged, Allie and I stayed up late watching movies. One film that stayed with me was *Stories We Tell*, a documentary about Sarah Polly's search for her biological father. I kept wondering how Allie's son, Oscar, would respond to the news of his real dad. Despite its subject matter, the movie didn't make Allie uncomfortable. That in itself made me wonder.

Allie also planned a ride on the Lehigh Valley Railroad (LVRR). I tried keeping my love of trains under the radar. You lose all credibility the minute people know you're a "foamer." But Allie had sniffed it out when visiting Woodside and not only accepted it, but graciously fed the beast.

In its heyday, the LVRR had been a profitable railroad transporting coal from Pennsylvania to the industrial centers of New England. Now a modest non-profit with limited rolling stock, it barely squeaked by as a tourist attraction. Still, it was a lovely layout and I liked the fact Allie had ridden it as a child. Regrettably, the steam engine wasn't running that day, but they did have an F unit whose porthole headlight and snub-nosed hood appealed to me.

But the highlight of the day wasn't the train; it was the bus full of Mennonite women that pulled up right before our departure. There were twenty in all, each wearing a pastel-colored bonnet and homespun dress that reached their ankles. The F unit may have been from the 40s, but the Mennonites were a century earlier. I watched in fascination as they clustered on the platform.

If there's anything better than doing stuff with the woman you love I don't know what it is. I was having so much fun visiting Allie I extended my stay a few extra days even though it cost money I didn't have. So much oxytocin flooded my brain I never wanted to leave. I just couldn't get enough of her.

\*\*\*

As we drove around Twin Rivers, Allie talked about the psychiatrist she was seeing. She'd been going to him for more than a decade, and spoke in glowing terms. From what I could tell, Dr. Ivankovich had a moderating influence on her. He was the one who walked her back from marrying me right away. Though he relented in letting her move to California he insisted she live separately until she saw how things worked out. I was relieved when told of the change.

That Allie saw a therapist was not just a good idea, it was a necessity. Love can only go so far in healing a troubled past. I was all for her seeking professional help. But the more she talked about Ivankovich, the more I wondered who this Svengali was that held such sway over her.

Allie saw him once a week, sometimes twice, with the occasional Skype session on an as needed basis. That seemed like a lot, but since Allie credited him for keeping her stable I accepted it without question.

You didn't have to know Allie long to realize she was troubled. Heck, half the time she'd tell you herself. But it took me longer than it should have to understand Allie was always at war with someone.

Whether it was her father, her ex-husband, her children, or her neighbors, she was always in some sort of fracas.

I didn't blame her, at first. As I've said, I was sympathetic to her stories. I began to recognize a pattern though. Someone was always being unfair, or didn't understand. That's when I realized Allie had a predilection for poking the hornets' nest.

As it turned out, conflict was her natural state; it was the medium in which Allie excelled. Whether fighting with her aunt over her mother's brooch, with Hirsch about finances, her sisters about their grandparents' headstone, or her neighbors about a perceived slight, she was often embroiled in conflict.

Part of the problem was Allie had difficulty regulating her emotions. In fact, most of the time, she didn't admit to having any. Allie's other shortcoming was that she was never in the wrong. Since she'd become my principal object of study, I was determined to understand her better, but I also wondered why Dr. Ivankovich wasn't doing more to help.

I certainly understood Allie's attachment to her shrink. But the more she talked about him the more I heard things that didn't sound right. For example, Allie told me Ivankovich was helping her establish boundaries, but when I probed further, I realized what she meant was that he was trying to make her more assertive. More assertive? Allie was one of the most assertive people I knew. If anything, she needed to dial it back.

It seemed to me that Ivankovich's time would have been better spent helping Allie manage what I considered her most pressing problems, beginning with her impulsiveness (i.e. instant marriage proposals), hyper-sexuality, and anger, which I had yet to experience. Yet apparently these symptoms didn't interest him.

Like a lot of people in long-term therapeutic relationships, I wondered whether Allie was being well served. She bragged Ivankovich confided in her as proof of their connection, but these were things he shouldn't have told her such as he was unhappy in his marriage, regretted having five children, and had had a vasectomy.

Some shrinks are happy to relieve you of cash in return for no demonstrable improvement. They're about as close to a licensed flim-flam artist as one can get. It didn't help that Allie suffered from something chronic and incurable. I didn't know whether Ivankovich saw Allie as an evergreen source of funds, but I had my suspicions. And that was before I learned he didn't like me.

Because Allie had trouble censoring herself she told me during one of our excursions that Ivankovich was against us getting involved.

"Why?" I asked. "I've never met the guy."

"When he heard about your hearing impairment he was concerned I'd have to take care of you."

"I don't need to be taken care of."

"I know. But he thinks my picker is broken. He says I choose men who can't take care of themselves. I told him he was wrong in your case. In fact, things got so heated I told him to back the fuck off."

I appreciated Allie coming to my defense, but none of this sounded good.

"The worst part," she continued, "was when he asked what you write about."

"What did you say?"

"I told him you wrote about unusual inventions that fail in the market. He said that's because you see yourself as broken."

"I what?"

"He says you see yourself as obsolete."

Of course, I was infuriated. This guy Ivankovich, who I'd never met, not only deemed me unviable, but an unworthy suitor for Allie, a woman far crazier than I'd ever be.

What really burned me though was he had a point. My hearing loss was crippling despite my efforts to counteract it. Additionally, I was unmarried, unemployed, and in my 50s - another way of saying I was obsolete. Yes, I was trying to turn things around, but the jury was out.

What stung most though was that Ivankovich had not only put his finger on my doubts, he'd shared them with Allie. That's when I realized I was in a three way relationship. It was me, Allie, and Ivankovich, and Ivankovich was calling the shots.

\*\*\*

By my last day in Twin Rivers I'd visited all of Allie's landmarks. I'd seen the house she'd grown up in, the house where she raised their children with Hirsch, and the love nest where her father conducted his affairs. But before I left there was one more place she wanted to show me.

101

On a country lane about ten miles outside of town, Allie pulled off the road near a single story farmhouse set back on a hill.

"This is where my father murdered my mother," she said.

I knew the story. One of Allie's nieces emailed me about it shortly after it happened. It began when Allie's mother developed Alzheimer's. Harry Katz had insisted on being his wife's primary caregiver even though he wasn't particularly good at it. For starters, he wasn't very caring. He also hated cooking and left his wife alone too much. Allie lived nearby, so kept an eye on things. It wasn't easy given the bad blood that had finally developed between her and her father. Still, Allie managed to visit most afternoons when she and her mother would watch cartoons together. It was one of the few activities her mother still enjoyed.

As Allie's mom declined Allie began noticing her father was having difficulty keeping up. He was in his 80s by now with health problems of his own. When she called her father's attention to how slovenly the house looked he lost his temper and kicked her out.

Three months later Harry Katz pulled the trigger. There was nothing impulsive about it. He'd been planning it for months. First, he poisoned his wife. When that didn't work, he shot her with a handgun before blowing his own brains out. Later an autopsy showed his wife was already dead when he shot her. It made no difference how he killed her, though. People said it was an act of love.

The murder-suicide was sufficiently titillating that the newspapers picked it up. The lead on the evening news showed a ServiceMaster van outside the house, presumably cleaning up the mess Harry Katz had made. As a last act of vindictiveness, he cut Allie out of his will. Two years later the locals were still clucking.

Not everyone was fooled, though. When Allie and her sisters emptied the house they found a box in their father's closet filled with sex toys and Polaroids of his conquests, most of them nude. It was hard to square the hero portrayed in the obituaries with the leering man they found in the box. But that was Harry Katz.

As it turned out, his timing was flawless. He owed everyone in town, including thousands of dollars to a local hospital for a recent operation.

Over the course of his marriage, Harry Katz had swapped spouses, fucked his neighbors' wives, and sexually abused his daughter. Who did the guy think he was? The noble scion of a well-bred dynasty intent on maintaining standards, or a red-nosed, watery-eyed satyr that

102

couldn't keep it in his pants? He may have been married 62 years but his wasn't a love story. It was something much darker.

If Allie had been wounded by her past she was positively traumatized by the death of her mother at her father's hands. People called it an act of love but she insisted on calling it what it was: a murder-suicide. Ever since, she'd abhorred handguns, exacerbated by the time her second husband threatened to kill himself with one. It sickened her just to look at one.

But the chief reason Allie was upset was because no one understood who her father was. I considered him a monster and was glad he was dead but he'd left his daughter more wounded than St. Sebastian. Allie needed somebody to love her, somebody to tend to her needs. I certainly had my problems, hearing loss being one of them, but at least I understood her. We were two wounded souls who could help one another. Now, if I could only get Ivankovich to agree.

# Chapter 22
## Guess Who's Coming to Dinner

There are some people whose gravitational pull is so strong they lock you into their orbit. Once there, you find yourself incapable of escape. That was okay because by this point I'd rather burn up in Allie's atmosphere than make a run for freedom.

After returning home from Pennsylvania our plans accelerated. Allie put her house on the market while I began looking for a loft rental in Oakland so she'd have a place to live.

I understood why Allie wanted out of Twin Rivers. There was nothing left for her there. Her parents had died, her two oldest sons were either drunk, high, or in jail, and both her ex-husbands lived nearby. The place was full of ghosts.

In the meantime, I'd kept in touch with the California Department of Rehabilitation. Every week they emailed me a list of jobs culled from their job bank. Most of the positions were for technical writers, an area where I had no expertise. My ideal job was working for a company writing press releases or speeches, but companies with this type of position didn't post on a state job board. Nor were they enlightened enough to hire a deaf person to work alongside their executives.

None of this bothered me because my love for Allie filled me with optimism. I knew if I just kept at it I'd solve my problem.

It was a golden time for us. It wasn't unusual to exchange dozens of text messages in a single afternoon. And though it didn't assuage my ache for her we developed strategies for dulling the pain. Allie liked streaming my radio interviews while she painted. I, in turn, hung a self-portrait she'd created on my bedroom wall. I also sprinkled her photographs throughout the house. True, I hid them when the kids came to visit, but gazing at Allie's face when I was alone gave sweet satisfaction.

I knew my daughters would have trouble with Allie because they had trouble with all my female friends, even the ones who were gay. No daughter wants their father in a romantic relationship with anyone save their mother. I wanted to honor those feelings, so Allie and I kept our relationship on the down low. Telling them would be easier once she'd moved here. In the meantime, I knew better than to rush things.

Since it was Allie's turn to visit she came in November for my birthday. Among the activities I planned for us was seeing the Hockney exhibit at the De Young Museum (though I didn't know it at the time, Hockney is deaf), taking her on a tour of Andrew Goldsworthy's installations in the Bay Area, and showing her a private beach I'd discovered. When I asked Allie if there was anything she wanted to do, she told me to be sure to schedule plenty of bedroom time. I didn't have to be asked twice.

I've joked about Allie being crazier than me, but the truth is I was counting on it. I'd made a calculation, as most people do in a relationship but are loathe to admit. I hoped Allie's craziness would make me look better. After all, I'd already held down a series of high profile jobs, made money, and had a book in bookstores. Hopefully, this would compensate for my current shortcomings, which Ivankovich, her therapist, regularly reminded her of.

By now I'd told Allie my sister owned the house I lived in. I'd also referenced my financial struggles. My mother had died shortly after my visit to Twin Rivers, leaving me enough money to pay my debts and give me a financial cushion for a year or two. Though I wouldn't inherit the money for another six months it went a long way to relieving the pressure. At least I wouldn't starve. Importantly, it would fund our life together.

*** 

It had been a long time since I'd celebrated my birthday with anyone other than my kids. Having Allie present filled me with joy. In honor of the occasion, I decided to invite my sister for dinner, and Allie made a cake from scratch to add to the festive mood.

The purpose of the dinner wasn't so much a birthday party as it was a chance to introduce my sister to Allie. Things had not been well between my sister and me for some time. Since being in love improved my outlook, I decided to make amends. On some level, I guess I was seeking my sister's approval. I was saying, "I know I've been difficult, but see the nice girl I've found? Thanks to your help, everything's worked out fine. Let's bury the hatchet."

Sometimes you do stupid things with the best of intentions. If time had proven anything it was that most branches on my family tree were rotten. Yet I thought a single dinner could repair that. Love had made me an optimist.

It didn't help that Allie could be uneasy in social situations, blurting out the first thing that came to mind. I'd seen her do it more than once. At a wedding reception she'd encouraged one of the bridesmaids to drop her top for the group photograph. Another time she told a table of strangers that while giving birth she'd mistaken the doctor's cry of "stool!" as his request for a chair. The story wasn't funny the first time she told it, less so the third.

I tried reassuring her, but who doesn't dread the first dinner with your boyfriend's relatives? Allie had reason to be concerned and not because of Tourettes.

My sister did not like people. Though she hid behind a gracious façade she suffered from a case of double-speak. You never knew what she really thought. Instead, she masked her feelings behind the big hello, the fake smile, and an artificial warmness. Nevertheless, it couldn't disguise the fact she radiated a feeling of "not-wanting-to-be-here" like heat off asphalt. Though my sister tried transforming herself into Mrs. Happy-Face it never quite rang true. It only obscured the damage beneath the surface.

The truth did occasionally peek through. Once, I heard her tell a friend who complained her date was too short that men "look a whole lot taller standing on a stack of cash." Ah, the truth disguised as a joke, I thought. Now we're getting somewhere.

One reason my sister's social intimacy was limited was her "10 minute rule." She could not sustain a conversation for longer than ten minutes. If a chat passed the double digit mark she grew uncomfortable, began to fidget, and escaped by saying, "I should let you go."

Let me go? She wasn't letting me go, she was running away!

For the longest time, I thought I was the problem. Then I noticed my sister built a guest house but never invited guests. What did that tell you? True, my sister would have been a lot more sympathetic if she hadn't been filthy rich, but that's the consequence of having money. I liked her a lot more when she was a poor middle class housewife struggling to pay bills. Now that she was Woodside-rich it was hard to sympathize.

The biggest problem was my sister didn't like me. She might go out of her way to deny this, but what else would you expect from someone who concealed their feelings? Her actions proved otherwise.

Born the third out of four children, my sister held a privileged position in our family growing up. She was not only the baby, she was the only girl. When I came along seven years later, snatching "the youngest" title, she never forgave me. Thank God I wasn't born female; I'd never have survived infancy.

Geoghegans tend to be dismissive of other people, but none so much as their own. When my sister realized she couldn't eliminate me, she changed her strategy. First, she ignored me. Later, when I began to speak, she treated me with disdain. Finally, when I was old enough to become a target, she invented diabolical tortures to practice on me. Seven years is a significant age difference, which meant my sister had no trouble pushing me to the ground, sitting on my chest and saying: "If the back of your head touches the palm of my hand, I'm going to slap you!" Only my sister could devise a punishment where the only two choices, resistance or surrender, resulted in pain.

A lot of this could be dismissed as sibling rivalry if it hadn't continued past the age of consent. When my college acceptance letter arrived, she tore it from my mother's hands exclaiming, "I knew he didn't get in!" When I sold my first book she said, "I can't believe how much they paid you." And in a fit of honesty after my precipitous hearing loss she told me, "Better get used to being poor. You'll never be rich again."

I told Allie she had little to fear from my sister; she would stay an hour and be gone. To soften the situation, I invited one of my sister's girlfriends, who I thought Allie would like. I'd even bought my sister's favorite wine to improve her conviviality. In other words, I was trying.

This didn't relieve Allie's anxiety, however. As dinner approached, I felt her grow tense. Since someone needed to maintain their cool, I focused on dinner prep and drank a beer. I'd already married one woman whose social skills meant I left her at home. Had I gotten involved with another?

Earlier that afternoon I polished my dining room table. Now I set four places using my best china and silverware. Adding candles, cloth napkins, and a sterling silver wine holder, I made the last minute decision to use my blue water glasses to give the place settings a bit of color.

Since my dining room window looked across the meadow at my sister's house, I could see when she set out to join us. When she arrived at the back door, I was ready.

With her high cheek bones and flipped bob my sister looked like Sally Fields even at 63. Since Allie didn't drink anymore, and my sister didn't fall for the bottle of MacRostie, we got off to a stilted start. Allie did her best to break the ice but my sister was barely there. This was not the kind of meal you wanted to have 100% sober, yet I was the only one drinking. To complicate matters, my sister's friend had a crush on me. I'd long since steered her toward friendship, but half way through the meal she ruffled my hair in a proprietary gesture that made Allie uncomfortable.

I'd always enjoyed small dinner parties that linger over wine but we finished in record time. Except for a moment when Allie planted an awkward kiss on my face marking her territory there were no disasters. Still, weird undercurrents threatened to swamp my party at any moment. Had my chair been an ejector seat I'd have punched out right there.

My sister and her friend almost didn't stay for Allie's cake. Feigning tiredness they each took a slice but left it on their plate, uneaten. A few minutes later as they got up to go my sister remembered the gift she'd brought. I hadn't expected one. As I say, the purpose of dinner was to introduce Allie and make amends. But my sister said she'd given the present a lot of thought and insisted I open it before she left.

As she handed me the gift I noticed it was wrapped in newspaper - not the fancy presentation she usually preferred. Working up the necessary enthusiasm, I untied the string, unwrapped the newspaper, and with as much ceremony as I could muster unveiled a bright blue roll of dog-poop bags.

Hostility comes in many colors. That night it was blue. There was no missing the message, though. I might be flying the flag of truce but the war with my sister was far from over.

# Chapter 23
# Giddyup!

One thing that may help you to understand my sister is that she prefers horses to people. Her equine affinity began at age four when she spent hours straddling a saw horse in our parents' backyard wearing western regalia. By age eleven, she was overturning lawn chairs to make a jump course which she cantered through while making whinnying noises. This is typical for a young girl, but at an age when most kids abhor vegetables my sister freely snacked on celery and carrots. She considered apples dinner and sugar cubes dessert, best served on flattened palm.

Horse fever usually passes once a girl attains adolescence, but not for my sister. That's when things got serious. She not only rode every day, she began competing in horse shows. My parents must have approved because they spent a fortune on her passion. She not only had her own horse, she had two, which I never understood since you can only ride one at a time. My sister racked up so many blue ribbons she didn't bother displaying them, though the same can't be said for our parents who proudly showed off her champagne buckets, silver platters, and loving cup trophies.

There's something about the way women love horses and it's not always good. I'm fine with horses for transportation or farm work, but the way my sister fetishized them put me off. She even built her house to look like a barn.

Horses are prey animals, big, dumb beasts that can't survive outside a herd. The best thing that ever happened to them was being domesticated by humans. They'd never have survived without us.

Obviously, this is an unpopular opinion, but you might judge me less harshly if you understood why I don't like horses. First, it doesn't help that their brain to weight ratio is unimpressive. They also spook for the palest of reasons. Something as minor as a plastic bag caught in an updraft, or a glimpse of their shadow, is enough to make them bolt. My sister knew this having broken her wrist riding so many times she had to have a pin put in. Once, during a jumping competition, she was thrown from her her horse and had to undergo a year's worth of cosmetic surgery. Twelve months later she still didn't look right.

Any half ton beast that can be led around by a nine year old can't be that smart, not to mention they're always taking a dump in front of you. But my sister could not form a meaningful relationship with any creature that had fewer than four legs. All of this would have been fine if she'd liked me, but she didn't. She lacked the empathy gene, just like our mother.

There were times when I could have used my sister's help. I had trouble hearing in family court when I was fighting to increase visitation time with my children; or with my accountant when I wrestled with bankruptcy. Had I known sign language I could have gotten by but I didn't. As it was, it wouldn't have taken much for my sister to help. Writing things down for me to read, or summarizing a meeting would have been enough. But my sister didn't consider helping a loving act; it was an obligation, an inconvenience, something she had to do. The few times she did offer assistance (largely at the suggestion of our shrink) she couldn't sustain it. The truth was, my sister may have been a lady of leisure but she had better things to do than deal with her deaf brother. That those "better things" involved riding didn't do anything for my love of horses. It didn't do much for my love of sister, either.

*** 

There's rarely one reason why a family is dysfunctional. In my case there were several. First off, I never really knew my siblings. My brothers are nearly two decades older than I am and were already in the armed forces when I was born. I also didn't know my sister very well. By the time I was six she was already in boarding school. When I turned ten she was away at college. This put me in the unique position of being raised as an only child despite having three siblings. It also explains why we weren't close.

The second reason was my mother and father's belief that the sole purpose of having children is to reflect glory upon their parents. In other words, we had to make them look good. When we succeeded, as

110

measured by grades, promotions, or money, we were given sips of praise. When we failed, we were criticized, ignored, or occasionally shown the door. Given this situation, my siblings and I spent more time pleasing our parents than getting to know one another. Home was like working in a corporation. You labored hard to stay on top.

This strategy didn't work for everybody. When my middle brother developed a drinking problem at age 16, he brought shame (and a grand theft auto charge) upon my parents. Their response? They kicked him out of the house. Twenty years later, after he stopped drinking and petitioned to rejoin us, he never fully regained his rights as a family member. His crime? Never having gone to college.

When my eldest brother quit his prestigious job and moved to Florida to write a novel, my parents didn't speak to him for a year. When my sister was rejected by the college of her choice, my father told her, "You'll just have to get used to being second rate."

Given how fragile our family connections were you'd think we'd have done more to nurture them. But hardly a year went by without one of my siblings being ostracized for failing to measure up. It was like living under McCarthyism. You never knew who'd be next.

My mother set the tone for our future marriages when, after 32 years of hers, she filed for divorce. My father was so incensed he refused to move out. Instead, he drew an imaginary line down the middle of our house, staying on his side for the next two years. It wasn't until a Sheriff's Deputy blocked our driveway so that he could serve my father an eviction order that he finally got the message and left.

After their divorce was final, my father refused to speak to my mother for the next thirty years. I'm sure he had his reasons but the main one was money. My mother never tired of pursuing my father for financial gain even when she didn't need the dough. The Inspector Javert of family court, she chased him down wherever he lived. Whether it was Connecticut, Florida, Vermont, or California she always got her man.

It wasn't clear why my mother needed the money. She lived a frugal lifestyle like the Connecticut Yankee she was. A cross between Miss Havisham and Ethan Frome, she barely weighed 100 pounds, most of it Maker's Mark. Intelligence was far more important to her than money. Even in her 90s, Mom had an excessively analytical way of looking at the world. Stripped of sentiment, devoid of compassion, it was fine for discussing foreign policy but less so when taking stock of friends or family. There was nothing my mother enjoyed more than debating the latest outrage as reported by the *New York Times*. That's not everyone's cup of tea. Still, she wanted her children well dressed, well spoken, well read, and well compensated. If not, well, there was the door.

My father also had a keen intellect, but intelligence was not as important to him as success. Having grown up poor during the Depression he spent his entire life trying to get ahead. Once he made it, as measured by success and wealth, his ex-wife spent her life taking it from him. In fact, my father was in one of his Lear-like rages over a lawsuit she'd brought when he suddenly dropped dead of a massive stroke. I could think of no fitter ending. Like I said, Geoghegans play rough.

The fact my father had a temper meant we kept our distance. Since we never knew when he might explode, we didn't get too close, especially since Dad handed out shrapnel indiscriminately. When he finally expired, I didn't feel that he died so much as God had deliberately misplaced him. I loved him, sure, but it was a relief he was gone.

The longest feud was not between my mother and father, however. It was between my mother and sister. I was of mixed emotions about this. It's not unusual for mothers and daughters to fight, but the way my sister dealt with the situation was to cut all contact. On the one hand her self-exile was a survival strategy. Still, it hurt my mother badly even though she was every bit as responsible for the break.

Mom had high standards, which included actively undermining each of her children's marriages because she knew they could do better. No wonder my married sister steered clear of our mom. It was a matter of self-preservation.

The situation worsened once my mother developed heart disease. For three years I shuttled between the Bay Area and Chapel Hill taking care of her. Mom wanted to remain in her house until the end, a wish I wanted to honor. But as she continued to decline she needed help cooking, cleaning, and shopping. The problem was whenever I hired the necessary help my mother fired them the next day. This happened two or three times, which was frustrating since my mother couldn't remember the simplest task, such as taking her heart medication. Inevitably, she'd end up in the hospital, and the whole unnecessary cycle would start again. It wasn't long before my two brothers washed their hands of her, but when Mom's caretaking fell largely to me, I was reminded of my family's shortcomings once again.

That the Geoghegans were incapable of loving one another was a constant source of disappointment. It not only influenced my marital ineptitude, it was the primary reason I refused to date. But as much as my legacy scared me, I was determined to overcome it. That's where Allie came in. With Allie, I could wipe the slate clean. I wouldn't be judged for my job, or material wellbeing, but loved for who I was. Plus, I'd be picking someone I not only had a connection to, but a history with. I knew it wouldn't be easy. Escaping your legacy is like trying to outrun your shadow. But Allie gave me hope, and hope was all I needed to give us a try.

\*\*\*

In August 2012, after an especially grueling trip to my mother's, I returned home with a chip on my shoulder. While I'd been dealing with my mother's poor health, my sister had been busy riding horses, working out with her trainer, and generally living the good life. Frankly, I was pissed.

One thing that preoccupied me was the realization that my sister, who lived just across the meadow, never came to visit. Yes, she occasionally dropped by if she needed something, but never of her own volition and never just to talk. I was the one who always initiated contact and when I did, I either ran up against her double-speak, or her ten minute timer.

It wasn't easy determining the validity of my concern given my increasingly diminished mental state. Nevertheless, I was convinced my sister didn't want a relationship. I'm a believer that if something is important you invest time in it. If it's not, you don't. The fact my sister never spent time with me seemed proof she didn't want to. That's when I decided to conduct an experiment.

What would happen if I stopped crossing the meadow? What would happen if I ceased all contact with my sister and her family? Would they care? Would they reach out to me? Would they even notice? It seemed a proposition worth testing.

113

Of course, what I wanted most my sister couldn't give me, but I didn't realize this. I thought I could change our relationship for the better if I could just demonstrate how little I meant to her.

My growing depression may have been biologically based but it was situationally amplified, and the situation with my sister wasn't helping. Still, determining the validity of my concern was of utmost importance. And so I commenced my experiment.

Not surprisingly, it worked! Months passed without hearing from my sister. Still, a part of me hoped I'd be proved wrong, especially since I lived next door. Little did I know nobody was coming. That's when my problems really started.

As my experiment played out, my mental health and financial situation continued to deteriorate. After the next trip to my mother's I returned so broke I didn't have enough money to get home from the airport. It goes without saying I didn't have the $500 necessary to get my dog from the kennel.

This time I came prepared though. I took advantage of my mother's declining memory to "accidentally forget" to return her credit card after buying her groceries. Of course, I planned on mailing it back to her once I got my dog out, but then I decided to buy a few additional things and before you knew it I was George Hurstwood in *Sister Carrie* who can't return the money because the safe door has closed.

The fact I'd been off my meds while scraping by financially contributed to my lack of judgment. But since I'd already crossed the line, I began using my sister's account at the local market to buy groceries without her knowledge. Not long after, I borrowed her credit card to buy gas and neglected to return it.

Resentment is a great source of self-justification. I knew what I was doing was wrong, yet I had no problem rationalizing it. It was payback for not wanting a relationship with me. Besides, they had so much money I didn't think they'd mind throwing a few extra dollars to me. The last straw came on New Year's Eve.

The day before my daughter's 9th birthday I got a call telling me my mother was in the cardiac intensive care unit at UNC Chapel Hill. Mom wanted to die on her own terms and had gone so far as to refuse medical help in the past. In this case, a neighbor found her unconscious, so she was unable to refuse the ambulance.

Ironically, my two brothers who lived closest to my mother were on their way to visit my sister and brother-in-law for the holidays. I'd been invited to Christmas dinner at my sister's house and then uninvited because, as I was told, "the evening's just for family." Since none of my siblings wanted to deal with my mother, I was the one to fly across the country and tend to her needs.

I arrived at Raleigh/Durham airport early the evening of December 31, 2012. It was impenetrably dark and pouring with rain but somehow, by the grace of God, I managed to find the hospital, even though the car's navigation system had conked out. While my two brothers were on the other side of the country yucking it up with my sister who, don't forget, hates guests, I spent New Year's Eve in the cardiac ICU with Mom.

I must say when I arrived she looked terrible. She resembled one of those recently thawed mummies they find in the Alps. Shrunken, confused, and gasping for air, she couldn't remember where she was, or how she got there. Just the sight of her rattled me.

She spent the next few days in the ICU followed by 20 days in rehab, which turned out to only be 10 because there was no way my stubborn mother would let them keep her any longer than she needed to learn to walk again.

The defining moment came that first night of my arrival after my mother had fallen asleep. It was 9:00pm and still raining. I hadn't eaten since yesterday and was starving. Most places were closed for the holiday, but as I was driving to Mom's house to spend the night I saw a McDonald's in the distance, its lights ablaze. The place was empty save for two local police officers who I ended up sharing my meal with. As I sat there eating a Quarter Pounder with Cheese on New Year's Eve, I found respite amongst strangers.

I couldn't help but notice their thick black utility belts, and holstered gun with a grip so large I couldn't see how they could hold it.

"How do you wear that thing all day?" I asked. "It must weigh a ton."

"It's not the belt," one of them said, forking a handful of fries into his mouth. "It's the vest. They're not only heavy, they make you sweat."

Later, as I tried exiting the parking lot, I drove my mother's car smack into the base of a streetlight. A few seconds later, glass from the overhead lamp rained down on the hood startling me. As I sat there listening to the engine tick, I wondered whether my life could possibly get more pathetic. After a few minutes, I went back in the restaurant and asked my new friends to write up an accident report for the insurance company.

"This is the only call we'll get all night that won't involve liquor," one of them said. We all had a good chuckle.

My sister never did cross the meadow except to get her credit card. Certainly, I'd given her good cause not to. Then again, she'd given me more than a few reasons to be upset. That's how some families are, though. Despite being related they're more at odds than at peace. Given my family, it's a wonder I reproduced.

# Chapter 24
# Dr. Squeaky-voice

Allie returned to Pennsylvania after my birthday where she spent the next month boxing up her belongings. In the meantime, we communicated by text.

I hadn't been kidding when I'd told Allie my family relations were lamentable. Still, she had the edge on me. As far as I knew, none of the Geoghegans were sexually abused, nor had we murdered any family members, though there was still time for that. There was one thing about Allie that concerned me though, one thing I increasingly worried about. She had a bad temper.

The problem with texting as your primary form of communication is that you only receive about half the information. The other half - intonation, facial expressions, body language - is lost. Allie and I had our share of textual misunderstandings. I dismissed them as "dust ups." But as their number grew they took on a darker character.

A conversation might start out harmless when, out of the blue, Allie would explode at something I'd said. I never could tell what would set her off. I certainly didn't intend to make her angry. Still, her temper was not only unpredictable, it escalated at breathtaking speed.

The first time Allie became angry I wrote it off as an anomaly. When it kept on happening I paid attention. One day she accused me of being sexist. Another day, I was homophobic. On Monday I wasn't doing enough to find a loft for her in Oakland. By Thursday I was doing too much.

Allie was proficient at administering what I call the slap and the kiss. The kiss was something she said, loving or complimentary, that sent me into a blissful swoon. This was often followed by the stinging rebuke. Sometimes it had a basis in fact but usually it didn't. What scared me was that I never knew what caused her angry response.

I was eager to please Allie, so her criticism surprised me. Not only was I unaware of the things she accused me of, but I assumed she was right because I loved her. My own philosophy was akin to *Star Trek*'s prime directive—it's okay to observe another civilization but not to intervene. Allie didn't share these feelings. She not only intervened, she launched full-on invasions.

As her angry responses increased in frequency I turned to my therapist for advice. Yes, I had my own Ivankovich: a chubby-cheeked, squeaky-voiced psychiatrist with the face of a Cabbage Patch doll. My sister had referred me to Dr. Squeaky-voice after my meltdown in Tokyo. I'd been seeing her on and off for seven years. For the most part, Dr. Squeaky-voice met my mental health needs just fine, but I may not have been the best judge.

An accomplished clinician, Dr. Squeaky-voice was a Professor at Stanford's School of Medicine as well as having her own thriving psychiatric practice. Her helium-tinged vocal chords belied her intelligence, but Dr. Squeaky-voice's squinty-eyed smile was almost always filled with compassion. She was just the right person to help me understand what Allie was doing.

I'd like to say I never held anything back from Dr. Squeaky-voice but that wasn't true. I told her the icky stuff, but there was no getting around the fact Dr. Squeaky-voice was my sister's therapist, too. She made it a point to tell me she was my advocate and I could rely on her. Still, I wondered how much got back to my sister especially since she was paying the bills.

Dr. Squeaky-voice may have reassured me our sessions were confidential, but it's impossible to erect a Chinese wall in human relations. Things inevitably spill over. For example, Dr. Squeaky-voice constantly reminded me how thankful I should be that my sister was letting me live rent free in her cottage, paying for my therapy, and covering the cost of my anti-depressants. I was thankful, but it was more complicated than that. And why was she reminding me? Was my sister complaining?

What I knew that Dr. Squeaky-voice didn't was that it was my brother-in-law's idea for me to live in the house next door, not my sister's, just as it was his idea to rescue me in Tokyo. Since I feared anything getting back to my sister, I kept my mouth shut about our poor relations. Still, Dr. Squeaky-voice was a pretty good therapist.

Dr. Squeaky-voice had a wacky side, though. She took me off Lexapro when she learned it was associated with hearing loss. Unfortunately, the drug that replaced it suppressed my libido even more. This concerned me given Allie's sexual appetite, so Dr. Squeaky-voice prescribed an antihistamine which she told me to take before sex since it would counteract my dormant desire. When Allie visited, I took the antihistamine as instructed and promptly fell asleep. This is what I mean by Dr. Squeaky-voice's wacky side. Who prescribes a sedative to someone getting laid?

Dr. Squeaky-voice was also keen on me getting government disability. I was against it on principle. I may have *felt* disabled at times but I didn't *see* myself as disabled. Furthermore, her insistence confused me. It suggested she didn't see me as a whole person capable of taking care of myself, yet that's the person I wanted to be. Had I been connected to the Deaf community I wouldn't have felt disabled or alone, but I wouldn't make that discovery for another few years. In the meantime, I struggled with my identity.

The important thing was Dr. Squeaky-voice's enthusiasm for Allie. She may never have met her, but she knew Allie was good for me. And yet, I wondered whether my sister was behind this enthusiasm. I knew my sister was eager for me to leave the cottage. Her ten minute rule had long since expired. Could encouraging me to start a new life with Allie be Dr. Squeaky-voice doing my sister's bidding? Christ, that sounded paranoid even to me, but I couldn't help wondering.

As I've said, some of Allie's texts could be scary. Like Joe Pesci in *Goodfellas* she could turn mean after being told she was "funny." As a result, every conversation became dangerous. When she did ignite, I found myself trapped in a minefield, unsure where to step next.

Anger management classes had taught me to retreat from tense situations. When I did, Allie came after me. When I tried getting to the bottom of why she was mad, she accused me of censorship.

"Do you want me to self-edit?" she'd cry.

If I said no her outburst continued. If I said yes we had another fight. There was no way to win.

To be clear, I have no problem with differences in opinion. But Allie's opinion involved a string of invective that threatened to undermine our carefully tended relationship. The most she would admit to when pushed was having a "sharp tongue." It wasn't her tongue that

119

bothered me; it was her irrational behavior. And so it was to Dr. Squeaky-voice I turned for help.

After a brief explanation, I handed Dr. Squeaky-voice my phone and let her scroll through a text exchange with Allie. She was quiet at first as she read the thread, but the further she got the more she shook her head. Finally, when she reached the end she handed back my phone and said:

"You've got a problem."

"How so?"

"She's projecting her fears onto you."

"What do you mean projecting?"

"You say one thing, but to her it means another. Even after you clarify your intention she doesn't get it because she's locked into her own interpretation. You may be the trigger, John, but Allie's anger has nothing to do with you."

"But I'm getting blasted!"

"Yes, I see that, but your texts are harmless. The problem is Allie reads too much into them."

"How can I stop pissing her off?"

"Given what you've told me it's not unusual for a woman like Allie to be triggered in unexpected ways."

"Can I prevent it?"

"Other than talking to her there's not much you can do. The problem lies with Allie."

"Is she always going to be angry?"

"Not if she recognizes the problem and gets help for it."

"I love Allie, Doc, but her temper is killing me."

"Maybe you should cool things for a while."

"Cool things?"

"This is something Allie has to do on her own. You can't change her. Do you think she'd be willing to explore therapy?"

Knowing Allie was in therapy with Ivankovich, and neither thought she had an anger problem, I doubted things would change.

"I don't know, Doc. She doesn't see a problem."

"Well, be careful. This kind of anger is a relationship killer."

I never liked arguing, probably because my parents did so much of it while I was growing up. Allie, on the other hand, loved drama. She'd been immersed in it from the day she was born.

Nobody's perfect, myself included, so I set aside my hurt feelings and pressed ahead with our plans. If sacrifice and compromise are the cornerstones of love, I was prepared to make both. Hopefully, given time, Allie would as well.

# Chapter 25
# Danabling

My oldest daughter had recently become a teenager. This meant Justin Bieber posters on her bedroom wall, boy-band magazines, and all her time spent on her iPhone.

This is normal behavior for a 14 year old girl, but Dana was not a typical kid. For starters, she's a hybrid: half Caucasian, half Japanese. This means she had long brown hair, beautiful skin, and a pronounced epicanthic fold.

That my daughter carried both American and Japanese passports while speaking each language fluently did not help her fit in to Marin. It may not have made a difference when she was little, but now that she was a self-conscious teenager her identity in a mostly white community was at issue.

At first, nothing seemed wrong with Dana except her constant carping about her mother. Even then, that's normal for a teenager. But beginning her eighth grade year, Dana began lobbying me to move back to Marin. Her primary reason: she and her mother weren't getting along.

I wasn't surprised there was conflict. I knew my ex-wife's parenting style wasn't well suited to our daughter's personality. But I discounted half of what Dana told me, knowing how unreliable teenagers can be. That's not to say I didn't find Dana's request flattering. I usually had to fight for the few hours I got with my kids. Now that one was asking to come live with me I was tempted to jump to her rescue. Instead, I listened more than I spoke, came to her mother's defense when appropriate, and counseled Dana to remain calm. If I'd been any more selfless I'd have ascended into heaven.

By the time Allie came to Woodside for her second visit, I was facing Dana's full blown campaign to move north. Dana could be emotional when she wanted. She could also be stubborn. I resisted her at first, but when she accused me of abandoning her she'd found my weak spot.

I'd only moved to Woodside to save money, and even then I worried about the distance from my kids. After two years of making the 100 mile round trip to see them every other weekend I was ready to move back. Fortunately, the inheritance from my mother allowed me to make the move, but Dana could only live with me if my ex-wife cooperated.

I'd always thought punishing someone for the rest of their life because you were once married was unfair. Still, my father had done it to my mother. Now, my ex-wife was doing it to me. I'd always wanted to be a part of my children's lives, but their mother found ways to keep me out. I couldn't blame her. You sucked it up in Japan when a marriage went bad, you didn't call it quits. But her constant reminders of how selfish I was to pursue a writing career, abandoning my family, and abrogating my financial responsibilities, even though I paid child support, wore me down. Five years after our divorce she was still furious. I began to share her terrible opinion of me.

The irony was I'd never had more time to spend with my kids, yet my wife's resentment ensured I never saw them less. Should it come as a surprise I was an easy mark for Dana's plea? Finally, after she told me she couldn't live one more day with her mother, I decided to investigate.

\*\*\*

Dana started eighth grade strong, but her grades soon began to plummet. Since I monitored her academics closely I complained about them during her visits. I pointed out she was getting A after A in a subject then would flunk a test. The A's told me should she could do the work, the F's told me she wasn't trying. The inconsistency was concerning.

Since Dana wasn't forthcoming, and my ex did her best to withhold information, I made an appointment to see Dana's school counselor. I'd met the counselor when I first separated from my wife, asking her to keep an eye on Dana. Since I never heard anything, I assumed she was alright. But given how little I knew about Dana's life outside of Woodside, school seemed a good place to start.

The middle school Dana attended was a classic example of cold war architecture. A single story, cinder-block structure, it looked like it could survive the center of a blast radius. The school office was cramped, the staff of three, grim-faced. The last thing they needed was another clueless father looking for the school to tell him what his ex-wife already knew.

When Dana's counselor skipped into the waiting room identifying herself as Barbie I thought I'd misheard. She asked whether I wanted coffee. When I declined, she waved me toward her office.

She was in her late thirties, but dressed far younger. That wasn't bad except her clothes suggested a medieval fantasy more Renaissance Faire than school administrator. This was California, so there was no telling how a person might dress. In Barbie's case it was knee high boots, black tights and a jacket cinched so tightly it barely covered her ass. As she skipped down the hallway flipping her hair her hand motion revealed more about her character than words could say. Once we were in her office I took charge.

"I'm here about Dana. She's having trouble at home and I'm worried it's impacting her schoolwork. I live in Woodside, but am thinking of moving back. I know you occasionally meet with Dana, so thought I'd check in to see how she's doing."

"We're very worried," Barbie said, her expression serious. "Dana's what we call an 'at risk' kid. We've been talking to her mother about getting her help, but as far as I know nothing's happened."

"What do you mean an 'at risk' kid?"

"Well, she's depressed for one, and a cutter. A couple of her friends also told us they're worried Dana has an eating disorder since she never eats lunch. Obviously, she's doing poorly in school, and you should be prepared for other risky behaviors as well."

"Like what?"

"Like drugs, alcohol, vaping, sexting, and unprotected sex."

"Vaping?"

Barbie explained vaping in a way that led me to believe she didn't understand it any better than I did. Then she dropped the bomb.

"Our biggest concern is Dana is at risk for suicide."

At first I didn't believe her. After all, the woman's name was Barbie, probably with a big fat heart over the "i". Obviously, she was not credible. But as she explained why my daughter was at risk of killing herself the blood drained from my face.

"Oh, I'm sorry. You didn't know this?" she asked.

I shook my head. "I had no idea."

I needed to get some air, but didn't think I could stand without falling. Barbie to her credit realized I needed a minute and gave me one.

As I sat there, my head in a whirl, I thought what's worse, a father who has no idea his daughter is coming apart at the seams, or one who has to be told by a woman named Barbie?

That afternoon I made the decision to move back to Marin. Dana may or may not have been at risk of killing herself, but one thing was for sure, I was not taking any chances.

# Chapter 26
# Complications

While sitting in the parking lot of Dana's school I furiously texted her mother. It was recess for fifth graders, who joyfully chased one another around the blacktop. Normally, just seeing them would make me happy, but I felt far from joyful.

As my fingers mashed the tiny keyboard I felt like I was composing the most important text of my life. Yet my ex so hated me I knew it might be days before she responded. In this case, I got lucky. She replied right away.

The Japanese are masters of indirection. The information Dana's mother supplied was so vague I couldn't tell how much she knew about Dana's situation let alone whether she was doing anything about it. There was no mention of meetings with the school, cutting, sex, drugs, or depression. It sounded like she might be taking Dana to a therapist, but if she was I'd never heard about it.

I was due back in court in a couple of months to contest my visitation schedule, but legal tactics weren't the solution here. Not only did I not have the money for prolonged litigation, even if I won my ex ignored the rulings. This left me pretty much where I began; starved for contact as well as information.

One reason I wasn't sure if Barbie was right was that I'd never found evidence of Dana cutting. Heck, Dana was afraid of spiders, how could she possibly cut herself? As for drugs, alcohol, vaping, and sex, that was purely speculative. Still, there was no denying Dana's normally high grades had tanked, and that's what parents in Marin cared most about.

I fired off an email to the psychiatrist Barbie recommended and made an appointment for Dana. I felt scared, but taking action emboldened me. If Dana's mother wouldn't deal with the situation, I would. I had no intention of letting my daughter suffer.

The long, beautiful drive back to Woodside mocked my mood. Later that afternoon my sister stopped in to ask if I could move out earlier. I'd planned on moving in February after Allie arrived, but as of today I planned on moving as soon as possible. My sister was pleased with the information, but before she left she mentioned one more thing.

"Oh, I forgot to tell you. Your youngest said she saw Dana kissing a boy after school and didn't think it was her boyfriend."

"When did she say this?" I asked.

"A month ago."

I don't know what was more surprising: that Dana was kissing boys now, or that my sister took a month to tell me.

\*\*\*

That night I wrote Allie a long email detailing everything that had happened, including my meeting with the school counselor, text exchanges with my ex, and my new belief I needed to move to Marin so Dana could live with me.

The reason I wrote Allie was obvious. She was my partner. I loved her. I wanted her input. I also knew she was experienced in dealing with troubled kids since two of her sons went off the rails in high school. But moving to Marin had not been part of our plan. The plan was for me to move to Alameda, a small island only a mile from the loft I'd found for her in Oakland. Though the distance between Oakland and Marin was only 26 miles, it was not the same as living next door. Nevertheless, I expected Allie would understand the gravity of my situation. Marin was just a bridge away. The next morning I received her reply.

*I'm noticing a pattern here that disturbs me.*

Huh?

*I need to see that you can be a parent that sets firm boundaries not just ignore red flags.*

What?

*You talk about moving to Marin without consulting me. I'm taken aback. Living in two separate communities does not work for me, yet no discussion has transpired between us. Remember, I have a big stake here. I'm moving across country. I can't control what you do, but if I don't get what I want I can move on.*

127

Her last paragraph concluded:

*Ivankovich says there's no shame in having a problem just in not confronting it. I'm not making the same mistake I've made before. The ball's in your court.*

Allie's response so surprised me I wasn't sure what to do. The attack felt personal, but it didn't make sense. She said I wasn't communicating yet I sent her an email explaining everything the same day it happened. She said I was making decisions without her, yet I was seeking her input.

The worst part was I was in an impossible situation. If I didn't move to Marin and move Dana in with me her problems could get worse. Yet if I did, Allie would dump me. No matter what, I lose!

Most people find it difficult to make a choice when selecting from two unattractive options. When they do choose, they inevitably feel disappointed. I wanted both Allie and Dana in my life, but Dana's situation was forcing me to make a decision. On the other hand, Allie's email was clear. I would pay the price for any decision that adversely affected her.

My world was crumbling. Dana was falling apart, my ex-wife was obfuscating, my sister couldn't get rid of me fast enough, and Allie was boiling mad. No wonder I felt under attack.

I paused long enough to wonder where Ivankovich was in all this. Did Allie write that email or did she have help? It was hard to know but I had my suspicions. I knew Ivankovich played a bigger role in Allie's decision making than I did. But I had an Ivankovich of my own, so I sought her advice.

Dr. Squeaky-voice shook her head disapprovingly as she read the latest digital exchange between Allie and me. If anything, she seemed more concerned than the first time. Handing my phone back, she said:

"Allie suffers from Intermittent Explosive Disorder."

"What's that?" I asked.

"It's a personality disorder characterized by anger out of all proportion to the circumstance."

I had to think about that for a minute. *Anger out of all proportion to the circumstance.* Hmm. That certainly described our many disconnects. Later, when I looked it up, I learned the acronym for Intermittent Explosive Disorder was IED - the same as Improvised Explosive Device.

If my hearing had been normal, Allie and I might have hashed out our differences over the telephone, but that wasn't going to happen. As things were, I had to decide between my daughter and my love life.

I'd seen plenty of guys pick new girlfriends over their kids. It always was an ugly choice. But if Allie couldn't understand Dana needed help, if she couldn't find it in her heart to compromise, then maybe it was better calling the whole thing off.

Dana might be broken, but that was no reason to reject her. I wasn't going to make the same mistake I'd seen made time and again. If I had to choose, I was choosing my daughter. Which is another way of saying I broke up with Allie.

# Part III
# Off the Rails

# Chapter 27
## Marin

Six weeks later I moved to Marin.

Beautiful, self-satisfied Marin with a mountain so perfect at its center it looks drawn by Hokusai. The people in Marin aren't as ridiculously rich as in Woodside, but the county remains one of the wealthiest in Northern California. As proof, it's a breeding ground for Teslas.

Nothing makes a man feel poorer than moving himself, especially when he could once afford a moving company. In my case, this meant renting a U-haul and hiring two day laborers who didn't speak English. It also meant buying cardboard boxes, packing them myself, and driving the truck like I was still in college. I wasn't 18 anymore, I was 56. The approach may save money but I had moved three times in five years. I was tired of it.

Packing up the Woodside house gave me a renewed appreciation for how much stuff I'd accumulated. I'd collected over 200 boxes of books, my father's desk, my parents' club chairs, and a Khmer head I could hardly lift. All of this had to be boxed up, carted off, and unloaded in an apartment so small there was no room for mice.

One sticking point was I hated the place I was renting. It was way out of my price range, with the only thing recommending it being proximity to my kids. The landlord's half-hearted attempt to class-up the place didn't help. Freshly painted walls of cheap sheet-rock couldn't hold a towel rack. The wood floor was so thin it buckled in places. To top things off, the apartment was so dark it seemed underground; which for the most part it was.

My first day at home I walked into the sliding glass door so hard I broke my glasses. It was the perfect demonstration of how deaf, blind, and dumb I felt.

I'd asked Dana to move in with me but hadn't set a date because I didn't want to antagonize her mother. I knew if I waited, it would happen on its own. Since I was only a block away Dana visited frequently. Meanwhile, I got the second bedroom ready for her arrival.

It had been over a month since I told Allie not to move to California. She took the news better than I expected. She was saddened, but claimed to understand. Frankly, it was a relief: Dana had become my main focus. Plus, Dr. Squeaky-voice's assessment struck a chord. I could only handle one out-of-control person at a time. That person should be my daughter.

It wasn't easy getting to the bottom of what was bothering Dana. I knew my ex didn't believe in therapy, but when I finally obtained the name of Dana's doctor and met with her, I could tell she was all wrong. Dana proved this by refusing to utter a word during our joint 50 minute session.

The more I observed my daughter the more concerned I became. It turned out that Dana and her mother had argued so much that neighbors had called the police. I didn't hear these stories from the main actors; it was Dana's little sister who told me. She was so nonchalant about it, it froze my blood. I wasn't sure what passed for normal in that house, but it didn't sound good.

*** 

I spent the first night alone in my new apartment. Since I was exhausted from the move I made a modest dinner, read for an hour, and turned out the light. Sometime after midnight Austin's tail started beating on the bedspread. My phone was buzzing. When I picked it up there was a text from Dana's mother.

This was the first time I could remember my ex reaching out to me since our divorce. Normally as cool as Mr. Spock, she sounded panicked. Dana was missing. She had blown off her pick up time from school and was still on the lamb eight hours later. She wasn't answering her phone, which would be cause for alarm except she'd texted her mother she wasn't coming home.

The situation must have been serious because the last thing my ex wanted was to need me for anything. I texted her back asking if she'd called the parents of Dana's friends. I knew my daughter's buddies, but her mother had poisoned so many of their parents against me I didn't feel I could wake them up in the middle of the night. Besides, I can't hear on the phone.

My ex texted she'd make some calls and let me know once she found Dana. Finally, at 2:45 am, I received a text saying Dana was at Dean's house. Dean had been the source of concern among Dana's peer group. They claimed he was suicidal, which may be attention-grabbing for all I know. But when Dean texted his friends earlier in the day that he was going to kill himself, everyone rallied at his house. Dana was his strongest supporter.

It's the kind of story that leaves you unsure how to feel. Should I be proud my daughter is helping this depressed kid? Or maybe it's just a pair of self-important teens whipping themselves up over something they have no business being involved in? I knew one thing. This behavior couldn't continue.

When I ventured outside it was a beautiful January night. It was both clear and cold as the moon cast a milky light. It was a weird feeling being up when everyone else was asleep. Still, I had to get Dana.

I'd never been to Dean's house but it was easy to find. When I pulled into the driveway, I left my lights blazing to make sure whoever was at home knew I was there. Then I put on my hazards for emphasis before banging on the front door like a police raid.

It took a minute before anyone responded, then a short, dark-haired woman appeared in the living room. Sleepy-eyed, and yawning, it was clear I'd woken her up. I couldn't care less. I was there for my daughter and it was partially this woman's fault I was out in middle of the night looking for her.

From what little I knew, Dean was the boy with two moms. One was a family therapist, the other departed for parts unknown. You'd think a therapist would know better than to host a bunch of eighth grade kids for a Friday night sleepover, but there's no telling what other people think is right.

Dean's mom opened the door and whispered something I couldn't hear. Then she pointed towards a door in the back before she too disappeared. What was I supposed to do? I didn't feel comfortable wandering around someone's house in the middle of the night. But it was late, I was tired, and I didn't feel like screwing around. I walked towards the door where she pointed, gingerly pushed it open, and stuck my head inside.

There in a room narrow enough you could almost touch the walls lay five eighth grade boys asleep on the floor. Curled up in the middle was my daughter. Fortunately, everyone was wearing clothes. The room was warm with body heat, and I didn't see any beer cans. The scene might be harmless except it smacked of kookiness. Where were their sleeping bags anyway?

Since all I cared about was getting my daughter, I carefully reached over and shook Dana awake. She looked surprised at first, but got the message when I jerked my thumb towards the door. I was rewarded with a contemptuous stare, but since she began to rise I let it go and exited the room.

Dean's mother had reappeared wearing a robe and stood near the front door. I took a position opposite her and briefly explained Dana didn't come home from school that day, which was why I was there at 3:00 o'clock in the morning making a fuss. Dean's mother seemed nonplussed and mentioned Dana told her she had permission to sleep over. That my daughter was a liar who goes AWOL was new to me, but anything was possible.

Finally, Dana emerged from the puppy palace and walked towards us half asleep. When she was only a few feet away I asked whether there was anything she wanted to say to Dean's mother, hoping for an apology. What I got was Dana, arms outstretched, silently breezing past while giving us the finger.

My problems had just begun.

# Chapter 28
# Cross Country

Dana had been living with me only a few weeks when I got trapped in a blizzard. It was February 2014 and I found myself on the other side of the country in Westport, Connecticut, on a day so cold it was impossible to stay outside more than a minute. I was intent on spreading my mother's ashes at Compo Beach despite the gale force winds. Snow and ice covered the shoreline making it difficult to reach the water, but since this was her last request I was determined to succeed.

My mother had spent many happy summers at this beach sunning and playing bridge. But when she died at 92 my siblings were so alienated from her they declined to hold a memorial service. My eldest brother wouldn't even send me her ashes unless I agreed to pay postage. Knowing how he felt, Mom was lucky she didn't end up at the foot of his driveway in the recycling bin.

You're never prepared to lose a parent even when they've overstayed their welcome. Mom was the strongest person I'd ever known. Tough and independent, she could easily have crossed the country in a Calistoga wagon. As a result, she lived alone for more than thirty years never needing anyone until the end. Even then she refused help.

Though she prized her intellect as her best quality, dementia had dimmed it in the last few years. She'd always been difficult, but once she lost her social filters she became downright ornery. I spent as much time with her as I could and then some but it wasn't as much as she needed. But by the end I was worn out. Of course, I thought she'd live forever. Being the pioneer-type she seemed invincible. But when she died it came as a surprise, and I'm sorry to say, a relief, too.

Since my mother wanted her ashes scattered at Compo I made sure it happened. Only six people attended: my middle brother, his wife, two of my mother's oldest friends, and Allie.

You're probably wondering why Allie was there. What can I say? It was the natural culmination of wanting two things and refusing to give up either one. Once the initial shock of Dana's behavior subsided, I wanted a companion with whom I could navigate rough waters. Allie may still have had an explosive temper, but I loved her too much to give her up.

Our small group huddled in the weak sunlight as a leaden sky threatened more snow. My brother, in a navy blue pea coat, hugged his wife, with Allie close to his side. Since no one could take the weather I kept my words brief. Why, heck, the Gettysburg Address was only 272 words. I aimed for half that.

When I finished speaking I scattered my mother's ashes in the wind, waited a moment, then emptied a small bottle of Maker's Mark as a chaser. Though I'd tried to gauge the wind most of my mother blew back on me, which was not surprising given our relationship. Thankfully, no one said anything. They were too busy dreaming of a warm car.

Lunch with my brother and his wife followed at a Chinese restaurant. It was a sad affair. The restaurant seemed only weeks from closing and this was the last time I'd probably see my brother. With a nearly 20 year age difference, no parents to connect us, and the geographical separation, it would be difficult to keep in touch. When it came time for Allie and me to drive to California I hugged my brother leaving an ocean of words unsaid.

\*\*\*

My trip east was brief given I needed to get back to Dana, but it did involve another notable event. I met Dr. Ivankovich.

As it turned out, Allie had one last session with her therapist before moving to California, so I tagged along. Ivankovich's office was in a single story office park fifteen miles outside of Twin Rivers. The parking lot was deserted when we arrived. When we entered the empty building the heat was turned off.

I was looking forward to meeting the man who'd discouraged Allie from being with me. I wanted to take his measure. Allie had her session while I sat freezing in the waiting room. Then, fifty minutes later, she reappeared with her therapist in tow.

Ivankovich was a clean cut, all-American type in the manner of a Dick Clark or Bob Costas. In his early 40s, he looked younger with short brown hair and a slight build. His khaki pants and crewneck sweater only reinforced his youthful image.

Allie got giggly when she introduced him to me. This threw me since it didn't seem the appropriate response. I knew how highly she valued this man's opinion, but he exercised a control over her that wasn't altogether healthy. Her awkwardness reinforced my concern.

"I really wanted to meet you, Dr. Ivankovich," I said.

"Please. Call me Bob."

"Well, Bob, I wanted to see how you feel since Allie is moving to California tomorrow."

"I'm okay with it," he said not missing a beat. "A lot has happened."

"Yes, but my hearing hasn't improved. Aren't you worried I won't be able to take care of myself?"

I was happy to cause this man some discomfort considering how much he'd caused me.

After an awkward moment of silence he responded,

"From what I hear, you're doing just fine."

Before I could reply, Allie made a noise to go. Ivankovich smiled, hugged her warmly then extended his hand towards me.

"Well, good luck to both of you. It sounds exciting."

As I shook his hand for the first and last time I hoped he would spontaneously combust. Much to my disappointment he was not even smoking.

When Allie decided to move to California I expected she'd leave Dr. Ivankovich behind. That didn't happen. Through the miracle of Skype Allie continued having her weekly sessions with him. I didn't say anything but I was unhappy. When Allie first told me about her many years of therapy I assumed it meant she'd worked through her problems. Little did I know it was more a warning than an indication of progress. It seemed like I'd have to put up with my nemesis a while longer.

\*\*\*

Long car trips are a test for any couple but the prospect of seven days in close quarters didn't bother me. I enjoyed spending time with Allie. For the most part everything went well. The only uncomfortable episode came three quarters of the way through our trip.

We were driving along Interstate 40 somewhere in New Mexico when we pulled off the highway to inspect a roadside sculpture. It was a life-sized T-rex and someone with a sense of humor had placed a mannequin in its jaws.

If you've never been to the American southwest it's worth going. Its fantastic rock formations and red landscape make the place look like Mars with breathable air. It may be desert hot and sparsely populated but that's part of its charm.

Allie snapped a photo of me looking at the dinosaur in pretend horror. I immediately posted it on Facebook along with the caption: *Roadside dino eats driving companion.* When I showed her the post, I expected her to laugh. Instead, she handed back my phone, looked at me in disgust, and said:

"Why don't you ever post pictures of us on Facebook?"

"What?"

"We've been in the car for five days and all you've done is post pictures of yourself in every state. You haven't posted one picture acknowledging us as a couple."

"That's not how I use Facebook."

"What am I anyway, your 'driving companion'? And how come you don't change your relationship status? Facebook says you're single. I thought we were in a relationship."

I felt the pit of my stomach go wrong. I tried explaining I didn't use Facebook the way most people did, which was to broadcast life updates. I used it to post humorous observations.

"That's fine if you want to keep us a secret," Allie said, turning away, "but I know what it means when your boyfriend doesn't post pictures of you."

"Allie, I'm not keeping you a secret. I've introduced you to my family, my friends. You've even met my children. And don't forget I posted that picture of you from my birthday. I'm not ashamed. I love you. I'm just not blasting it on Facebook."

The bad feeling lasted the better part of two states and was still poisoning the air when we checked into a Motel 6 near Flagstaff. Clearly, Allie was someone who enjoyed a "good fight" but given I'd grown up in a household filled with them I didn't share her pleasure.

That night, while she was in the shower, I checked her Facebook page. Mostly she used it to promote her paintings with the occasional photo of her sons or her dog. As I scrolled through her feed one thing was clear: she hadn't posted a picture of me either. Didn't that mean Allie was guilty of the same thing she accused me of? Given we had 700 miles to go it was best not to ask.

# Chapter 29
## Sugar and Spice

Living with Dana was a chance to make up for lost time. After being apart for five years, we were finally under the same roof. It felt good.

But I soon learned I was not prepared for life with a teenage girl. Dana left strands of hair in the sink; mascara marks on the counter; and never cleaned the bathtub. I could forgive her for squeezing the toothpaste from the middle of the tube but not for leaving the cap off. On top of that she never replaced a roll of toilet paper and regularly left wet towels on the bed. The fact she'd leave a cup of tea on an end table until it burned a ring in the finish was enough to drive me crazy. In other words, my daughter was a slob.

Part of the problem was she acted with impunity, and though I tried teaching her basic life skills she didn't seem to care. She never washed a dish, did the laundry, or made her bed. None of this behavior was allowed when I was growing up. Why should she get away with it?

I was so confused by my daughter I studied her like a lab experiment. Dana was plenty bright, but if her executive function was any lower she'd be in Special Ed. Once, I watched her try to light a match, which she honest-to-God couldn't figure out. When I showed her how, she lit the wrong end of an incense stick. Another time I was amazed to see her sew a button on her pants. When I examined her handiwork, I realized she'd sewn it on backwards.

Dana also had a tendency to break things. Once, she spilled nail polish remover on my dining room table, which damaged the wood beyond repair. It's one thing not to clear your place after dinner and quite another to ruin the carpet and three towels when putting highlights in your hair.

Dana's habit of losing things also surprised me. She made ear buds disappear like a magician palms quarters. Gift bracelets and necklaces were lost within days, sometimes hours, of receipt. At first I thought it was carelessness, but as her possessions vanished I wondered if it was a developmental problem. I mean, what do you do with a kid who shatters the screen of a tablet computer a week after getting it, or rips a cabinet door right off its hinges? These were the risks of living with Dana.

I certainly didn't lack for nagging. Still, nothing I did had much effect. Some things I wrote off as roommate adjustment problems. Then I noticed how forgetful she was. It wasn't just that Dana forgot what I told her, she forgot important things: not a day went by when she didn't either leave her iPhone, her charger, her make up, or her hairbrush at home. I expected her to give me a hard time about keeping her room clean, but when she couldn't remember to bring her phone to school I thought apart of her brain must still be squishy.

One of Dana's most embarrassing habits was that she swore without compunction. Among the awful things she called her mother was "evil, psycho, demon cunt." Not that I'm squeamish. My father practically invented the "f" word. But was this something her mother put up with? I had no idea.

There are few things crueler than a teenage daughter. They have no problem telling a parent exactly what's wrong with them. Unfortunately, they're right at least half the time. One day, while putting away laundry, I noticed a tangle of multi-colored lace in her drawer. When I investigated further it turned out to be half a dozen, not very clean, thongs, which I immediately threw out. Because Dana's organizational skills were poor, weeks passed she noticed anything missing. When she did, I received her full fury.

"Dad!" she screamed. "Were you in my room?"

"Yes."

"What the fuck! You're violating my privacy."

"Fourteen year old girls are not allowed to wear thongs in my house," I replied. "Besides, you're not entitled to privacy until the age of consent."

Dana looked at me as if I'd clubbed a baby seal then let loose a string of expletives so foul a rapper would blush.

It wasn't as if there weren't consequences to Dana's behavior. I took away her phone; banned television; and changed the password on our wi-fi. When that didn't work, I barred her from Snapchat, Instagram, and Tumblr, which she could only access on my phone. She remained undeterred.

By April the situation was out of control. Dana's grades had dropped so far her school warned me she might not graduate. And yet I could barely get her to study, let alone meet with the tutor I'd hired. When I received a letter from the state informing me she'd missed so many classes she was officially a truant I sank into despair.

Dana's decline was so fast, so unexpected, and so unpredictable that it took me by surprise. It was like being clobbered by a tidal wave. Before she'd moved in I'd bought a shower curtain with the optimistic phrases: "Be Fearless," "Follow Your Dreams," "Find Your Passion" splashed across the front. I'd hoped the messages would seep into my daughter's brain when taking a shower. Now my shower curtain seemed an advanced case of parental lameness.

Finally, one morning, Dana refused to go to school. She'd pulled this stunt before, so I knew she wasn't sick. Still, how many mental health days can an 8th grader take? Lying in bed, she pulled the covers over her head and moaned she'd rather die than go to school. I tried reasoning with her, but after thirty minutes I called the police. That day, Dana went to Kent Middle School in the back of a squad car.

***

Why was Dana having so much difficulty? Was the divorce responsible, or was it something else? I was pretty sure she never witnessed any fights between her mother and me, but kids have a way of sensing these things. Besides, her mother had shared her opinion about me, which couldn't have helped.

One Sunday afternoon, I was at home reading the newspaper when my phone started to buzz. I wasn't sure who was trying to contact me. When I looked at the screen there was a notice from Tumblr saying three new photographs had arrived. That was strange: I hardly used Tumblr, and nobody ever sent me anything. Nevertheless, I tapped the icon and waited for the pictures to load. When the first photograph filled my screen I had no trouble discerning what it was. It was a close up of some guy holding his enormous red dick.

I was stunned at first, even more when I realized it was my daughter's Tumblr account not mine. After some quick detective work I saw that she'd been conversing with some twenty-something idiot on an Air Force base in Oklahoma. What's more, their conversation was strictly pornographic. I'm not sure what surprised me: that my 14 year

142

old daughter knew what these acts were, or that she expressed a desire to perform them. What was worse? I soon found photos of my daughter no father should ever see. The trap door of disappointment opened beneath me.

Dana was in her room playing her guitar while this was going on. Usually, I loved the sound of her sweet, tremulous voice, but the photos on my phone were the kind of performance that must be stopped.

When I asked Dana to come into the living room, she appeared the picture of innocence, dragging her guitar by its throat.

"What's this?" I asked, showing her the guy's photo.

"Looks like a penis, Dad."

"Why is this guy sending dick pics?"

"Ha! That's funny, Dad. You got dick pics."

"He's not sending them to me. He's sending them to you!"

"Let me see that!" she said, grabbing my phone.

She looked quickly at the screen and deleted the first picture. When I grabbed the phone back she started to scream.

"Give me that you shit head!"

"Look Dana, you're sexting this guy and I want it to stop."

"Are you crazy? I'm not sexting."

"Do you have any idea what can happen? They can arrest you for disseminating child pornography. Second, this guy can post your pictures all over the web. Do you want your friends at school to see these?" I waved the phone at her.

"Fuck off, Dad. That guy doesn't have pictures of me."

"Oh, yeah?" I said. "Then what's this?"

I showed her one of the many gynecological photos she'd taken. Dana looked surprised, but only for a moment. Then she bolted from the room.

I followed her until she ran into the bathroom, slamming the door in my face. Then I heard the lock turn. I was confused about what was going on here. Was Dana hiding in the bathroom because she was embarrassed; trying to avoid punishment; or needing time to cook up a story?

When I knocked she didn't respond. I took a minute to decide what to do. Normally, a father would never intrude on his 14 year old daughter in the bathroom. But the longer I stood there the worse feeling I got. I knocked again, this time harder. When I got no answer I threatened to break the door down. Finally, Dana turned the lock and the door swung open. That was when I saw all the blood.

There was so much of it, Dana looked like Carrie in the horror movie. My brain went numb before I pulled myself together. My daughter had made a dozen horizontal incisions on each arm running from wrist to elbow. The incisions had filled with blood, which now dripped like tiny rivers onto the white tile floor.

The black art of cutting was not something I was familiar with, and frankly it freaked me out. This was exactly what Barbie had warned me about, and though I'd dismissed her concern, she turned out to be right. Over the next several months Dana became proficient at cutting. I never knew, when I tried parenting her, whether she would run for a razor, or disappear for the day.

In the meantime, I was just a frightened single father concerned his daughter was bleeding to death. Wrapping her arms in a bath towel, I guided her out the front door. The Emergency Room at Marin General was less than a mile away. I only hoped it wouldn't be crowded.

# Chapter 30
# The Dutch Boy

Meanwhile, Allie settled in at The Dutch Boy.

The Dutch Boy was named after the Dutch Boy paint factory in East Oakland. The factory had closed in the 70s and been converted into a live/work space. It was now a magnet for artists who needed room but couldn't afford much rent. It seemed the perfect place for Allie to paint.

Allie had rejected the suburbs as a place to live, fancying herself an edgy urban creature. The Dutch Boy certainly delivered on this. Wedged between Amtrak and BART, it sat in the middle of an industrial wasteland in the worst part of Oakland. To give you an idea just how bad that part of town was, the Dutch Boy was surrounded by a chain link fence, eight feet high, with razor wire running along the top. The only way you could get out was by unlocking one of the ludicrously heavy gates, which were big enough to guard Fort Knox. Though the fence kept the riff raff out it had the unfortunate effect of making you feel imprisoned, which in many ways you were given the neighborhood.

My sense of white privilege, deeply ingrained from growing up in Fairfield County, Connecticut, did not serve me well in a pluralistic environment. For starters, I constantly worried about being robbed, shot, or carjacked every time I visited. To be fair, East Oakland was undergoing gentrification. Still, the Dutch Boy was stranded in a godforsaken no-man's-land of trash, grit, and crime.

Since it had once been a factory the Dutch Boy looked like you might expect: a box three stories tall. It was painted an adobe red to soften its industrial character, but you couldn't hide its purpose. Thirty years later lead paint so contaminated parts of the building they remained off limits.

If Oakland represented bohemian, certain parts were more akin to a war zone. It was easy to tell from Allie's window on which street folk were mentally ill, suffered from substance abuse, or wanted to rip you off. And that was just the tenants. For example, Allie lived next door to an apartment that was such a hoarder's paradise the Collier brothers could have been subletting. A few doors down, a man in his 20s raised parrots and designed inhalant devices for a marijuana company. There was also a sculptor who drank too much, and a tatted-up pair of lesbians whose Pomeranians barked at me.

You had to be a little crazy to live at the Dutch Boy. Prostitutes and their johns parked under Allie's window at night while homeless men, meth tweakers and junk scavengers kept things lively by day. One guy, who lived in an RV at the end of the street, was welcomed by residents because he chased the hookers off at night. He was a friendly guy, unless he'd been drinking. It was always best to note his condition before approaching.

All of this struck me as bleak. Still, there were aspects to the Dutch Boy I liked. One is that a rail spur ran right by Allie's door. Every couple of nights a slow freight rolled by with its headlight shining. I loved its smell of diesel fumes and listening to its engine labor under all that weight. Allie understood, and let me stop what we were doing to watch the train go by.

It's a measure of how much I loved her that I made East Oakland if not my primary residence at least my second home. It wasn't Connecticut. It wasn't even Marin. But it was a sign I could adapt and that's what mattered to Allie.

\*\*\*

One thing I admired about Allie was that she was adventuresome at heart. Within a month of moving, she'd discovered a local Vietnamese restaurant that served excellent Pho, had taken me to Phat Matt's for barbeque, and discovered a neighborhood food truck serving delicious Mexican cuisine at a reasonable price.

Unfortunately, the Dutch Boy scared the pants off my kids. It was just too foreign, the neighbors too scary, for a pair of Marin girls. We had our successes though. Allie took Dana and her sister to see *Frozen*, which they loved. While my daughters sucked down Cokes and gobbled Twizzlers Allie and I held hands in the dark, rolling our eyes at the saccharine sweetness of Disney.

Dana hadn't calmed down as much as spread out her misbehavior. On alternate weekends when the girls stayed with their mother I went to Allie's. It was those Fridays, however, when Dana chose to disappear, forcing me to cancel my plans and spend the evening searching for her. I hoped she wasn't doing it to frustrate my romance, but who can parse the mind of a 14 year old?

Because of this, Allie and I once went three weeks without seeing each other. True, she was out of state part of the time, but it was hard to justify. According to Google we only lived 26 miles from each other. Interstate 80 may have been a notorious bottleneck but traffic wasn't the reason I couldn't see Allie. Dana was.

When I wasn't transporting my daughter to and from school, I guarded her at home, yet she still managed to escape. It's a bad feeling not knowing where your daughter is. I eventually wised up enough to download her contacts into my phone. Later I supplemented them with her friends' parents' information. Still, it was no way to operate.

Allie gave me plenty of advice, since she'd raised three boys, but Dana continued to strain our relationship. Soon I felt trapped between loving Allie and parenting Dana. Of course, I wanted to love them both, but someone always suffered.

Then, when things couldn't possibly get worse I was contacted by California's Department of Child Protective Services (CPS). This is the state agency responsible for children's welfare. The first thing I thought was, "What about mine?" Then, I wondered who had filed the complaint. The school? My ex? Dana? When they arrived at my door it felt like a visit from the East German Stasi.

I prepared a list of everything my ex and I were doing to help Dana. She had a weekly appointment with a therapist, a monthly appointment with a prescribing psychiatrist, went to Dialectical Behavioral Training seminar every Wednesday, and had a tutor Tuesday nights. In addition to catechism on Mondays and Japanese school on Saturdays we'd surrounded this kid with so much support it was a wonder she could breathe.

It was hard enough dealing with Dana, but now I had CPS breathing down my neck. And the worst part of it was I felt ashamed. I'd never in a million years thought I'd be the kind of parent to attract such scrutiny. After all, wasn't CPS for child abusers, junkies, and welfare moms? I might be struggling, but I'd never let my children suffer. Besides, I was doing my best to help Dana. Was CPS telling me I'd failed?

Nothing toughens you up like being a parent, but what more could go wrong? I learned never to ask that question again because when the answer arrived it was not only worse than I imagined, there was nothing I could do about it.

# Chapter 31
# Work

My book had been in stores for almost a year. Press interviews and author talks were all behind me. I'd gotten some positive reviews, which was encouraging, but the *New York Times* hadn't reviewed me at all, which I found disappointing.

Positive reviews are nice but publishers want a book to sell. Sadly, the American public are not book buyers. They're not even readers as I understand the concept. The US ranks 22nd in a global survey of the time a nation's populace spends reading. Incredibly, only half of US adults report reading a book in the past year.

The sad truth is that in a nation of 350 million people a hardcover book only needs to sell 50,000 copies to be a success. That's only 1.4% of the country's population. Sometimes a book makes the bestseller list selling even less. Considering 80 million people bought a ticket to *Jurassic World*, and 12 million bought the video game *Mario Kart*, books don't sell anywhere near other forms of entertainment. In other words, they're more Etsy than Amazon.

The way the industry works publishers are more willing to take a chance on an unknown author than buy his second book if the first one didn't sell. That's because in the absence of data publishers can believe an author's first book will do well. But at 10,000 copies my sales weren't good enough to justify publisher interest in a follow up. I'd always figured the highest hurdle would be getting your first book accepted; once published you'd be on your way. Now, that seemed misguided.

Life doesn't stop because you're deaf, crazy, or in love. Now I was settled in Marin I needed to find work. Money wasn't the only reason I needed a job. Allie and I were talking about me getting a Cochlear Implant (CI). Cochlear surgery is fabulously expensive. The only way I could do it was with health insurance and the only way to get that was to have a job.

I'd been courting a bookstore in Marin for a year. It was only a mile from my apartment and I shopped there regularly. I'd scored an appointment with the store's manager, a young, hip guy who gelled his hair until it stood up like a brush fire. When I arrived, the smell of coffee filled the store. I noticed one of the shelves displayed my book face out; a nice touch that made me feel welcome.

I followed the manager to the cookbook section where we sat on folding chairs for our interview. He did his best to make me feel comfortable, but the store's background music drowned out most of what he said. Oh sure, I caught a preposition here a pronoun there, but not enough to construct a sentence.

As I strained to listen, I debated what to do. I really wanted this job but was afraid to show weakness. Finally, when I realized I couldn't take the chance of missing something important, I worked up the courage to say:

"Would you mind speaking up a bit? I'm having trouble hearing over the music."

"Of course!" he chuckled. "I'm a soft talker."

I could have kissed him for that.

Though he tried speaking louder his voice soon trailed off. After a minute, I was back to not hearing him. I'd told the manager about my hearing loss. Still, the last thing I wanted was to demonstrate just how bad it was. When I still I couldn't understand him, I threw caution to the wind.

"Would you mind if we moved outside? It's quieter out there and I don't want to miss a word you say."

Once again the store manager graciously complied. But when we moved outside construction in a nearby store drowned out everything he said.

Poor hearing wasn't my only problem. I'd learned that gainful employment automatically disqualifies me for disability. This didn't concern me as much as it did Dr. Squeaky-voice. She was the one who insisted I file. The last thing I wanted was to be considered disabled, so when Social Security rejected my claim I was relieved.

Dr. Squeaky-voice wanted me to appeal the decision but I was reluctant. I knew if I got the bookstore job I'd no longer qualify for disability. That was okay with me since I wanted to make my own way. But a voice inside me wondered what would happen if I got this job and lost it because of my hearing? I'd not only be unemployed, I'd have blown any chance to apply for disability.

It's amazing how long people can talk without realizing you don't hear a word they say. I guess its human nature. Most of us would rather talk than listen. All someone with a formidable hearing impairment had to do was stick the occasional "uh-huh" in the appropriate place and we skated by. Despite my best efforts though, I was convinced when I left that morning I hadn't gotten the job. But an email from the bookstore manager was waiting for me when I arrived home. As a former headhunter I knew hiring decisions take time - the only ones that come quickly are rejections - so imagine my surprise when I opened the email and read that the bookstore wanted to hire me.

Now, if I could only do the job without hearing, everything would be fine.

# Chapter 32
## Beauty in the Breakdown

Working in a bookstore is a noble profession even at $11.00 an hour. One thing I noticed right away was how nice the staff were. They knew about my hearing impairment and went out of their way to help me. I not only didn't have to answer the phone, or work near the latte machine, someone also turned the background music down a notch. There was still one thing I couldn't hear though, and that was the customers.

It's hard to miss how angry people get when you ask them to repeat themselves. Most people will say something twice; more than that invites irritation. If they wanted a book whose title I knew I might decipher their request, but if it was an author I didn't know, I didn't stand a chance. I made one poor guy ask where the bathroom was so many times everyone in the store knew he had to go. By the end of the week I dreaded customer interactions.

Working in a bookstore made me realize just how problematic my hearing was. Watching people's mouths without understanding what was coming out triggered a sweaty panic I never got used to. No matter how hard I tried their words were invisible.

By my second month I slipped into a depression. That makes it sound like putting on a comfortable pair of shoes, but the truth is it happened so gradually I hardly noticed. I certainly didn't wish for mental illness, but it tiptoed in like a cold before pneumonia.

After six weeks of not hearing customers, sadness took on a life of its own. At first I kept a list to remind myself about life's pleasures. Later, when I was feeling despondent, I changed its name to "Reasons Not to Kill Myself." Even daylight savings didn't release me from the dark and heavy weight.

Sometimes depression is a logical reaction. Other times it's brain chemistry. In my case, it was probably both. There was a time when my skills had been valued, but the world no longer needed me. My skills, my interests, my me-ness were obsolete. I was headed for extinction.

Depression has been described as like falling down a rabbit hole. You end up in a world where nothing is the same. Distorted thoughts, compromised cognition, and wrong thinking become commonplace. In my case, I have a helper - a small voice that tells me I'm no good. Normally, I keep this voice in check. It might pop up to embarrass me now and then, but I don't dwell on it. But my run of bad luck had emboldened this voice to speak up.

We often have a narrative running through our head like subtitles in a movie. It's not always clear where it comes from. Sometimes we've internalized it from our parents, other times we get it from our spouse, or a boss. Often the narrative is negative: "You're a loser, a failure, you're just like your father."

Everybody has some version of this but mine had turned into an endless stream of negative self-talk. Mental health practitioners call this rumination. I called it "self-loathing moments," or SLMs.

Self-loathing moments were memories of every stupid or embarrassing thing I'd ever said or done. It turned out I had an uncanny ability to remember such things decades after they'd happened. I replayed these memories over and over until they plowed a trench so deep in my brain I couldn't climb out.

For someone who wanted to be a good person, it's amazing how bad I felt about myself. I may have walked into the bookstore wearing a smile every day, but it was a mask hiding my true feelings.

"I'm selfish. I'm irresponsible."

"I've abandoned my family."

"I'm a loser who gave everything up for a writing career that never happened."

"I'm broken... damaged... beyond repair."

The voice may have been small, but it didn't lack for conviction. It was a determined messenger throttling my confidence at every opportunity.

When people talk about "hearing voices" they usually mean schizophrenic hallucinations. In my case, the only voice I heard was my own. But that voice took on such malevolent intent it could only mean me harm.

How do you calm a restless mind trapped in recrimination? It might've helped had I recognized the problem but the very thing driving me insane rendered me incapable of fighting back. Instead, my self loathing moments ran wild until eventually they reached the point where they were the only thing filling my head.

***

With a newly minted PhD in self-loathing, my life took on a darker cast. My worldview became so negative I saw the worst in everything. Depression, like hearing loss, isolates you. It prevents you from asking for the help you need. Things you might normally do to defeat it, such as exercise or socializing, are impossible. I spent more energy hiding my depression than fighting it.

I was so embarrassed by how I felt I kept it secret. Nobody knew, not my daughters or my friends and certainly not Allie. The reason was simple. Most people see mental illness as a moral failing. Depression isn't like that though. Depressed people aren't lazy, or self-indulgent, they're trapped inside their heads unable to free themselves. It's like being buried alive. Given societal views it's easier to admit a hearing loss than admit you're depressed and that's no exaggeration.

Dr. Ivankovich already thought I was wrong for Allie, and the last thing I wanted was to give him more ammunition. It didn't help Allie had no clue how to talk to a depressed person. One morning, after dropping Dana at school, I felt so poorly I lay on the couch all day. Later that afternoon, feeling guilty, I texted Allie my confession. Her response?

"Get up and do something!"

"Walk it off" was something a Little League coach might tell you after getting beaned by a baseball but it doesn't help a depressed person. Of course, it's never easy. Depressed people wallow in despair rather than seek help. It's the sickness that refuses a cure. But don't blame us. Depression is like falling in quicksand. The more you struggle the faster you sink. Sometimes it just feels better to lie still.

As March turned into April I remained stuck in February. I found it harder to get up in the morning and easier to go to bed at night. If you had read my mind, it looked like a satellite image of a hurricane gathering strength.

All you have to do for atrophy to occur is nothing. My life soon came to a complete halt. I still took Dana to school, made her meals every day, and went to work, but in all other respects I was the walking dead. I may never have had a dog talk to me, seen something that wasn't there, or communicated with a ghost, but in every other respect I was bat-shit crazy.

# Chapter 33
## Slippery Slope

It was clear I could no longer work at the bookstore. Not only could I not hear the customers, I couldn't get enough hours to make a living. Since I was only a part-time employee I didn't qualify for health insurance. Without it, I couldn't get a cochlear implant.

Given my state of mind, looking for another job was a Herculean task. I could barely get out of bed in the morning. Still, I was determined to find work. I wanted to prove to Allie I was worthy of her love. I chose to ignore that my hearing made it impossible.

After giving it some thought I decided a limousine service offered the best chance for employment. Driving doesn't require a lot of hearing, and since most people hate chatty drivers I wouldn't have to talk to the customers. Plus, the economy was booming. Limo jobs should be plentiful.

A Google search generated the top five transportation companies in San Francisco. The leader, Breuer Transport, asked to be contacted only by email, so I started with them, and bingo! they were hiring. After a brief online questionnaire, I was scheduled for an interview.

Breuer Transport was located in San Francisco south of the Bay Bridge. The company's headquarters was a former customs warehouse on the city's waterfront. The area reeked of 20th century technology long since abandoned. To prove it, a huge Navy ship sat mothballed next door. I should fit right in.

Breuer's warehouse was cavernous. Filled with high-end motor coaches and black jitney vans, it was so dark you could barely see. The smell of motor oil combined with the sound of pigeons flapping in the rafters made the place feel like a garage, which it was.

The scene would be depressing in the best of moods but given how negative I felt the place seemed downright menacing. Full of machines and empty of humanity the warehouse was so unwelcoming I had to steel myself to go in.

Once inside, I noticed three 40 foot containers sitting next to the entrance. One was marked "Dispatch," the middle one "HR," and the third, "Operations." I headed for the container marked HR, climbed the stairs, and entered a waiting room.

The container inside was divided into a tiny warren of offices. Though the interior was partially finished, it gave the impression that just enough money had been spent to make the place habitable. A few worn chairs and a tired copy of *Time* magazine graced the waiting area. Otherwise the place was empty.

After a few minutes, a disembodied voice called out and directed me to an office near the back. I stepped through a doorway into a room so small there was only room for a desk, a chair, and the person occupying it. A nameplate read: Glenn W. Healy, HR.

Healy had a shock of white hair the color of dirty snow and a too tight suit that strained across his middle. He was finishing lunch but introduced himself, waving me towards a folding chair leaning against the wall. The only way I could fit in his office once I opened the chair was by angling it in the doorway.

"So, tell me," Healy began. "Why does a guy from a fancy place like Marin want to drive a limo?"

The question didn't surprise me. I'd been working on the answer for days. What did surprise me was that Breuer's head of HR spent the next ten minutes trying to talk me out of the job. Of course, I missed half of what he said, maybe more, but the gist was clear. He was trying to get rid of me.

I refused to concede. Breuer paid $15 an hour plus tips, promised a 40 hour work week, and offered health insurance. When Healy wound down, I launched my pitch.

"I'm a writer, Mr. Healy, who needs flexible hours." I handed him a copy of my book. "I've got a 14 year old daughter at home, so I need something that pays around $40,000 a year."

I watched Healy's face closely. He remained unmoved.

"I've lived in the Bay Area for twenty years and San Francisco for nine. I know my way around."

Still nothing.

"I also know Breuer caters to a high-end clientele. Given my background, I understand how your customers want to be treated. I also know how difficult they can be, which doesn't bother me in the least."

I was starting to make a dent, so I kept going.

"You know, I used to use Breuer limos when I headed an ad agency here. The only difference is now I'll be riding up front."

Healy chuckled. I took this as my opportunity to close him.

"And I'm one of the few guys you'll see this week who can take direction, pass a urine test, and doesn't have a felony conviction. Give me a chance Mr. Healy, I'm sure you'll be happy. If not, we can part friends."

"Right," Healy said, wiping his mouth. "Go next door to Operations and get scheduled for a driving test. Assuming you pass the background check, you've got a job."

"Ok, but in the interest of full disclosure there's one thing I want you to know." Healy raised an eyebrow. "As you can see, I wear hearing aids." I turned my head side to side so he could see the devices in both my ears. "I'm okay in one-on-one situations like this, but I have trouble if there's too much noise." I paused to let this sink in. "I assume Breuer has some sort of a computer in their cars. If your dispatch can issue me instructions via computer, I shouldn't have trouble. You just don't want to call me on my cell phone. I can't hear well on that."

Healy appreciated my candor. "That should be doable," he nodded.

I had no business applying for this job given depression had both hands wrapped around my throat but I refused to give in. As luck would have it, Breuer's training program started in a week. I'd finally caught a lucky break.

\*\*\*

In the meantime, I continued working at the bookstore. But since they only wanted me Sundays, I was at a loose end the rest of the week. Soon, I graduated from lying on the sofa to spending all day in bed.

I'd never spent a day in bed. Normally, just the thought would horrify me. But I was so depressed I didn't have a choice. Part of me knew things were bad. I'd stopped writing, which wasn't good, but it wasn't until I stopped reading that I knew I was in serious trouble. Of more concern, the skin condition that had plagued me in Woodside had now entered the flesh eating stage. My body was so riddled with scabs I couldn't look in the mirror.

It was also around this time I became obsessed with living in a van. I'd always known I'd end up homeless, but rather than live in a remote cabin like the Unabomber, I decided living in a vehicle was more practical. As it turned out, there's a sub culture of people living in vans with numerous blogs devoted to the practice. I learned about which vans are best to live in, where to park at night, and how to find shower facilities.

At some point, I told Allie what I was doing and her reaction was classic:

"The one thing guys living in a van all have in common are no girlfriends," she told me.

I laughed when I heard this but she was giving me a message. Since I loved Allie I took what she said to heart. Once, she told me it wasn't until her second husband threatened suicide with a pistol that she decided to divorce him. This wasn't surprising given her father murdered her mother with a handgun, but it did seem cold. It wasn't until later I realized how little concern she had for her husband's mental state. Maybe she had boundaries after all.

The problem with Allie's honesty was she spoke the truth in such an unvarnished fashion it was sometimes hard to take. She was not always right either. Once, after seeing how neatly I hung my clothes she asked whether I was "on the spectrum".

"All the men I date are a little spectrum-y," she added. "That might explain Dana's dead-eyed look."

My daughter had a dead-eyed look?

Another time over dinner she let slip how disappointed she was when we first met because I had circles under my eyes and was a bit overweight. Okay, that may be true, but I didn't need more reasons to hate myself. I was doing just fine on my own.

The thing about Allie was she had the uncanny ability to reflect my worst fears. She'd already pushed the not-being-able-to-care-for-yourself button, but when she started complaining that my hearing was "draaaaaaining," she was stomping on my fingers while I was hanging off a cliff.

Dana wasn't helping either. My daughter was misbehaving so badly it was hard to keep up with her. In addition to failing grades, cringe worthy outfits, sketchy friends, and more time spent in front of a mirror than I thought healthy, she was still going missing.

One afternoon we agreed I'd pick her up after school, but when I arrived she was nowhere to be seen. I texted, asking where she was, and received an almost instant reply telling me she was in the grocery store across the street and I should ask for the manager. When I did, I was escorted up a narrow flight of stairs to an attic office. There, sitting opposite my 14 year old daughter, was a policeman. She'd been arrested for shoplifting.

My first thought was "how in the hell am I going to explain this to Child Protective Services?" but I put that aside to deal with the matter in front of me.

A tall slim can with gothic lettering sat on a table. It turned out to be the energy drink my daughter had taken without paying. The police officer was trying to extract information from Dana but she was not cooperating. In fact, she had clammed up, replacing her usual expression with the dead-eyed stare Allie was referring to.

I was still trying to understand how my daughter learned to channel the look of a hardened criminal when the policeman turned to me for help. He explained Dana was being charged with a misdemeanor and would have to appear in juvenile court. She'd be assigned a probation officer and would probably have to perform community service. When the policeman finished I apologized on Dana's behalf. Then the manager informed us Dana was banned from the store for a year.

During the car ride home, I tried thinking of something constructive to say. When I couldn't come up with anything I blew my top instead.

"Jesus, Dana, what were you thinking?"

All I got was a sullen look of indifference.

That weekend, when Dana's little sister heard what had happened, she waited until her sister left the room before waving me over.

"Dad, Dad!" she whispered in my ear. "Can we put Dana in a foster home?"

I actually had to think about it before shaking my head. Given how I was feeling, it wasn't such a crazy idea.

# Chapter 34
# Limo Man

The inheritance from my mother paid for the black suit I needed to drive a limo. In addition, I bought five white button down shirts and six pairs of black socks. I even bought a shoe shine kit so my shoes looked impeccable. I may have felt like shit but I was determined to look my best.

On my first day of training I woke up at 5:00am and made the hour long drive to San Francisco. The roads were empty at that hour, the city still asleep. I watched as the homeless underneath the Bay Bridge began to break camp. This could be me in a few months unless I made this job work.

When I arrived at Breuer I was told to wait in the drivers' trailer. The trailer was tucked in the far corner of the warehouse. Not much bigger than a shipping container, it held several faux leather sofas, a small kitchen with a fridge and a TV so loud it prevented me from understanding what the other drivers said.

It was customary to keep the lights off inside the trailer so everything was dark. A few drivers slept on the sofas, man-spreading with their heads tipped back. Since they intimidated me I picked an empty sofa and feigned interest in the morning newscast. I didn't want anyone talking to me for fear of betraying my hearing loss.

At precisely 7:00 a large young black woman with a hair weave so long it reached past her bottom opened the door and called for trainees to follow. This was Aisha who, as luck would have it, was to be our instructor. It's safe to say Aisha didn't have an advanced degree in anything but she was just as impressive without it. She not only knew how to drive a gigantic motor coach, she knew how to handle people. And though she had a no-nonsense attitude that made you behave, she radiated a warmth and understanding that was inviting. I immediately took to her.

Aisha herded five black women, one black man, and me onto a Breuer jitney which she drove to a hotel just off Union Square. We headed inside to an upstairs room that was reserved for our training and took seats around a conference table.

In the beginning, I thought it wise to keep my mouth shut. The majority of Breuer's trainees had already driven buses either for casinos or local transit authorities. Only one trainee besides me was there to drive a limo, and that was only until a dispatch position opened up.

As it turned out I was the only white person in Breuer's training program. I'd never been in the minority before and felt nervous. I didn't need to be though. On the first day a trainee named Joseph reached out to me. He had a scratchy voice and a marvelous, dry-roasted chuckle. Even though I understood only half of what he said he was one of those people you just want to spend time with. Short, with shiny hair he treated with something, Joseph was relaxed and friendly. I followed him like a puppy.

Over the next four weeks I got to know each of my fellow trainees, all of whom had interesting stories. One woman, who was highly argumentative, sported long fingernails and a witch's brew of hair. She took every opportunity to tell us she had too much experience to be in a training program. What she didn't understand was that Breur wanted us to learn how to do things the Breur way. Aisha saw to it she was gone by the end of the week.

We spent most of our first day watching a training video that was distinguished by the fact there wasn't a single person you'd want to fuck in it. Around mid-morning I realized my suit pants still had the chunky security tag attached to the leg. I was mortified. Either no one had noticed or my fellow trainees were too kind to say, so I ducked out at lunch, headed to a nearby Macy's to have it removed, and dashed back to class.

I wanted to do this job well but it wasn't easy given how I felt. Half of me wanted to be a limo driver while the other half wanted to stay in bed. After surviving my first day, I headed to the Dutch Boy for the comfort of Allie.

The next day I was almost fired. Though I'd planned for an hour long commute, I misjudged the traffic to San Francisco. To make matters worse, there was an accident on the Bay Bridge that brought everybody to a halt. By the time I arrived, Aisha and the bus had left.

I checked in at dispatch. After confirming I'd missed the bus a tall skinny white kid with a shaved head stepped up to the window and screamed: "Late trainees make for bad employees!"

I tried not to cry but I was so depressed it felt like the big bad wolf blowing in the door on my house made of straw. Nevertheless, the dispatcher had a point.

My head was spinning but I didn't admit defeat. No limo job meant no money, no health insurance, no cochlear implant and no Allie. I couldn't let that happen.

I've always been good at coming up with solutions in tight situations. Though my thought process was funky I tamped down my panic and looked at my watch. That's when I realized it was only 7:15. Class didn't start for another 15 minutes. If I drove like hell, I could reach the hotel before class began and pretend I'd planned on driving to work that day. It ended up costing me $50 to park but it was worth it. I saved my job.

\*\*\*

Not hearing is like not being able to read. You constantly worry you'll be found out. Fortunately, once my classmates caught on to my problem they started covering for me. They repeated instructions I didn't understand, told me where to go and what to do, and answered Aisha's question when I failed to hear her. Gratefulness spread through me like a warming glass of scotch.

Though my hearing seemed the problem the truth was the hearing-world wasn't very nice to me. It constantly denied my deafness and made few if any accommodations. Virtually no one changed their communication style even when I advocated for myself. Of course, I contributed to the problem by hiding my deafness. Worse, I had zero knowledge of sign language, the Deaf community, or Deaf culture, all of which could have helped. Instead, I relied on the technology of my hearing aids, which increasingly failed me. In other words, I wasn't only deaf, I was ignorant, all in the misguided hope that I could get by in the hearing world. It would take me years to learn otherwise.

My fellow trainees may not have had the benefits I did growing up, but they were far more savvy in dealing with discrimination. Years of white privilege meant I was a fish out of water without my protective bubble. That the drivers at Breur understood this, accepting me without reservation, seemed the kindest act in my swiftly darkening world.

Breuer placed a high priority on having a clean, orderly appearance. I shared their philosophy but liked a little flair. One day, Aisha scolded me for wearing a black tie with a pattern on it. Ties should be solid black or nothing, so she made me take it off. Still, I noticed Breuer made allowances for eccentricity. Though my tie wasn't regulation, there was a driver (one of the few white men besides myself), who wore a bowler hat while working. Since he'd been there many years I assumed he'd earned the privilege. Still, it was an encouraging sign. The next day, I bought a solid black tie.

One of our homework assignments was to memorize the names and locations of the city's top hotels. I excelled at this, having stayed at most of them. Still, I kept my pride to myself; I didn't want my colleagues knowing my background. All I needed was to watch Joseph park a $600,000 motor coach in a space so tight there was no margin for error to know he was better at his job than I was at mine. The last thing I wanted was for my colleagues to think I felt otherwise.

Our second week, class was held in the Breuer warehouse. We learnt how to inspect our vehicles for dents, scratches, or broken taillights. This "pre-flight" check was important because we were responsible for any damage caused during our shift. No one wanted to pay for the carelessness of another driver. Besides, an accident could get you fired, so we took the inspections seriously.

One thing I learnt that week was that throwing up in a limo is pretty common. This surprised me. I figured our customers were the kind of people who didn't barf in the back seat, but Aisha told me this was not the case. In fact, she encouraged everyone to carry paper towels and latex gloves when on the job.

Halfway through the program, the head of driver training took us to Napa on a day trip. The goal was to show us our clients' lifestyle so we could serve them better. I relished the distraction, not because it demonstrated Breuer trained its drivers better than anybody else (which they did), but because I wouldn't have to drive that day. Given my depression made driving an uncertain act, the lowered expectations of a field trip suited me just fine.

Not all days were spent in Napa. Some days, I was tapped to drive. Otis, the man who rode with me, was a phlegmatic guy in his 60s with a graying soul patch and a dark-colored Trilby on his head.

Otis wasn't the kind to get ruffled. He was too cool for that. But my driving shook him up so much I worried he was going to fail me.

"You're too close to that car! Signal before changing lanes! Watch yourself in traffic!"

One reason I was nervous was I couldn't hear Otis' instructions from the back seat. I explained about my hearing, but Otis was the one who seemed deaf. Things got better when I hit upon the trick of repeating everything he said to invite correction. Still, I frequently screwed up. Even though I drove just fine alone, I was a mess when watched.

Despite feeling intimidated I was a diligent student. I was conscientious and enthusiastic, but just beneath the surface I was coming apart. When you do something because you think you should rather than because you want to it creates a stressful dichotomy. I got so anxious before work I had to take an Ativan just to get out the door. I may have attended Choate and Amherst, been a CEO, and published a book, but I felt like a failure. The malevolent voice inside my head was running wild.

Finally, it was graduation day. Breuer's four week training program had ended. It was another beautiful California morning: clear, blue, and golden, but I didn't see it that way. As far as I was concerned it might as well have been a cold, grey February in New England.

As a reward for completing the program we were treated to lunch at the Ritz-Carlton in Half Moon Bay. It was a five star establishment on a beautiful piece of property overlooking the Pacific. Aisha drove us there in a shuttle bus. Everyone felt like celebrating.

As we filed into the hotel dining room I thought of the picture we made. Joseph, a small black man, followed by four black women and me, all dressed like pallbearers. Strangely enough, I was the most self-conscious, though not for the reason you might think. My fellow trainees may never had been to the Ritz-Carlton but I was all too familiar with it. The problem was, I wasn't there as a guest, I was there as a limo driver. It was just too far to fall.

165

# Chapter 35
## Fixing My Ears

Understanding how things work gives me comfort, which is why I tried to figure out Breuer's strategy.

Back in the 90s the company was king of the stretch Hummers. Since then it had moved from the high volume, low margin business of custom limousines to luxury motor coaches. The change appeared to be working.

Limos were a low end, dog-eat-dog business with numerous carriers using the exact same town cars and stretch limos. There's not much margin taking kids to the prom; the real business is busing corporate employees to work. Breuer concentrated on this high-end segment, leaving limo service to others. In fact, limo driving had become such an afterthought I didn't see one town car or stretch in Breuer's fleet. Instead, they owned a dozen metallic-black Mercedes-Benz GL5 SUVs with Bluetec technology - whatever the hell that was. Their strategy was to deploy these SUVs at peak times around the city so someone with a Breuer phone app could contact us. They called the concept iCars but it was clearly an attempt to be an upmarket Uber.

The more I thought about it the more Breuer's strategy made sense. Uber was killing the taxi and town car markets, but the luxury end was up for grabs. It seemed like a smart way to go, which told me something about the company I was working for.

My first day as a driver felt like the first day of school. I prepped my kit bag with latex gloves, a roll of paper towels, and a spray bottle of Febreze. I also brought the regulation Thermos all drivers carried. If I looked the part maybe I'd feel better. My intentions were good, but the voice inside my head told me otherwise.

Since I never wanted to be late again I showed up forty-five minutes before my shift started. I also decided never say no to a job, and work until 2:00am if necessary. I even spent $200 on the useless GPS system the company foisted upon us even though the iPhone map app was superior.

On my first day I was disappointed to learn that dispatch couldn't text to a driver's phone. Worse, the computers were wonky, which meant we had to call in for instructions. Next I learnt there wasn't any business.

My first two days (which were mostly nights) I didn't get a single client. This was weird, but Breuer was paying me $15 an hour to cruise the city whether or not I carried passengers, so I went with the flow. Other iCar drivers were hip to the problem and invented ways around it. Some drivers parked near the downtown hotels and solicited clients on their own. The most popular hangout was the lobby of the Inn at the Presidio where a friendly concierge let them drink coffee for free and steered the occasional fare their way. This defeated the whole purpose of iCars but we wanted the tips.

The worst part of the job was that it was lonely. There was no one to talk to. That was until I met Kevin. Kevin was an iCar driver in his 20s; he had short brown hair and a Boston accent and looked like a young Mickey Rourke. There was something deep and unexpressed inside of Kevin. Maybe it was his intelligence, or something darker. Whatever it was, I found him sympathetic.

Somebody had told Kevin I'd written a book, and since he wanted to be a playwright he buttonholed me during our pre-flight inspections. I'd told Mr. Healy about my book, but among my fellow drivers I'd kept it a secret. Kevin was so earnest though I had to respond, and when I did he showed me the ropes.

Kevin explained the best way to get fares and how to goose a tip. He also showed me which parts of town to avoid and where to get fares after midnight. Sometimes, late at night, when things were slow, we used the iCar app to find one another. Then we met up in an empty parking lot off Van Ness and talked until the sun came up. Late one night, when Kevin realized I hadn't had a customer all day, he gave me one of his - the limo driver's equivalent of 'leave no man behind.' To find kindness in an unexpected place made me love Kevin, if only temporarily. It was one of the few times a positive emotion punched through my cloud of despair. When I learnt he'd been working 14 days without a break, a clear violation of company policy, I kept it to myself.

\*\*\*

167

Driving a limo was an important step in the plan Allie and I had put together. It fulfilled the requirement of getting a job that paid enough to earn a living while providing health insurance for a cochlear implant.

Since Allie had been encouraging me to get the implant I'd researched the operation. The surgery is so standardized they have you in and out in three hours. That didn't make the procedure any less scary. It starts with a surgeon making an incision behind your ear so he can place the implant flat against your skull. Next, he threads the implant's long wire tail into your cochlear nerve, then sews you up. Four weeks later, after your incision heals, you're "activated," which means the implant is turned on. This is done by placing a battery pack on the back of your head which uses a magnet to attach to the implant. In addition to serving as a power source, the battery pack contains a microphone and the software necessary to wirelessly transmit an audio signal to the implant inside your skull. The implant in turn converts the signal into electrical impulses which your brain reads as sound.

I was told the operation had a high success rate but certain things concerned me. First, threading an implant into your auditory nerve ensures you lose what residual hearing you have left. In other words, they have to make you deaf before you can hear. True, I didn't have much residual hearing, but I desperately guarded what I had left.

Additionally, once you're activated human speech doesn't sound like human speech, at least not at first. For some people, it sounds like beeps. For others, it's robotic. Either way, the thought of being deaf for a month then hearing only beeps until my brain sorted things out was unnerving.

Besides, cochlear implants look like hell. The battery pack is a big chunk of plastic, larger than a conventional hearing aid that sticks out of your head like a bolt on Frankenstein. The operation can also have side effects. A small percentage of people experience facial paralysis. Others have their taste buds numbed. In most cases these disruptions are temporary but not always.

Finally, there was the price. A cochlear implant operation easily topped $100,000. The price was obscene but implant makers have a captive audience so they can charge what the market will bear. A manufacturer will tell you that the high cost of their device supports ground breaking research. But the truth is most hearing devices don't break new ground they just include more bells and whistles to justify their price. Worse, a wealthy infrastructure of audiologists, trade associations, hearing doctors, and profit-hungry manufacturers promote CI operations at the expense of the Deaf community, Deaf culture, and sign language.

As it turned out, I was misinformed about the success rate of cochlear implants. The results were more mixed than I was first led to believe. Some implants cause infections, others painful headaches, while still others barely improve hearing. Then I learned that many children who are born deaf are given an implant even though they can never learn spoken English. If anything, the implant *slows* their ability to acquire language and learn. Many of these children would be far better learning sign than using an implant to replicate a language they can never hear or pronounce correctly. When I inquired why deaf kids were given implants rather than taught sign I learned it was yet another example of the hearing world dictating terms to the deaf. No wonder so many deaf people were angry. The hearing world may have been well intentioned but it was wiping out their culture in the misguided belief they were making things better.

Take Tommy for instance. Tommy was a lovely middle aged man I met one Saturday at the Northern California Hearing Association's cochlear support group. I'd attended the group to research the operation and Tommy was the first person I met who told me between sips of coffee that the operation had paralyzed half his face. I found this disturbing, even more so when he confessed he'd gladly have the operation again because it restored his hearing. It was Tommy's choice to make and I didn't begrudge it. He seemed happy enough but I wasn't sure it would work for me.

And then there was Sandy. Sandy was an in-your-face guy I met a few weeks after Tommy. Short and muscular, he wore a bright red polo shirt stretched so tight across his chest it looked like it might rip. Sandy purposely shaved his head to show off his twin implants. A practiced bomb thrower, he walked up to me during one of the breaks, rolled his shoulders, and said:

"Hi, I'm Sandy. I'm loud and I'm proud."

This seemed a weird thing for a deaf person to say and Sandy's wiggling of his shoulders only made it more so. The problem was I was self-conscious about my hearing. That the solution was prominently displayed only made me more so. Sadly, it wasn't until much later I realized I'd misjudged both Tommy and Sandy. Sandy's Deaf pride could have been particularly useful to me but I was still intent on denying my deafness. It just goes to show I continued to identify with the hearing world.

The last thing you want to hear about a CI surgery is that "results may vary." Unfortunately, they do. It takes anywhere from 3 to 12 months after an operation to fully recover "some portion" of your hearing. Even then you're unlikely to get it all back. Some people regained as much as 80% or 90%; others, less than 50%. Either of these results was better than what I had but the lack of consistency was discomforting.

One thing was clear. I couldn't go on living like this. I may still have heard some things if not others but I didn't know how to sign and my hearing would only get worse. In other words, I was trapped between the hearing and the deaf and neither world would have me.

As I explored implant alternatives I looked into sign language. I was told it would take at least two years to become fluent, which, given my age and lack of someone to practice with, was unlikely to happen. Importantly, I'd grown up among the hearing. They were my tribe. But since I could no longer function amongst them what choice did I have? A cochlear implant seemed my only solution, or so I believed at the time.

After my research, I concluded I wasn't deaf enough to justify the risks. Allie disagreed and coaxed me along. When I finally gave in, I did it more to please her than a desire for an implant. I only hoped she'd still love me when my face was paralyzed.

\*\*\*

As I've said, Allie had a vision I was trying to conform to: getting a job, fixing my hearing, helping Dana, and moving to Alameda (an island near Oakland in San Francisco Bay). Since the school year was almost over, Dana would soon be leaving for Tokyo to visit her grandmother. That made May the ideal month for me to look for an apartment near Allie. The problem was I felt so crippled I couldn't do it on my own. Allie grudgingly agreed to help but I could tell she wasn't happy. Once again, I suspected Ivankovich had influenced her.

I'd tried talking to her about the negative voice inside my head but she was dismissive. Since then I'd stopped saying anything that might undermine her opinion of me. Instead, I reminded her of how much progress I was making. Not only did I have a job with health insurance, I was financially solvent. Soon, I would be moving to Alameda. I was full of good intentions.

But Allie hated the word "intention." It was something she learned in her AA meetings.

"People don't 'intend' to do something, they just do it!" she told me. "Actions are all that matter. Intentions are just unfulfilled promises."

But, hey! I was checking all the boxes. Wasn't that what she wanted? Still, Allie had complaints. She told me I wasn't involved in her art that we needed to do more things together, that I didn't touch her enough. I made an effort to correct these, but it wasn't easy given the demands Dana, work, and a raging depression made. In the meantime, I continued unraveling.

Then one day, around 11:00 in the morning, Breuer's computer system broke down. Suddenly, I had four hours to myself.

My first thought was to contact Allie about the exhibit at the De Young she wanted to see. It would be a great way to spend time together. The idea so excited me I kept making typos as I texted her.

"Hey, just got four hours off! Want to see that exhibit at the De Young?"

"What about your apartment?" she texted back. "I'm seeing it at 1:00?"

"Forget about it!" I responded. "You've wanted to see this exhibit for weeks. Let's live!"

"So your time is more important than mine?" she texted back.

Wait. What?

Her follow up arrived seconds later.

"Seeing the apartment is no longer important because you want to see an art exhibit?"

"I thought YOU wanted to go?"

"That's not the point. The point is you think your time is more important than mine."

"I'm just trying to please you. I thought you wanted to do more things together?"

Foolishly, I engaged Allie in debate because I wanted my actions understood. Nothing I said made a difference. It only made her madder.

"I tell you what," she wrote back. "If the exhibit's so important, you go. But forget about your apartment. I'm taking my dog for a walk. My time is as important as yours."

For the first time in our relationship, I allowed myself to be furious. Allie had pushed me to the point where I was so mad I sent a text without thinking.

"I'd really like to punch you in the head."

Though I was pissed off, I thought this over-the-top pronouncement would be understood as a true measure of my anger rather than my intention. But you can't rely on texting to convey nuance. Allie took it as a threat and blew her top.

Though I knew I'd gone too far, I was no longer interested in self-editing. That night instead of going to the Dutch Boy I turned my phone off and headed to Marin. Silence is a form of punishment but it also protected me from my girlfriend's unreasonableness.

After all, my time was as important as hers.

# Chapter 36
# Coming Unglued

Rain must fall into every life which is fine except when it's a monsoon.

Some days were so bad I went to sleep at 7:00 leaving Dana alone to watch TV. Other days, I lay in bed fantasizing about being killed by crossfire in a robbery.

The voice in my head had become a shame machine. As I lay in bed it whispered, "Kill me now! Kill me now!" as I imagined a row of spikes swinging down from the ceiling.

I tried fighting depression but like a drunk on New Year's Eve I was more impaired than I realized. As I turned inward Allie looked to my shrink for help. She was still using Ivankovich but decided she should supplement him with Dr. Squeaky-voice. I drove her to her first session to show my support. But when I heard her say, "not very well" in answer to the Dr.'s question, "how are things going?" I worried.

During our trip home I merchandized my progress. I wanted Allie to know that even in the grip of depression I was trying; that my feeling for her was strong. When I glanced at her she seemed unmoved. What more could I do for her? I was coming apart at the seams.

\*\*\*

One afternoon, an hour into my shift, I stopped for lunch at a place Kevin had shown me. It wasn't much to look at, but the food was cheap and plentiful. Since I calculated lunch in terms of how many hours I had to work to afford it, I'd become a regular.

When I ordered I handed my debit card to the cashier, who ran it through the register then told me it wasn't authorized. Thanks to depression, I hadn't checked my bank statement in months, so I drove to the nearest Wells Fargo to inquire within. A lady there informed me that "unusual activity" had been recorded on my card. Specifically, she pointed to charges I didn't recognize, which included iTunes purchases, Uber, and multiple cash withdrawals.

At first I thought it was fraud, but the more I thought about it the more I realized all three charges had something in common: they were things Dana liked. Obviously, I never bought music for the reason I couldn't hear it. As for Uber, I'd set up an account but never once used it. And cash withdrawals? Well, Dana had borrowed my debit card several times to buy ice cream at the store across the street, which turns out to be the same place where the withdrawals were made.

Sometimes you blame your kids for stuff they haven't done. I had the opposite problem. Dana had done so many wrong things I had trouble keeping up.

When I got home that night, Dana was sitting on the couch watching *American Horror Story*. I was so tired the last thing I wanted was a confrontation, but I couldn't put it off until morning or my anger would dissipate.

"Dana, we need to talk."

No response.

"Have you done your homework?"

No response.

"Dana?"

"What?"

"Have you done your homework?"

"Yes."

"Where is it?"

"Can't you wait until this is over? It's really good."

"No, I can't wait. I want to see your homework… now!"

"Check my bedroom," she said without taking her eyes off the screen.

Since Dana was a poor liar, I went to her room to see if she'd even taken her books out of her backpack. I had to determine whether she'd done her homework before confronting her about larceny. Otherwise, the homework would never get done.

As usual, Dana's room was a mess. I quickly scanned the floor looking for her backpack, which is when I spotted something so obvious I knew what it was though I never expected to see one in my daughter's room. Next to the object lay a metal jar that looked like it contained lip gloss except for the marijuana leaf embossed on its lid.

174

"What is this?" I said, walking into the living room with the lip of a used condom pinched between my fingers.

"I don't know," Dana said, looking up for the first time.

I could tell from her panicked expression I'd caught her red handed. It was so rare I had tangible evidence of her misdeeds that I overcame my squeamishness at handling such a disgusting object. The truth is I expected her to be mortified, so I dangled the condom in front of her to get a reaction.

"Dana!"

"It's none of your business.

"Of course it's my business. You're my daughter."

"Where'd you find it?"

"In your bedroom. Do you want to explain what's going on?"

"I had sex, no big deal!"

"Dana, you're fourteen!"

"What's that got to do with it?"

"And what the hell is this?" I showed her the silver container.

"I don't know," she lied.

I unscrewed the cap and took a whiff. It reeked of pot.

"So let me get this straight. You brought a boy home from school, fucked him in your bed and then got high?"

"No, we got high first."

The casualness of her admission left me flabbergasted. I'd never have had the guile to say such a thing to my parents, yet Dana didn't care.

I watched my daughter watch television if only to confirm the conversation was over. Then I went to my bedroom to think.

Only the day before, Dana and I had had a great time grocery shopping. We'd goofed around in the store stuffing every possible item into the cart she might like. But this was a whole new level of misbehavior, a level I'd not been aware of. Barbie had warned me and I'd ignored her. Now I was paying the price.

The fact I had to have a serious conversation with my daughter was terrifying. And yet, sometimes we rally when it's most unlikely. After organizing my thoughts, I went back to the living room, turned off the TV, and sat next to Dana on the couch.

"OK, look. I wish you weren't having sex," I said, making eye contact. "I think you need a level of emotional maturity before you can have a loving relationship. You're still too young for that."

Dana began to speak but I held up my finger.

"Obviously, that horse has left the barn. What I'm now concerned about is your safety. I don't know this boy. I don't know if he treats you right, or has an STD. For all I know he just want to brag to his friends."

"He's alright," Dana muttered.

"I know I can't stop you from having sex though I'd like to. But at least you had enough sense to use protection. I commend you for that. The last thing I want is for you to get pregnant. That would be a disaster."

Dana nodded her head.

"So, think about what I've said and we'll talk tomorrow. In the meantime, I'm going to bed. I'm exhausted."

Dana said nothing, just picked up the remote and turned the TV on.

My daughter may not have masterminded a school shooting but it felt like the next best thing. She was already taking Lexapro, seeing a therapist, and enrolled in a "teens at risk" program but none of it was working.

Had I done this to her? Was this the legacy of divorce? The voice in my head said yes. Still, I was at a loss what to do.

That I loved my daughter more than anything else I had no doubt. But I was beyond being worried for her. I was already fighting depression. Now, Dana's actions made it worse. In the meantime, all I wanted was to sleep. Maybe things would feel different in the morning though I doubted it. For now, sleep would have to do.

# Chapter 37
# The Great De-accessioning

According to Allie's plan, once school was over and Dana left for Japan I was to move in to The Dutch Boy with her. That shouldn't have been difficult since I'd left most of my furniture in Woodside. But there was a wrinkle. My sister wanted my remaining stuff out of her cottage, pronto. Knowing my next apartment was likely to be smaller than the one I was in, I made the considered decision to purge my belongings. This became known as the "great de-accessioning."

How far can you shrink your life and still have one? I didn't know but I was going to find out. Disgust with all my stuff reflected my negative outlook, but I was not alone in this. Both Allie and my sister encouraged me to get rid of my belongings, as did a friend who claimed enlightenment after a similar purge following his divorce.

Just the thought of moving all my furniture again was paralyzing, so their suggestion seemed helpful. The great de-accessioning would not only rid me of my belongings, it would create a smaller, more manageable footprint in which to live. I was not getting rid of excess stuff so much as erasing my former life. The truth is nobody cares about your belongings. What may seem precious to you is junk to everyone else. This doesn't matter unless you're forced to get rid of it all at once. When you do, I'm here to tell you it hurts like a son of bitch.

They say that abruptly getting rid of your possessions indicates a predisposition for suicide. In my case the experience was so painful I wondered if it was a cause. To cushion the blow, I told myself disposing of everything was character building. It would make me a better person. If Allie was all I needed then ridding myself of excess belongings was like Cortes burning his ships on the beach. There was no turning back.

Once I arrived in Woodside I started having second thoughts. It was hard seeing the de-accessioning as anything other than what it was: another failure disguised by a rationale. If I acted as planned, I'd go from sleeping on a four-poster bed to a press-board monstrosity from IKEA. It may not sound like much but it smelled like defeat to me.

The first thing I realized was I needed an organizing principle, a means to decide what to keep and what to get rid of. It didn't help I had so much furniture every decision felt like Sophie's choice. Unfortunately, I was incapable of rational thought. My belongings may have been inanimate objects made of wood, fabric, and foam, but my mind seized at the thought of losing them. Never again would I host a sparkling dinner party replete with witty repartee, excellent food and my custom made dinner table that sat twelve. Just the thought depressed me.

Only later did I realize that if I'd kept those pieces I'd have to replace if I got rid of them, such as my bed, I'd have been fine. But my brain didn't function properly, so I decided to get rid of everything. The Salvation Army had never seen anything like it.

If there are two things I hate in books it's dream sequences and lists, so feel free to skip this section if you want to. First to go was my four poster bed with matching night tables; followed by my Thai elephant chair, my dining room table and my father's dictionary stand—a gift from my mother. Next went my coffee table, which I had designed, two custom made club chairs and twin end tables.

I didn't stop there, however. I dumped two dozen custom-made suits; my Thai spirit house; my Mars globe; and a cigar box filled with my favorite childhood toys. These included a yellow baseball player swinging for the fences; a Boy Scout penknife; a herd of dinosaurs; and a silver metal Jaguar whose trunk and hood opened in a way that still captivated me fifty years later. Some of this stuff had been around the world and back with me. Now, I dumped it into garbage bags and left it unceremoniously on the sidewalk.

But I wasn't finished yet.

Next, I decided to get rid of my archive: five three-drawer filing cabinets as tall as I was and considerably wider. This included everything I'd ever written since junior high school including all the research for my published book, several unpublished novels, dozens of short stories, and a file of every idea I felt worth pursuing. These cabinets represented my intellectual legacy but they took up a lot of room and weighed a ton. There was no place for them in my future life.

And still I continued.

I threw away every article I'd ever published along with the research. Over a hundred files with future story ideas disappeared in the trash. Allie was there to help but she cared just enough to strip mine those things she wanted for herself. Otherwise, she was in a hurry for me to finish.

By far the hardest thing to throw away was my books. Even as a kid I loved books so much that a single crease in a paperback cover was cause for heartbreak. Assembled over a lifetime, they were a personal reference library forty years in the making. I quickly learned, however, that my books were worthless. Nobody would buy them. When I drove to Green Apple books in San Francisco I was told they didn't even want them for free. I was so furious I left 100 boxes on the sidewalk in a fit of pique and drove off. Later, I anonymously dropped another 100 boxes at libraries around the Bay Area.

Next to dispose of was my record collection, which included my prized Billy Holliday 78s. Amoeba Records offered so little for something that meant so much to me I left my records on their counter without taking the money. Later that night I abandoned a box of three hundred CDs in front of San Rafael's Goodwill like a baby at an orphanage.

It wasn't the economic value of these things that mattered, it was their emotional legacy. So what if my furniture defined me? An object may not talk, but it can tell you where it comes from, speak of your feelings for it, and remind you of the role it's played in your life. Unfortunately, what is precious with memory and meaning means nothing to anyone except you.

The last thing I got rid of was my dog. I loved Austin but the majority of landlords won't accept a canine, so I made arrangements to give him to a family in Woodside. They had three sons and more land than I could dream of so it was a good fit. The only drawback was telling my daughters.

\*\*\*

Once I'd divested myself of all my possessions, I had one last thing to do. I crossed the meadow to my sister's house where I presented her with a check for $20,000. It was reimbursement for all the expenses I'd incurred during my two year stay including my meds, sessions with Dr. Squeaky-voice, and a greatly discounted rent. It was my way of making amends; of saying thank you for putting up with me. Hopefully, it would wipe the slate clean.

When my sister saw the amount she was surprised.

"This is very generous," she said, waving the check in the air. "It will almost cover refinishing my floors."

I briefly wondered how someone could spend $20,000 refinishing floors that were only four years old but I didn't want to know. Instead, I told my sister The Salvation Army would be by to pick my things up at the end of the week. Then I made for the door.

"Whoa! Wait a minute!" she said. "Nothing gets taken until my guys have a chance to go through it."

I wondered what she meant by "my guys." Was it her gardener who came every Friday? The women who cleaned her house? Or the groom that took care of her horse?

Getting rid of my stuff made me sad, but someone picking through it made me feel worse. If the great de-accessioning was meant to cure me of possessiveness it did a poor job. Then again, they tell you never to make an important decision when depressed. Now I know why.

# Chapter 38
## Moving Day

Finally, it was moving day!

Despite Allie's promise to find me an apartment, she'd failed. Since I couldn't keep paying such exorbitant rent we decided I'd put the few belongings I had left into storage and move in with her until I found a place of my own.

The prospect of moving was hard to face. My resolve was weakening and I was tired and out of sorts. The great divestiture, only a few days old, felt like a colossal mistake. My thoughts were so negative, dark and destructive it was a miracle I could function. No one, not Dr. Squeaky-voice, not Allie, nor my daughters, knew how much trouble I was in. Still, I had things to do. It was moving day.

Since it was the last day of school, I made Dana a nice breakfast, which there was only a 50% chance she would eat. Making three meals a day when you're clinically depressed is nothing short of miraculous, but that's what I did because a daughter's needs trump depression.

I was also in my role as timekeeper. I knew exactly how long it took to get her to school. But Dana was forever late: I constantly had to push her out the door. Finally, ten minutes past the time we should leave I asked whether she'd made her lunch. When she said no, I yelled for her to do it.

A few minutes later, I was in the middle of making my bed when I heard Dana scream hysterically. She was in the kitchen. When I went in I expected to see she'd accidentally chopped a finger off. Instead, she was holding the refrigerator door open.

"There's nothing to eat!" she wailed.

This was untrue. We'd recently stocked the fridge with items of her choice. The grocery bill exceeded a hundred dollars. Nevertheless, she was shouting so loud I worried the neighbors would complain.

"What am I going to dooooooooooo?"

As I stared incredulously my body flooded with adrenalin.

181

"Can I pleeeeeeease have moooooooney for lunch?"

That's when I snapped.

"Dad?" Dana said, sensing the change.

My mind went numb as I took a menacing step towards her. It was easy cornering her in the Pullman-sized kitchen. Her face registered alarm as I went into full predator mode. Dana called my name questioningly one more time before I reared back and slapped her across the face.

"Dad!" she said, rubbing her cheek. "What did you do that for?"

For one brief moment if felt good to have slapped her, then I was instantly swamped with regret. I wasn't sure I could answer her question, other than to say I was fed up with her bullshit, but slapping her was no solution.

I immediately texted Allie and told her what happened. If I had any hope of conquering my anger I needed to own what I'd done, but her response surprised me.

*Is that all?* she texted. *Once I bit Hirsch's nose so badly he needed stitches.*

Within minutes Dana was on the phone with her mother demanding to be picked up, even though home was a five minute walk. The next morning, she left for Japan.

I felt terrible for slapping my daughter, but I'd be lying if I didn't admit to relief that she was gone. Still, the incident couldn't have come at a worse time. Allie was on her way to help with the move and I still had to get the truck and find two laborers to help with the packing. It may have been moving day but I couldn't stop my hands from shaking. The voice in my head was right: I was a bad father after all.

\*\*\*

I was still agitated when Allie arrived. My breathing was ragged; my mind unsteady. The only way to get through the move was to focus on one step at a time. If I did that I might survive, but it seemed doubtful.

The first thing I did was go get the truck. When I arrived at the rental place the man in charge told me there was no truck for me. It took a moment for me to absorb this information since I had made a reservation. When I asked what happened, he told me he'd left a message on my phone even though my voicemail says not to since I'm deaf. I was already agitated so it was easy to start yelling, "I want a truck, God damn it! You better find me one." He was reluctant at first but once he saw how crazy I was he picked up the phone and started dialing.

After several calls he located one, but there were two problems. First, the truck was way bigger than I needed; second, it was thirty miles away. I didn't have a choice. I'd taken the day off from work and couldn't get another. So I piled into my car and started driving north.

As I merged onto 101, I was so disassociated from my actions it was like an out of body experience. My senses were dull and my thinking slow-witted. Since I didn't feel competent to drive I forced myself to pay attention. I didn't get very far before colorful lights illuminated my rear view mirror. The Highway Patrol wanted to talk.

I pulled off the highway and waited for a CHP officer to approach my car. When I lowered the window, she asked whether I knew why she had stopped me.

"I've no idea, officer."

She explained she had pulled me over because the registration sticker was missing from my rear license plate.

"From what I can see someone's peeled it off," she said. "Happens all the time. You can get a new one from DMV but I have to cite you."

The officer was nice enough but that didn't stop me from hyperventilating. I didn't want to arouse suspicion, so I fought to control my breathing. When she turned over the ticket my hand was visibly shaking.

When I finally arrived at the rental depot I was more than an hour behind schedule. I had to double check I was at the right address. It wasn't just in the middle of nowhere, it didn't look like a place of business. Then I noticed a single Budget rental truck in the parking lot so maybe I was wrong.

I bumped the horn and a mechanic in a blue jumpsuit walked out from the garage. He unlocked the gate and handed me a clipboard with paperwork. Meanwhile, I was looking at the truck. It was 26 feet long, big enough for the contents of a four bedroom house.

"Do I need a Class C license to drive that thing?"

"It'd help," he said.

I couldn't tell if he was kidding.

By the time I got home I was two hours late. Workers were packing up the last of the kitchen while Allie finished the bedroom. As per my instructions, she'd put my personal belongings into several boxes. She'd even labeled the contents. Clearly, she'd done a good job, only I didn't think so.

I was so jittery I ripped open each box and began rooting around to see what was inside. When I saw Allie hadn't sorted my belongings the way I wanted, I insisted on taking everything out and repacking it.

"What are you doing?" she asked.

"Reorganizing."

"I've already packed your boxes. I wrote the contents on the flap."

That I'd lost all perspective goes without saying, but I needed to separate what went to Allie's and what went into storage. It probably didn't matter. If I accidentally put something I needed in storage I could always get it later. But for some reason I can't explain it felt like the most important thing in the world, so I emptied all of Allie's carefully packed boxes and started over.

When she saw what I was doing she became furious.

"I refuse to help anymore!" she barked.

And you couldn't blame her. I was acting like a madman. But when Allie threw my plans into confusion my mind couldn't handle it.

It didn't help that we were late. I still had to drive my stuff to the storage place, unload, and drop the remainder at Allie's before driving the truck to Santa Rosa before 6:00. It was at least a hundred miles, most of it in traffic. Still, when Allie refused to help, it felt unnecessarily cruel. On top of that, it put me further behind schedule.

Nothing went smoothly after that. While backing the truck up at the storage facility I accidentally smashed it into the building, costing $1,000 in repairs. When filling the truck with gas, I misjudged the turn and rammed it into a concrete piling guarding the fuel pump, costing another $1,000.

Finally, as I was returning the truck, I had one last item to dispose of: my sofa. I didn't need a sofa in my new life. Allie had plenty of them. Besides, it was worn and dirty. So before returning the truck, I manhandled it out the back and left it in front of a cement plant in Sonoma. It was the saddest goddamn thing I'd ever seen.

*\*\**

By the time I reached The Dutch Boy it was 8:00pm. I was so exhausted I could hardly stand. On top of that, my nerves felt stripped of their protective coating.

Allie wasn't talking, so I went to bed. As I was getting ready, she walked into the room and asked:

"Is there something I should be doing different?"

I barely registered the question.

"I know age takes its toll, but am I wearing the wrong kind of clothes? Should I be doing something to make myself more attractive?"

Allie thought the reason we weren't having sex was that something was wrong with her. There was nothing wrong with her; it's just the same could not be said for me in my present condition. Since I didn't want to have this conversation right then I mumbled something about her being fine and turned on my side. When she sat down next to me I couldn't help but notice the desperate look in her eye.

"It's so much worse than I realized," she said, voice quavering, eyes tearful. "I had no idea things were this bad."

I wasn't sure what she was talking about. Did she mean my hearing, me, Dana, or something else? A few weeks before, I'd specially ordered a gift for Allie: a t-shirt with the original blond-mopped Dutch Boy hoisting a paint brush into the air. I'd even wrapped it. It was a small gesture but the only kind I could afford right now. I wanted Allie to know that despite everything I still cared for her, and though I might not be able to show it in the way she wanted everything would be okay if she just hung in there.

I climbed out of bed and went to where I'd hidden the t-shirt, then slowly, gently, handed her the package. Allie smiled when she saw what was inside, then put the t-shirt on before wrapping her arms around me.

I desperately needed to sleep. In just a few hours I had to go to work. Tomorrow was another big day, but, as it turned out, for all the wrong reasons.

# Chapter 39
# Gone Tomorrow

When I got up the next morning one of my hearing aids didn't work. Sometimes moisture got trapped inside and the device cut out on me. After drying it overnight it usually worked fine. But when I popped it into my ear I could tell it wasn't functioning. Need I say this concerned me?

I knew I couldn't fly a dual-engine plane on only one engine. That my remaining engine powered my weakest ear only added to my discomfort. Since there was nothing I could do, I made an appointment to have my hearing aid checked the next day. I also scheduled a hearing test since it was long overdue. Then I headed to work.

I was driving a 12 hour shift that day, from10:00 in the morning till 10:00 at night. Somehow, I managed to go the entire afternoon without a single client. Since I had a corporate event that evening I felt things should even out. Still, it was no way to run a business.

I was told the event was pretty straightforward. We were to pick up a dozen executives and drive them to South San Francisco for dinner. When they were finished, we were to drive them to their hotels. It seemed easy enough, but I was glad my buddy Kevin was among the assigned drivers. He knew about my hearing and when our boss finished the briefing he relayed his orders to me. This was perfect because without my right hearing aid I was having trouble understanding anybody, including Kevin. At least he was watching my back.

My instructions were to pick up four clients at the Oriental Mandarin. When I arrived fifteen minutes early my clients were already waiting. I welcomed each executive as they got into my car. They knew one another, which was good because once they settled in they'd talk among themselves rather than with me. By this point, I lived in fear of someone asking a question. There was no doubt I wouldn't understand, so I lowered my head, pulled in my aura, and prayed no one talked to me.

Once my G-Tech was loaded I convoyed with three other iCars to the restaurant. After dropping the executives, we had two hours to kill, so Kevin and I looked for a place to eat.

During our meal Kevin pointed out I couldn't stop scratching, which was true. My skin condition had degenerated to the point where my sleeves were bloodied. Fortunately, I was wearing a suit jacket, but when I took it off Kevin winced at the sight of red spots against my white shirt.

It was 9:30 by the time our clients emerged from the restaurant. They'd been drinking and were convivial. But instead of getting into their assigned cars they got into whichever car was nearest. This was a problem.

Of the three men and two women that entered my car none were going to the Oriental. In fact, they were all going to different hotels. When I asked which hotel they were staying at, they all spoke at once. I didn't understand a thing they said. I asked them to repeat themselves, but when I still didn't get it right the car became quiet.

I should have brought a pad and pen for my clients to write down their destination, but it was the one thing I hadn't anticipated. If someone threw up I was prepared, but not for a change of address. How lame was that?

Since I knew most of the hotels in San Francisco I eventually figured it out. The head honcho in the back seat, however, changed his mind halfway through the ride and gave me new instructions. No matter how hard I tried, and I tried so hard tears stung my eyes, I was unable to understand what he said. All I could tell was he was getting upset. Before I knew it everyone in the car was yelling to stop.

I pulled over to the sidewalk, at which point the head honcho got out and began flagging a taxi. It was a dark empty street, so I got out with him, leaving my other passengers behind.

"Sir, I'm happy to take you to your destination," I said. "I just don't hear very well. If you tell me where you want to go I'm sure I can get you there."

But the guy was furious. He wouldn't even make eye contact. I kept apologizing and offering to take him where he wanted but when a cab showed up he hopped in and sped away. After that all my passengers miraculously wanted to go to the same address.

The mix up had shaken me. It not only showed how bad my hearing was, it proved my hope of working as a limo driver was delusional.

When I arrived at The Dutch Boy I was in even worse shape than the night before. Since Allie was giving me the silent treatment I didn't mention what had happened and headed upstairs.

It hadn't escaped my attention that for the past 24 hours Allie had been treating me like her heroin-addicted son: she was leaving me to my own devices, refusing to get involved. I knew I wasn't good company but her withdrawal hurt. Given my condition I needed love, sympathy, and support, but none of these were forthcoming. Allie had already mentioned that she and Ivankovich had been talking about establishing firmer boundaries but where did that leave me? Nowhere good, that was for sure, so once again I sought comfort in sleep.

*** 

The next morning, I got up early and headed to my audiologist. While I was in my car I received a text from my boss.

*What happened last night?*

I turned cold as I read what he'd written. My boss was a good guy but I shouldn't be doing this job and he was paying the price. The head honcho in my car had complained as only an incensed executive can. I was officially on probation. Even with both hearing aids I was unlikely to do much better. I simply couldn't hear someone in the backseat telling me where to go.

This was one reason I hadn't had my hearing tested in a while. I didn't need an audiogram to tell me how bad my hearing was. Last night's performance was reminder enough.

I'd been going to the same audiologist for ten years but it was not my favorite place. If you've never had your hearing tested it's quite off-putting. The test booth looks like something the Israelis put Eichmann in when he stood trial. The acoustical tiling has a 1950s feel and their evenly spaced pinholes create a hypnotic effect. The whole experience is disheartening.

As I sat alone in the booth an audiologist spoke to me through half of an uncomfortable headphone.

"A narrator is going to say a series of words," she explained. "I want you to repeat back what you hear."

I'd been through this drill many times and the explanation was no comfort. It's like a dentist telling you you'll feel a pinch.

As an upbeat voice enunciated each word I closed my eyes to concentrate. Then I repeated back what I heard.

"Say the word: Plane."

"Pain?"

"Say the word: Beach."

"Each?"

"Say the word: Ball."

"All?"

"Say the word: Great."

"Ate?"

Tears slid down my face as I missed every word that she said. I knew I was guessing but without the context of a sentence it was impossible to understand individual words. Despite trying my best the words didn't make sense.

Next up was sentence comprehension. This time the narrator said a simple sentence which I was to repeat back. Halfway through the exercise I stopped responding.

I waited for the audio to play itself out. Meanwhile, the audiologist watched through the booth window. She was trying to look professional but she was stricken by my tears. When the narrator finally stopped, I exited the booth saying I needed to use the bathroom. Once alone, I tried to compose myself. Then I met with a different audiologist to repair my hearing aid.

As I sat across from her I mentioned my right device wasn't working. She plugged it into a computer to test the circuits. After studying the screen for a moment she looked at my audiogram and sighed.

"There's nothing wrong with your hearing aid but your audiogram shows you've experienced another precipitous hearing loss."

I was shocked at the news, especially since it was a much bigger problem than a broken hearing aid.

"My hearing's worse?"

"Yes," she said. "Once you've had one precipitous hearing loss the chance of another increases."

"How bad is it?"

She took a moment to read the numbers then gave me a weak smile.

"Your right ear has 12% speech discrimination and your left ear 24."

Then she turned away to study her computer and muttered under her breath, "You can't get by with this."

Surprisingly, I heard her every word.

***

It's not hard to pinpoint when thoughts of death turn from fantasy to a logical course of action. It occurred while I sat in the parking lot of my audiologist's building.

My latest test made it clear I was severely deaf. Even with my hearing aids I could only distinguish about 30% of what was said - not nearly enough to function. It was just a matter of time before severe became profound.

I'd resisted accepting my situation but my audiologist's casual appraisal smacked of truth. Another way to put it: there was no future for me. I was finished, washed up, shit out of luck, and flat out of options. I'd failed my daughters, my job, my writing, and Allie. I'd not only sacrificed my family for selfish pursuits, I'd deep-sixed my career, betrayed my wife, and given away my dog. I didn't even have a place to call home.

The last thing I wanted was to be thrown on the ash heap but that's where I belonged. Now, I had to do something about it. Which is just another way of saying, "Johnny get your gun. It's time to pull the trigger."

# Chapter 40
# The Glock Retirement Plan

It was an obscenely perfect day as I drove south on 101. The California State Highway Department's drought-resistant favorite's oleander, agapanthus and Spanish lavender were in full bloom. It felt like an insult.

People consider suicide selfish, which is surprising considering nobody wants to kill themselves, they just want to stop the pain. I'd done the math and realized my kids were better off without me. They'd receive more money from my life insurance than if I dragged things out staying alive. Plus, they wouldn't be embarrassed by having a hearing impaired father.

Shame is a powerful emotion. It makes people do things they wouldn't normally. Given I was soon to be unemployed, broke, and deaf, suicide was a logical response to my situation. Of course, no one in their right mind wants to die but that's the point. I wasn't in my right mind.

If the act of suicide is impulsive, the steps leading to it are anything but. I'd already researched the best place to buy a gun and as luck would have it the store was only one town away. I'd even picked the beach where I would end my life: far from civilization but close to nature, it was accessible only to the few who knew how to reach it. Pristine and peaceful, it was the perfect place to end your life. I could be there in less than an hour.

Silicon Valley has a thousand strip malls and The Gun Bank was in one of them. With its stucco exterior and casement windows it could have been a nail salon except for the sign over its door with a sniper's crosshairs between the words Gun and Bank.

As I sat in the parking lot working up the courage to go inside a tiny voice raised a Whoville cry of protest. I paused long enough to dash a text off to Dr. Squeaky-voice, telling her I was concerned about my mental state and thought I should be hospitalized.

A moment later she responded, *Where are you?*

When I texted back, *The Gun Bank*, she sent me a single exclamation point then went dark. When I heard nothing more I exited my car and headed towards the store.

As I've said, nobody in their right mind chooses to kill themselves. It's not an easy decision even when you're crazy. But the voice inside my head said it was time to die. Since I felt like earth's lowest life form my long list of shortcomings merited a fatal comeuppance.

I crossed the parking lot as a scrim-like curtain dropped in front of me. My vision narrowed and I felt no connection to my actions. The Gun Bank was a low-ceilinged space crammed with boxes and diminished by fluorescent lighting. Nearly fifty handguns lay holstered on a wooden table, each attached to a thin cable like cell phones at Best Buy. The walls were covered with assault rifles including Bushmasters, Rugers and other names I didn't recognize. It's scandalous how many guns were for sale.

The moment I walked in I felt unwelcome. Three men standing in a corner exuded an intimacy so clubby it was off-putting. I knew there must be an etiquette to this place but I wasn't sure how that dance went. The vibe was so weird I'd have left right away if I hadn't been determined to buy a gun.

Finally, one of the men, a younger, less well-groomed version of the cowboy actor Sam Elliot, separated himself from the pack and asked if there was something he could do for me.

"I'd like to buy a gun," I said, with all the confidence I could muster.

"Whatcha want it for?" he asked in a challenging voice.

I knew "blowing my brains out" wasn't going to get me very far so I gave him an answer I'd rehearsed.

"Self-defense. Home protection."

What I really wanted was privacy to explore the guns for myself but I could see that wasn't going to happen. Protocol dictated Sam Elliot personally show me a selection of handguns even though I didn't feel like being "sold." It was just too intimate a purchase for that.

The first gun he chose was too small and plastic-y for my taste. He demonstrated its action, sighted it at eye level, and talked about its merits. But its cheap, silvery finish said it belonged in a purse. I didn't tell Sam Elliot this because he already thought I was a pussy. Still, the next two guns he showed looked like Hasbro made them.

Selecting a gun to kill yourself is not easy and not just because there's so much choice. My thinking was compromised enough that basic decision making had come to a halt. Not only were my thoughts distorted, my personality felt like the poorly tuned signal on a satellite TV.

Still, I was keen on making a selection. What I bought had to have dignity. It had to feel right. It couldn't be silly or demeaning. Unfortunately, there was nothing amidst The Gun Bank's selection that fitted the bill. Finally, I worked up the courage to inquire further.

"Do you carry the Walther?"

Sam Elliot squinted like it was the wrong question.

"Only the .22. California law prohibits selling any other version for a bunch of silly-ass reasons."

This was a disappointment. I'd had my heart set on the Walther PPK because it's the same gun James Bond uses. If I was going to kill myself I might as well do it in style; but unless I was willing to drive to Nevada I was out of luck.

While I looked at more handguns a telephone started to ring somewhere. One of the other men answered it, spoke for a second, then gestured to Elliot it was for him. Sam, not one for apologies, mumbled something and left to take the call.

I used the opportunity to dance my eyes down the counter hoping to see something I liked. Suddenly, amidst the sea of plastic I spotted what I wanted.

"What's that?" I said after cowboy returned.

"That's a 9mm Beretta."

I hesitate to call a handgun beautiful but this one had the sleek, manufactured lines of what a gun should look like. Its handsome silhouette, eight inch barrel, and oily-black color seemed well suited to its task. I motioned to the gun in a questioning manner and cowboy shrugged as if to say, "Pick it up."

When I handled the Beretta it had a weight I found satisfying. It was also covered in small metal nubs, giving it a sensual feel. At first, I worried it might be too heavy to aim; then I realized there wasn't much chance of missing my target. Best of all there was nothing plastic-y about it. This was a gun you could kill yourself with.

"How much?" I asked cowboy.

He motioned with his chin. "Price on the grip."

When I took a look it said $760.

By this point I was operating on what scientists call the reptilian brain. Even then, a small, rational thought managed to float its way up towards my frontal lobe.

Isn't that too much money to spend on killing yourself?

I may have been suicidal but I wasn't crazy. $760 is a lot to pay for something you'll only use once.

"Do you have anything cheaper?" I asked, wondering how I became so price sensitive.

"Not in a Beretta," he huffed.

Then he gave me a look that said my time was up.

"Fine, I'll take it," I said, calling his bluff. "But show me how to load it first."

# Part IV
# Redemption

# Chapter 41
## Arrested Development

They say nobody knows how their life will end, but that's not true. Mine ended in The Gun Bank on the last day of June and I never got it back.

"Whoa, hold on partner," Sam Elliot said, raising both hands. "You need to complete a gun safety questionnaire first. Won't take a minute. Six year old could do it."

The store clerk handed me a pencil and a multiple choice test and escorted me to a chair with its back towards the window. The test was ridiculously easy. Even in my befuddled state I had no difficulty answering the questions.

Meanwhile, the atmosphere in The Gun Bank underwent a change. I could tell something was up, just not what. It could have been the boys in the corner were making fun of me. Whatever it was, I ignored it and concentrated on the test.

I sensed their arrival rather than saw it. Watching a TV drama unfold from the comfort of your home is quite different than experiencing it firsthand. As I held up my completed test half a dozen policemen stormed the store. I couldn't tell the exact number - they were mostly a blur - but so many cops flooded The Gun Bank there was hardly room to stand. Naturally, everyone froze save Sam Elliott who for some reason was pointing at me.

When the invisible hand of the state finally shows itself it lacks a certain restraint. Since I'd finished my test I made the mistake of standing up, which was when a hand grabbed the back of my neck forcing me to kneel. My arms were then pulled behind me, handcuffs cinched my wrists, and I was left on the floor in a penitent position. Strangely enough, I still held my gun safety test, on which I thought I'd done rather well.

I'd no thought of resisting. I was more embarrassed than anything else. I mean who wants to be arrested in the middle of a gun store in broad daylight? Yes, I might have been homicidal but my target was me. I didn't wish harm to anyone else.

It's scary when you set an action into motion the results of which you cannot control. The speed of my arrest, not to mention its violence, scrambled my brain. It's bad enough wanting to kill yourself, but getting caught in the act made me wish I were invisible.

Once I was in handcuffs everyone in the store relaxed. I kept my head down and my eyes on the floor in a conciliatory posture. Then one of the cops slipped his hands under my arm and lifted me to my feet.

"I'm going through your pockets now. Will I find anything I don't like?"

"No, sir."

I didn't like the feel of another man's hands in my pants but I was in no position to complain. A moment later, the officer took something out of my wallet and showed it to me.

"What's this?"

He held up a tiny ceramic frog the size of a hearing aid battery.

"It's a good luck charm. My mother-in-law gave it to me. I guess it's not working today."

"I wouldn't be so sure of that," the cop said flatly.

When he finished emptying my pockets he held up my car keys. "May we search your vehicle?"

I knew the best way to deal with policemen is to be compliant. That way they know you mean them no harm.

"It's a blue BMW. I parked it out front."

While my car was being searched, Office Moore, who I identified from his name tag, told me they're going to move my car so it wouldn't be towed. Then he sat me down in a chair. While the cops milled about I overheard a conversation taking place on the police radio. I understood my fate was being discussed but I was too numb, not to mention deaf, to follow it. Then I heard the words, "Let's take him to county."

I knew this wasn't a good thing but wasn't sure why. County funded institutions rarely have enough money. That's not a judgment it's a fact. The homeless, the mentally ill, the addicted and the imprisoned don't vote, so they receive only the bare minimum of service mandated by law and sometimes not even that.

A few minutes later Officer Moore escorted me out of the store and put me in the back of his police cruiser. It was too small a space to sit comfortably. The plastic bench was so low I had to angle my knees to fit yet they were still jammed up against the front seat. Meanwhile, the handcuffs were killing me.

A black wire partition separated me from Officer Moore, who climbed into the front seat and turned the ignition. Since suicide is a personal choice it didn't feel right to me to be arrested. Still, I was remorseful and wondered whether there was any way to get out of my plight. Maybe if I told Officer Moore I'd changed my mind he'd let me go, but my fate was no longer in my hands.

As we merged on to 101 I had no idea where Officer Moore was taking me. It was still a beautiful sunny day but I might as well have been at the North Pole for all the good it did me.

This was the first time I'd ever been arrested, the first time I'd ever been handcuffed, and the first time I'd ever sat in the back of a squad car. It was a big day for firsts, none of them good.

While I contemplated my situation I wondered how the police knew I was planning to kill myself. Did Sam Elliot figure it out and report me? Did Dr. Squeaky-voice take action? It was a mystery.

Though I knew it was pointless, I decided to tell Officer Moore what was in my heart.

"Officer?" I began. "I want to apologize for any inconvenience I may have caused you and your men."

"Don't worry about it," he said, not wanting to converse.

Of course, he was right. A ride in a police car was the least of my worries. A much bigger problem lay ahead.

\*\*\*

The Emergency Psych Services unit at the Santa Clara Valley Medical Center was not a welcoming place. You entered its lobby through a locked metal door set in a cinderblock wall with no visible windows. The lobby was large, sterile and empty save for a solitary bench nearest the door. On the opposite side of the vast linoleum space was a thick bulletproof window, behind which an admitting nurse sat. Next to the window was another locked metal door leading God knew where. The security reminded me of a prison.

Officer Moore sat me on the bench and asked whether I'd behave if he removed my handcuffs, to which I responded, "Yes."

While he uncuffed me I noticed a second policeman holding my personal effects in a clear plastic bag. It's amazing what's important when you're crazy. When I saw the second officer I asked Officer Moore whether I could borrow my cell phone.

"Make it quick," he said.

I had no idea how long I would be here but my instinct was to launch a cover up. The first thing I did was text Allie to say I'd be away for a few days. Next, I texted my boss at Breuer saying I was in the hospital and couldn't work that week. After that, Office Moore took my phone, an interior door was buzzed open, and an orderly guided me through it.

Nobody explained what was happening. Even if they did, I was so far gone I probably wouldn't have understood. After I was buzzed through the door I entered a gigantic room shaped like a lecture hall. There was a large central area with an anteroom off to one side. The room itself was filled with nearly two hundred La-Z-Boy recliners. Each chair was covered in turquoise-blue vinyl with a flannel sheet stretched across it.

The orderly led me to an alcove, made up one of the recliners, and beckoned me to sit. What was this place? I wasn't exactly sure. Other than the orderly, there didn't appear to be any medical personnel. About half the chairs were occupied but just as many sat empty.

I soon decided this place must be a holding tank for crazy people. I didn't want anything to do with the insane. I tried to steer clear of them on the street. Now I was locked in a room full of them. Perhaps they wouldn't notice me if I remained silent.

It's no exaggeration to say my brain felt like it had been through a cheese grater. Maybe that's why I was intent on repudiating crazy people when I was clearly one of them.

I wasn't sure what to do next. Reclining in the La-Z-Boy made me feel vulnerable, but I didn't want to be the only prairie dog sticking his head out of its burrow. Since I was worried my hearing aids would be stolen I clutched them in my hand. Then I closed my eyes to make everything disappear.

I wanted out of this place more than anything and I was worried I wouldn't hear if someone came to get me. Still, I couldn't resist my boiling brain. I curled up into a ball, mouth agape, and let a cry escape

I'd never heard before. Then the kindest possible thing happened. I fell asleep.

Later that afternoon, an orderly woke me to say I had a telephone call. While he led me to a pay phone I slipped in my hearing aids. One phone was dangling off the hook but when I picked it up no one was there. I said hello several times just to make sure then hung up. It wasn't possible that anyone knew where I was. The police hadn't asked for my contact information and I hadn't told anyone. I thought it must be a mistake.

I was still hugely agitated though, so I thought of something to comfort me. Visions of a Beretta like a rich chocolate cake swam through my head. Just imaging the gun helped to ease my pain. Then I fell back to sleep.

An hour later an orderly pressed a yellow sticky into my hand. It was a message from Allie and though it wasn't her handwriting its sentiments were clear.

*Allison called. She said she's thinking of you and will try to contact you tomorrow. She wants you to get better and to know she's here for you.*

Her words were so sweet, so comforting, I felt my first positive emotion in a long while. But I still went to sleep dreaming of a Beretta.

# Chapter 42
# Hillcrest

It was four o'clock in the morning when an orderly woke me. I'd been asleep for seventeen hours. I'm not sure why I was out so long. Maybe my mind was sheltering me from the storm. If so, I was grateful.

The place was quiet, the lights dim. I tiptoed past the humpbacked figures sleeping in their Lay-Z-boys. I wasn't being polite, I just didn't want to risk triggering a zombie apocalypse.

The orderly opened a locked door and led me into the lobby where two attendants waited with a gurney. They silently motioned for me to lie down. After strapping me in they rolled me out to an ambulance idling quietly in the darkness.

It only took a minute to get where we were going. It wasn't far and there was zero traffic that time of night. Thankfully, they weren't using the lights or siren.

As we pulled into a circular drive I read a sign that said: *Hillcrest Behavioral Health Center*. "Behavioral Health" is code for what used to be called the loony bin, the funny farm, the booby hatch, the bug house. In plain English it means the insane asylum. I'd been heading here for a while, yet I was surprised when I arrived.

*** 

Anyone who's ever mistaken a 9mm Beretta for a tongue depressor knows a county mental health facility is not a good place to be. I was uninsured and no private hospital would take me, which meant whoever was determining my fate had no choice but to send me to a cut-rate institution. This place may have been housed in a suburban office park but there was no mistaking what it was: a modern day Arkham.

Once I was wheeled inside a nurse took my belongings. After that, she handed me a set of scrubs and told me to strip. Since I was losing my mind, the last thing I wanted was to surrender my identity, so I

201

refused to change. It wasn't just that scrubs are unflattering, they make you look like everyone else. Since everyone else there was crazy that was not a good thing, so I insisted on keeping my clothes. The nurse just shrugged, saying, "Suit yourself," and handed me my room assignment. Then it was time for my tour.

* * *

The psych ward at Hillcrest was hugely depressing. It was a single locked corridor running the length of the building. Its cinder block walls were painted the same chocolate color as its couches. The fluorescent lights made everyone look sickly.

There were sixteen of us on the unit with five bedrooms at one end and four at the other. The nurse showed me my room which was a double. I was relieved to find it was empty.

The first thing I noticed was that the blinds on my window, like all the blinds on the ward, were closed. That wasn't the weird thing, though. The weird thing was the blinds were sandwiched between two pieces of plastic. You not only couldn't open them, you couldn't open the windows either.

The nurse explained there was a communal shower down the hall with an attendant who watched through a window. Men and women were supposed to take turns using the shower, but there was not much demand since mentally ill hygiene leaves a lot to be desired.

The nurse showed me the common area halfway down the corridor. One room had a few chairs for visitors; the other had a TV that was never turned off. Next to the common rooms was an alcove with a Dutch door. According to the nurse it was the medical closet where drugs were dispensed. A couple of female patients were sleeping in front of the door. Why they did this was never explained.

I noticed there was only one exit off the unit, which was kept locked at all times. A few people had keys but none worked on the ward which meant the rest of us were locked in. Those that came and went suggested an outside world in which I couldn't partake. If I was ever leaving that was my way out.

It didn't take long to realize Hillcrest was a prison with everything that implied: limited space, poor air quality, and no sunlight. They'd not only forcibly removed me from the outside world, they'd insured I

202

couldn't escape. After a look around I headed to my room to avoid the reality. Bed seemed the safest place to hide.

*** 

My first morning at Hillcrest, I asked for pen and paper to write down my thoughts. I was desperate to understand what was happening to me. I knew I could figure it out if I just applied myself but it was harder than I thought.

The composition book I was given had a black speckled cover like the ones we had in school. The pencil was the same golfers get to fill out their score card. Since it was only a few inches long it couldn't be made into a weapon. That was okay; I just wanted to write with it.

My first thoughts were questions:

*Why am I here?*
*Where is my girlfriend, my shrink, my family?*
*How do I get out?*

I was given so little information I was afraid but if I could assemble enough data I might figure things out. Normally, I excelled at this kind of thing. Now, it felt my life depended on it. If I was going to get out of there, I needed to pay attention. Otherwise, they might keep me forever.

*** 

The biggest problem with Hillcrest was there was nothing to do. They'd confiscated my phone and computers weren't allowed. Though I was allowed to check phone messages once a day I had to be careful. The battery in my cell was close to dying and I didn't have a charger. There was a payphone on the unit but I couldn't hear well enough to use it. Most of all, I worried about my hearing aid batteries. They, too, were close to expiring. If I couldn't hear well enough to advocate for myself I'd never get out.

I found an activity schedule posted on a glassed-in bulletin board in the hallway but when that came down mid-week the schedule was taken down and nothing replaced it. One of the common rooms had a TV, but since I didn't watch TV I wasn't about to start.

One blessing was a box of books locked in the medical closet. I had to request permission to look through it. When I did, the box turned out to have a pitiful selection. There were multiple copies of the Bible, and the AA handbook as well as some religious tracts. Other than that pickings were slim.

I noticed a paperback copy of Tina Fey's *Bossypants*, *Half the Sky*, about women in China, and George Orwell's *1984*. I wasn't particularly keen on Tina Fey and didn't think *1984* should be recommended reading on a psych ward but I grabbed both along with *The Big Book* to help me feel closer to Allie.

I was familiar with Hollywood depictions of insane asylums. I grew up watching *Shock Corridor* and *Shock Treatment,* both of which depict asylums as grim repositories for the criminally insane. They had nothing on this place, though. For one, they were just movies. Secondly, no one here was acting. We were all stark, raving mad.

As a result, you couldn't talk to most patients. They weren't high functioning enough. Some were full blown psychotic: hearing things, seeing things, speaking gibberish. One lady had both her eye sockets tattooed so her face looked like a skull. Another patient had a Bible and spent the next few days walking in the shape of a cross while speaking in tongues. Still other patients stared blankly ahead while clocking mile after mile wandering the corridor.

As I've said, crazy people intimidate me. Then I met Karen, a short, sweet fat girl who gave me a friendly little wave. When she invited me to sit next to her at lunch, I thanked her by touching her shoulder but she recoiled so violently I was startled. Later, she explained she had a fear of being touched. She also confided she'd been here before.

I had just enough pulse to realize how horrible Hillcrest was. I may have been clinically depressed but I was not psychotic; locking me in a prison full of people who talked to themselves would not improve my mood. I kept thinking they'd made a mistake. These aren't my people, I don't belong here. The hard thing was getting anyone to listen.

Each day I woke up hoping to be released. I wanted out so bad it was more important than food, water, or money. But once you're in the system it's hard to get out. That's why Dr. Squeaky-voice, Allie, and my sister were so important. They were the only ones who could spring me from this place. I was counting on them for help.

But nothing happened. Instead, I made notes in my composition book trying to figure out what was going on. One thing I noticed was the food was execrable. The absolute minimum had been spent providing us three meals a day, all of them inedible. I began skipping meal time and living off the bananas they handed out as snacks.

There's no lobby for the mentally ill to receive better treatment, so what they get is marginal. In keeping with Hillcrest's cost containment I was told the medicine I was taking was too expensive. When the nurse gave me new medicine, its efficacy unproven, she failed to wean me off my old meds first. I was hoping compliance rather than complaint would get me out of there, so I said nothing.

The smell of the place was also excruciating. The antiseptic they used was so pervasive it triggered my gag reflex. Breathing through my mouth helped but I was dying for fresh air. It was also always cold. Even my wool sweater didn't keep me warm. I couldn't imagine what it was like wearing the paper thin scrubs.

By day three I'd figured out Hillcrest wasn't a therapeutic facility. There was no daily meeting with a shrink, no arts and crafts, and no group therapy. The place was strictly for confinement. The staff noted our whereabouts every 15 minutes to make sure we didn't kill ourselves. But how was I to demonstrate I was getting better if I couldn't meet with a psychiatrist?

One thing I did to demonstrate my sanity was to shower every day. I also started joking with the staff in hopes that humor would get me out. The staff didn't run the place, though, psychiatrists did, and they were nowhere to be seen.

After three days I'd received only one text from Allie. When I didn't receive another I worried she'd gone dark. I still had the note the orderly gave me and read it every day for strength. A visit from Allie would have boosted my morale but I found her lack of communication confusing. I was powerless to do anything except wait.

***

The only person I saw every day was a discharge coordinator named Enid. She was impossibly young, with a clipboard and a harried manner. Her job was to help me put together a discharge plan so when I was released I didn't end up back there. She was also the only person who explained what was going on.

"Why I am in here, Enid?"

"You were brought in on a fifty-one fifty."

"What's that?"

"It's a California law saying a person who's a danger to themselves can be confined for 72 hours."

"You mean I'm stuck here for three days?"

"Yes."

"Then they'll let me out?"

"That depends."

"On what?"

"On how the doctors think you're doing."

"Anything else?"

"And having a discharge plan."

Enid asked for my shrink's contact information and the name of someone who could house me once I was released. I gave her Dr. Squeaky-voice's number as well as contact information for Allie and my sister.

My discharge plan was only half the battle, though. The other half was a positive evaluation by the unit psychiatrists.

The first two days went by without me seeing a doctor. On my third day, I finally met with a shrink. She was a short, sour woman wearing bifocals and a scowl. As it turned out she was the unit boss, though I didn't know that. She wore a sari with one sleeve draped over her arm and moved with a purpose that brooked no dissent. Neither compassion nor understanding seemed on her menu.

The interview took place in the common room for visitors. She was assisted by a staff member who acted as unofficial interpreter because her accent was so thick I had trouble understanding her. He was a young man with a baby face who, when he learned I'd worked at Lucas, couldn't stop asking me questions about *Star Wars*. I glimpsed at his ID badge to figure out where he was in the pecking order. If I could leverage the Force to get out of there, I would. As it turned out, he was too junior to help, other than to repeat in unaccented English what the head shrink had said.

It soon became apparent the doctor found three-way communication annoying. My guess is she felt it undermined her authority. She was surprisingly argumentative for someone interviewing a person who had just tried to kill themselves. She also had little patience for hearing loss even when I explained it was the chief reason I was there.

Since my fate depended on her diagnosis, I kept my cool. Still, she was so annoying it was hard to remain composed. After a few questions about my background, she zeroed in on the bookstore that didn't hire me.

"Why didn't you sue them?" she asked.

"What good would that do?"

"It would give you recourse."

"Who sues a bookstore over a minimum wage job? It would cost more to litigate than I'd ever earn. I want to work, not go to court."

"That's what I would have done."

"Yes, but you're not deaf," I said, a bit too harshly.

The shrink said something in reply which I didn't understand, so I looked at *Star Wars*-boy, who repeated it. When I still didn't get it, I asked him to say it one more time, but the shrink had had enough. She stood up in a huff, flipped her sari over her arm and snapped, "Never mind!"

*Star Wars*-boy looked apologetic.

The next day, my discharge coordinator informed me she had spoken with both Allie and my sister and neither would take me. It was shocking news. I had thought for sure one of them would say yes. In fact, the only reason I'd given Enid two names was to demonstrate I had places to go. Now that they had rebuffed me I was out of options. Did Allie and my sister want to trap me at Hillcrest indefinitely, or were they washing their hands of me? Perhaps that explained why I was not hearing from them.

I asked Enid to try a friend in Marin but he was leaving for Europe the next day, so couldn't oblige. I'd counted on getting out of there before the Fourth of July. If not, the staff would depart for the long weekend leaving me trapped for another three days. Enid hadn't told me the worst news, however. That was still to come.

"John, you should know the doctors have reclassified you."

"What's that mean?"

"You're now a fifty-one fifty-two."

"What's that?"

"It means they've placed you on a fourteen day hold."

My heart sank. "Fourteen days? But why? I'm getting better."

"It's because you tried to buy a gun."

"Enid, I have to get out of here! I want to go home."

It didn't help that Allie's refusal to take me meant I had no home. This left me in an impossible jam. If I insisted on being discharged the unit shrinks would think I was uncooperative and keep me there. But if I didn't make a fuss they'd keep me there anyway. One thing was clear, the longer I stayed at Hillcrest the more I was coming unglued. I'd put on my best face in the hope of being discharged but every day there made it harder to stay sane. If being held prisoner didn't drive you crazy, the food, the scrubs and the smell would.

That night I was so dispirited I went to bed at 7:00. To stay conscious a minute longer would have been ruinous to my health. There was no way I could last fourteen days in that place. I had to get out. If not, there was no telling what might happen.

# Chapter 43
# Trapped!

When I reread my notes from the previous day I could see my logic was improving. Still, I had lots to figure out. My two biggest questions remained: where was Allie, and how did the police know to arrest me?

It was possible someone at The Gun Bank thought I was acting strangely and called the cops. The only other person who knew where I was was Dr. Squeaky-voice. I'd texted her my location but after receiving her exclamation point had heard nothing more.

Then I remembered she once told me the protocol for dealing with a suicidal patient was to not get involved and call 911. I assumed this was what she did. Still, I would have appreciated a chance to resolve the matter in a less confrontational way, especially since I'd been asking for her help.

What I was really struggling with was Allie. After receiving her lovely message from which I'd derived strength, I'd heard nothing more. My sister was similarly missing.

When Thursday arrived I got a text from Allie explaining she couldn't visit because it was the Fourth of July. Even in my compromised state I knew it was an excuse. That my sister offered no comfort didn't surprise me but Allie's abandonment was a blow. There I was, arguably at my lowest point, swimming in despair. I thought for sure I could count on her.

Later that day, Enid handed me a brochure for a private residential treatment facility she said Dr. Squeaky-voice recommended. That was the first time I'd heard my shrink was still involved and only then it was second hand. Unfortunately, the facility had no beds available. Worse, you had to interview to get in. I couldn't do this, being confined to Hillcrest, so what good was it to me?

I did what I could to swallow my anxiety but like acid reflux it kept coming up. I'd placed a lot of hope in getting out before the Fourth. I knew if I didn't the staff would take off for the holiday leaving me trapped for another three days. It didn't look like it was going to happen, but if I saw skull-faced girl wandering the halls one more time I was going to lose it.

By now my clothes were so dirty I had to have them washed. As a reward, I was forced to wear their scrubs. It was one more step in succumbing to the place. Now, I looked like everyone else.

The highlight of our day arrived in the late afternoon when they set us loose in the courtyard. The courtyard was a small fenced in area off the lunch room - a covered concrete patio surrounded on three sides by the facility and on its fourth by a metal gate. We were allowed to circulate for 20 minutes each day when the staff remembered. All you could see was a sliver of sky and the crown of a palm tree rising in the distance. Still, it was amazing to be outside. To feel the sun upon my face, to bask in the warm, afternoon glow was restorative. It was the first time I'd felt human in a while.

The other thing I appreciated was the floor staff. Mostly Pilipino, with the occasional West African sprinkled in, they had an easy manner and charming accents, ideal for the caring of crazy people. Their job was difficult and thankless but their positive attitude made you want to hug them all the more. I particularly appreciated how ready they were to joke around. By the end of my first week I told them I was checking on them every fifteen minutes to make sure they were alright. They found this hilarious, stamping their feet and laughing unabashedly in a way that made me join in.

In the meantime, I found other opportunities to demonstrate my sanity. When I learned the World Cup was on I commandeered the TV and made the staff watch it with me. I don't have the sports gene but it was worth making an exception to kill a few hours with my caretakers. They were so enthusiastic about soccer it was infectious.

*\*\**

By the end of my first week I'd seen three different psychiatrists, none for more than five minutes. I made a note in my composition book:
*How can they tell I'm getting better if there's no continuity?*
My second psychiatrist was more pleasant than the first, but what did she know about my problems? Did she even realize I was deaf? I

couldn't help but feel the shrinks at Hillcrest were on the bottom of the career ladder. Why else would they be there? Any Silicon Valley psychiatrist worth their salt was either in private practice or working at Stanford. Hillcrest was hardly an endorsement of their skill.

Finally, on Friday, the start of the Fourth of July weekend, I met my third doctor. He was a handsome man with short black hair and a gentle demeanor. When I explained my problem he nodded sympathetically. Slowly, gently, with the greatest of warmth, he explained that he too had a hearing loss. To my amazement, he turned his head to show me the scar where his cochlear implant was. He even let me touch it.

We commiserated over how difficult it is to function professionally with a hearing impairment; how nobody changes their communication style to help you. As I described how my hearing loss led me to want to kill myself he leant across the table and gave my hand a sympathetic squeeze.

I felt at once this man understood me. He explained he didn't consider his deafness a problem as much as the way the hearing world treated him. In fact, there were many aspects to being Deaf he said he enjoyed.

It was too late to release me before the weekend but surely this fellow deafy, a member of my tribe, would recommend my discharge come Monday. But when Monday rolled around commencing my second week of confinement Enid told me the bad news.

"Sorry, John, they're not discharging you."

My disappointment was palpable. "What's the problem?"

Enid explained I can only be discharged if the head psychiatrist, Ms. Never-Mind, consented, and she didn't. Furthermore, I needed to have someone willing to take me in, and as things stood, no one would.

I was walking down the hall ready to succumb to insanity, when a petite, well-dressed woman I'd never seen before walked up carrying a briefcase.

"Mr. Geoghegan?"

"Yes?"

"Could you pronounce your name for me, please?"

"Gay-hay-gan."

"Hello, Mr. Geoghegan. I'm Arlene Sennett, an attorney with the Mental Health Advocacy Project. I understand you're a patient at Hillcrest on a 14 day hold."

"That's right."

"Well, the Mental Health Advocacy Project wants you to know you have the right to appeal that decision."

"I do?"

"Yes, you do. The Superior Court of California holds a hearing at Hillcrest every Monday for patients who contest their confinement. If you want, I'd be happy to take your case. I can hear your side of the story and prepare your appeal. There's no charge for my services."

I wasn't about to question this angel of mercy but the fact she had found me felt like a miracle. There was nothing I wanted more than to get out of that place. It was all I could think about. Yet my best efforts had been for naught; Hillcrest seemed determined to keep me. Maybe this lawyer was my answer.

Ms Sennett and I sat in the visitors' room as I explained my hearing problem. She was calm, quick-witted, and well spoken. She asked a few questions and made a few notes, but the whole process took less than 20 minutes. Then she told me to meet her by a door at the women's end of the unit at 11:00.

As it turned out, the door, which I'd never noticed, led to a conference room with a table where three judges sat. Ms Sennett and I were at one end of the table while a representative from Hillcrest sat at the other. I couldn't hear much of what she said but was amazed how well she presented my case given we'd spent so little time together.

The most senior judge, a woman about my age, asked me a few questions regarding my hearing which I struggled to hear. Then it was Hillcrest's turn to present.

When the Hillcrest representative began talking I was scandalized by what I heard.

"Patient demonstrates poor insight into his illness. Patient is also argumentative and lacks proper hygiene."

This could not have been further from the truth. I knew what was wrong with me. I was going deaf and there was nothing I could do about it. Had I known sign language, and had the support of the Deaf community, things might have been different, but I didn't. In the meantime, I couldn't hold a job, my daughter was out of control, and my publishing career had cratered. On top of this, my girlfriend had an anger management problem and my family wanted nothing to do with me. If that wasn't insight into my problem I don't know what is.

Besides, I had the best hygiene on the unit and that included the psychiatrists.

But the presiding judge didn't let the Hillcrest representative get very far.

"Is the patient suicidal?" she interrupted.

"No, your honor."

"Has he a treatment plan in place?"

Ms Sennett intervened. "Yes, your honor. He's agreed to attend the Las Alamedas treatment facility."

"Then I see no reason to keep him." The judge gaveled the table. "Patient to be released."

I sat there for a moment stunned. Finally… incredibly… I was free. Was it that easy? Now, I needed to figure out what to do with the rest of my life.

# Chapter 44
# Freedom

Though I was supposed to be discharged at noon Hillcrest didn't complete my paperwork until 2:00pm. It may not seem like much, but I was anxious to retrieve my car keys before the police station closed. In fact, I was so desperate to get out of there I was still wearing their rubber-bottomed socks when I climbed into the taxi.

The first thing I did was tell the cab driver to take me to The Gun Bank. Then I peeled off my socks, put on my sneakers, and settled in the back seat. I may have been dumped on the streets of San Jose with no money, no car, and no place to stay but I was happy to be free.

I could see the driver in the rear view mirror. He was balding with a circle of scruffy side hair and an unkempt beard. I didn't feel like talking until - too late! - he caught my eye.

"Were you in that place?"

"Not anymore."

"Woah! That's hardcore. What's it like?"

"It's no Hilton. But don't worry, I'm better now."

"I'm not worried," he said, sounding like a conspiracy theorist. "Half the people are in there because the government wants it."

"Next time you can be my roommate."

My biggest concern was my car. The last I knew it was in The Gun Bank's parking lot 20 miles away. But the police had moved it I knew not where. Since it was my only means of transportation, not to mention my primary domicile, I needed to find it.

I told the taxi driver my car was parked somewhere near The Gun Bank, so we had to drive around and look for it. What I didn't tell him was I didn't have any cash and the one debit card I had might not work.

I'd solved one problem, though. I didn't have a car key until five minutes before when, miracle of miracles, I remembered I had a duplicate plastic key hidden in my wallet. I'd never once used it in the ten years I'd had the car but when I checked my wallet's secret compartment it was still there. I raised my fists in victory and stuck my chin out like the prow of a ship. Now to find my car!

Most prison convicts have someone to greet them when they get out but that was not my situation. I was on my own. If my suicide attempt was a cry for help it was a spectacular failure. Instead of rallying people it had done the opposite. My sister, my girlfriend, and my shrink had fled for the hills, leaving me with an unquenchable desire to understand why. It's bad enough wanting to kill yourself; discovering nobody gives a shit only magnifies the hurt.

As we zipped up 101 I checked my cell phone. There was hardly any juice left but I decided to text Dr. Squeaky-voice.

*It's not right that neither you, my sister, or Allie haven't contacted me,* I typed. *I was in that place eight days! I'm pissed.*

Dr. Squeaky-voice replied right away, saying she understood how I felt.

*It's best if you do this alone,* she texted. *Don't ask your girlfriend or family for help. No more hostile dependency.*

*They abandoned me!* I texted back.

*You can only express gratitude for your sister's help. She felt overwhelmed. There are no villains here. Just mind your business and focus on healing.*

I shook my head. Since when is it a good idea to leave a suicidal person on their own? That my shrink thought this was the best course felt like an excuse. But my sister and my girlfriend wanted nothing to do with me. It's hard enough losing the woman you love on top of your family, but losing them while losing your mind is a double whammy.

I wasn't looking for sympathy when I tried to buy that gun. I had zero thought of how killing myself might affect others. But people's reactions speak volumes. I thought they'd wrap me in a warm embrace after my arrest. Instead, the opposite held true. I'd repelled them. Yes, it was my fault, but that didn't stop me from feeling hurt.

I suspected Dr. Squeaky-voice knew more than she was saying. Granted she was in an awkward position given that my sister, Allie, and I were all her patients. Her blithe, go-it-alone advice made me trust her a lot less, but at least she admitted to calling 911, which was why I got arrested. Though I'd have preferred an appointment with her to a jail cell, I can't say I was surprised.

Dr. Squeaky-voice concluded her message by telling me my sister would no longer be paying for my sessions. If I wanted to continue seeing her, I'd have to make other arrangements. That was fine. I recognized the value of a good therapist at a time like this; it just wasn't going to be Dr. Squeaky-voice. Ever again.

***

As the taxi approached The Gun Bank I averted my eyes; it was the last place I want to see. As luck would have it, my car was parked half a block away. It felt like winning the lottery.

I handed the cab driver my debit card and held my breath. I wasn't sure if it would work after Dana's purchases were challenged. But I was relieved to hear a receipt being printed, indicating the transaction had gone through. In fact, I was so grateful I gave the driver half the total as a tip. In thanks, he banged fists with me and said:

"Don't let 'em catch you again, brother."

"No worries," I said. "They're not even looking."

When I inserted my plastic key into the ignition I was in for another stroke of luck. My car started without a problem. I put the blinker on and pulled into mid-day traffic.

I didn't have much time. I had to get to the police station before it closed to retrieve my keys. The only way to get there though was by making a u-turn in front of The Gun Bank. I'd really hoped to avoid that place but I had no choice. When I made the turn, so much bad feeling radiated from the building I swerved to avoid it. Once safely past, I headed for the town center.

One thing I'd noticed since they'd released me was that the world seemed different. It was brighter than I remembered and the people stranger. It was as if I'd been dropped on an alien planet, only I was the alien.

I was relying on my cell phone to get me to the police station. When it finally died I panicked. It's not easy for a severely depressed person to problem solve, but I was only a few blocks from the police station, so I regulated my thoughts and looked for the parking lot.

When I inquired about my keys I was told they were in the property department, which was open until 4:00. But for some reason the person who ran it had left early. I couldn't get my keys until morning. No biggie, I could come back. In the meantime, I needed to buy a cell phone charger for my car. Since I'd passed a Rite Aid on my way over, I headed there to make the purchase. Within half an hour, my phone was functioning again.

By 5:00 pm I was starving. With money, a car, and a working phone I could afford to relax. There was a branch of my favorite pizza joint nearby, so I went there for a beer and a slice. Dr. Squeaky-voice once warned me booze and meds don't mix but I'd spent a week in the nut house. What could one beer do?

My next problem was where to spend the night. I had an interview at Las Alamedas, the private residential facility, the next day, but I needed a place to crash until then. I foolishly texted my sister asking whether I could stay in her guest house. When there was no response, I considered my options.

Dr. Squeaky-voice had recommended the Menlo Hotel, so I drove over to check it out.

When I asked how much a room costed, I was told it was $450 a night not including tax. There was no way I was spending that kind of money even if Dr. Squeaky-voice said I should "treat myself," so I slept in my car instead. Normally, I'd have considered this hitting bottom, but after my stay at Hillcrest it seemed an improvement.

The next morning, I woke up early and cleaned up at a gas station. Though it's true I'd have chewed off my ankle to get out of Hillcrest, I wasn't ready to be on my own just yet. There were several reasons for this, chief among them being I'd not ruled out killing myself. I was less determined, of course. Still, it was an option. I was also thinking of disappearing. I might just hop in my car and head east without telling anyone. If Dr. Squeaky-voice thought I had a "hostile dependency" then maybe I should opt for a hostile *independency*.

But this plan lacked credibility. For one, my kids were in California. Even though things sucked, I had no intention of giving them up. Additionally, I'd spent 20 years in the Bay Area. Starting over somewhere else wouldn't solve my problem. I was angry though, and felt seriously misunderstood. It was tempting to make a run for it.

\*\*\*

My interview at Las Alamedas was set for ten. When I arrived in Palo Alto, I noticed it was a home circa 1920s in the residential district. Curiously, there was no signage.

At the top of the doorstep standing next to a roller bag was a tall, willowy girl. Her name, I soon learned, was Oona and she'd obviously gone to some trouble to make herself look nice. She wore a black and white wraparound dress and wedge sandals that, added to her height, threaten to tip her over. Her nose was slightly too large for her face but it only added to her charm. Her blonde hair, done up in a French bun, made her look more sophisticated than her twenty-something years.

"Is this Las Alamedas?" I asked.

"Yes," she said, brushing the hair from her face.

"I have an appointment."

"Ask for Helena inside."

Even though I didn't feel like talking, I took a chance. "Do you live here?"

"Uh-huh."

"I'm thinking of moving in. How is it?"

"It's great. I did really well."

"You look okay."

"Oh, no, I'm a mess but thank you anyway."

"I'm a mess, too. I just got out of the booby hatch and never want to go back. I need some place to get better."

"You'll like it here. They give you lots of freedom. And the staff is great. They really want to help."

"Are you being discharged?"

"No," she laughed. "Just moving to a less strict house. But this is a good place to start."

There was a vulnerability to Oona as if she hadn't completely healed, and she was surprisingly knowledgeable about residential treatment, suggesting this was not her first time. It might be hard to get worked up about my problems - I was past my prime - but it was sad to see such hurt in the face of someone so young and lovely.

The woman who interviewed me was warm and sympathetic. Weirdly, she reminded me of Allie's sister, who I once met briefly and didn't like. I made a few jokes to show I wasn't crazy and twenty minutes later she had a bed for me. The only problem was it wasn't available until tomorrow. That meant I had 24 more hours on my own, just enough time to collect my toiletries and clothes for a 30 day stay. It also meant another night in my car unless I could spring for a motel.

Normally, gathering my belongings wouldn't be a problem, except everything I needed was at Allie's. That meant I had to go to The Dutch Boy which, given everything that had transpired, was not something I wanted to do. But since the only personal effects I possessed were in my pocket I didn't have a choice. If I wanted my stuff I had to see Allie.

Driving past The Gun Bank would be welcome in comparison.

# Chapter 45
## Beauty Hides the Thorns

Clearly, Allie had dumped me. How else could you explain her failure to communicate let alone visit me at Hillcrest? Now, sitting in my car, I sent her a brief text requesting a time to pick up my stuff.

I planned on keeping my visit short. All I wanted was to get my boxes and get the hell out of there. Since I had a key to her place I was hoping she'd schedule a time to get my stuff when she wasn't home. Given she hadn't spoken to me since before I was arrested that would be the honorable thing to do.

When Allie replied her text was short, formal, and to the point.

*Please come by at 11:30.*

Devoid of emotion and brutally brief, this is how people communicate when the romance is over. No response at all would have hurt less.

***

Everyone feels bad about certain places. They avoid the building where they were fired, or an ex-girlfriend's old haunts. I felt this way about The Dutch Boy only it was off the charts. The building may have been an inanimate object but it radiated so much malevolent energy it felt like The Gun Bank. It was all in my head, of course, so I ignored it and pressed on. Still, it wasn't easy going someplace I wasn't wanted to meet the woman who no longer cared for me.

As misfortune would have it, I was fifteen minutes early, so I sat in my car and waited. The area was deserted, the towering gates locked. The only person I saw was the RV guy sitting in a lawn chair sipping a beer. It was half past eleven.

A few minutes later, Allie appeared in my side view mirror exiting her apartment. I waited to see if she would hop in her Fiat and leave.

Instead, she took up a position behind the gate and stared in my direction. When she made no move to leave, I warily exited my car.

Love has a momentum. You can't turn it off like a switch. The sad truth is I still loved Allie but I was so hurt by her withdrawal I wanted to cauterize the wound. This explains my instinctive, crab-like walk towards The Dutch Boy. Head down, protectively hunched over, I refused to make eye contact. Still, I noticed she was looking at me with an expression more sympathetic than angry.

"I'm not mad at you," she said. Then repeated: "I'm not mad."

Then, she reached through the gate and rubbed the top of my head like I was a wayward child.

Allie misunderstood my body language. I was hunkered down not because I was afraid she was angry, but because I was protecting myself against the fact she no longer loved me. It wasn't surprising she misread the situation but it was revealing her first reaction was about herself. After all, I'd just spent a week in the county insane asylum.

Of course, I misread the situation too, mistaking her concern for evidence of love. Briefly, hope rekindled.

I'd expected Allie to leave my boxes on the loading dock so I could collect them without seeing her. But the loading dock was bare. Instead, she beckoned me inside.

When I entered her loft, Allie directed me to the couch then sat next to me, inching closer until she was curled up by my side. This confused me. What was she doing? I just wanted my stuff. A moment later she slipped her arm around me.

It was apparent Allie wanted to talk even if I wasn't interested. She'd had her chance. It was too late. But there were a few questions I wouldn't mind her answering. Like, why did she dump me? And why hadn't I heard from my sister?

Allie's conversation had never been linear. You always had to piece it together. That I had to do so with a compromised brain heightened the difficulty. Nevertheless, I wanted to know why she had abandoned me.

"Why didn't you get me out of Hillcrest?" I asked.

"Ivankovich said you were where you needed to be."

"What does Ivankovich have to do with this? He's not my shrink."

"He was the only person I could depend on when you got arrested."

"Don't you understand? You were key to me getting out of there! That place was a nightmare!"

"I know those places. They're not so bad."

Allie showed little sympathy for what had happened. She also refused to admit abandoning me. Instead, she kept channeling Ivankovich.

"You left me in an insane asylum for more than a week! I'd still be there if I hadn't found my own way out."

"What about me?" she said. "I didn't know what was happening! I had to figure it out for myself."

"It's not the same thing," I said. "You were free. I was locked inside a nut house!"

But Allie was too engaged with her own problems to have much compassion for mine. The most she would allow was that my actions threw her into extremis, for which she sought counsel.

It soon became clear Allie didn't want to hear about Hillcrest. So I changed strategies, hoping she would explain her actions if I just listened. And I was right, the strategy worked. Allie soon revealed she'd learned about my arrest from Dr. Squeaky-voice, who'd called her. She then contacted my sister for more information. So much for keeping my news on the down low.

Somewhere in her narrative, Allie blurted out the reason my sister didn't visit me was she was "tired of paying for everything." This surprised me. True, my sister had paid for a lot, but I'd ceased being a drain six months ago. Furthermore, I'd given her a check for $20,000 as reimbursement. As far as I knew, she'd made a profit. Still, "tired of paying for everything"? All the woman had to do was visit me at Hillcrest. That didn't cost a dime.

I sensed Allie was not telling me everything. She was leaving something out. When she revealed the missing piece I was so surprised I didn't know what to say.

As it turned out, her conversations with Ivankovich and Dr. Squeaky-voice revolved around how much of a danger I represented. Ivankovich, who'd met me once and even then only for two minutes, was worried I might kill Allie.

"A danger? Why would you think that? I wasn't dangerous to anyone but myself."

But Ivankovich wasn't the only one recommending Allie steer clear of me. Dr. Squeaky-voice said the same thing, informing Allie of my history of "domestic violence."

I'd already told Allie I was ashamed by how I treated my wife. But a "history"? Sure, I'd pushed her a few times and slapped her twice. Though I was wrong to do this, I never beat her. There was never any police involvement, no hospital visit. And wasn't that privileged information anyway? Who was Dr. Squeaky-voice working for anyway? Me, my sister, or Allie?

Dr. Squeaky-voice was so concerned that I might be a danger she told Allie to get rid of my boxes so I'd have no reason to visit.

"FedEx them to his home," she urged.

The problem was I didn't have a home. I was temporarily living with Allie. But this fact escaped Dr. Squeaky-voice.

While Dr.'s Ivankovich and Squeaky-voice warned Allie to have nothing to do with me, my middle brother, the one who helped spread my mother's ashes, called her to gossip. Believing he might shed some light on the situation, Allie asked whether he thought I was capable of murder.

After a moment, my brother said: "Yes."

Who knew I was such a desperado? Even my family thought I was a killer. When Allie called my sister to discuss the situation, my brother-in-law intercepted the call, thanked her for everything she'd done for me, and cut off further contact. Allie took this as confirmation I was a danger.

In my heart I knew I wasn't capable of murder. I'd never kill Allie, or anyone else for that matter. But if I was officially dangerous why was Allie talking to me?

It was hard to make sense of any of this, other than if Allie told Enid she feared for her life no wonder Hillcrest wouldn't release me. Of course, I should have anticipated Allie's reaction when I walked into The Gun Bank. For Allie, the death of her mother at the hands of her father was still raw. The fact I tried to buy a handgun, the same weapon her father used, made it worse.

After an hour, Allie surprised me by taking my hand and leading me upstairs where she proceeded to fuck my brains out. I'd have found this even more confusing if I wasn't still in love with her. Instead, I took it as a sign I still had a chance.

Afterwards, at Allie's instance, I took only enough clothes for a week and left the rest at The Dutch Boy. When I tried returning her house key she refused to accept it.

Later that night she sent me a brief email.

*This respectfully concludes the romantic portion of our relationship. I hope our friendship will continue.*

So much for cauterizing the wound. The next day I was admitted to Las Alamedas.

# Chapter 46
# Las Alamedas

Las Alamedas looked like every other house in Palo Alto. A three-story jewel box of stucco and timber, it sat on a modest piece of land a gardener maintained to within an inch of its life. Only a short walk from town, its location was as desirable as its sales price dear. In other words, what had once been affordable had now become a prized piece of real estate.

The peaked-roof residence had five bedrooms: one downstairs, three on the second floor, and another in the attic. It also had two full baths, which tended towards overuse given there were eleven of us living there. In addition to a large kitchen, there was a dining room, a living room, and a gazebo out back; everything you needed to feel at home.

The house blended in with the neighborhood but who knew what the neighbors thought? Not every street in Palo Alto boasted a building full of loonies. I asked the staff what Las Alamedas meant but nobody knew. Later, I looked it up and discovered it's Spanish for tree-lined boulevard. Since there weren't many old growth trees around I suspected it was real estate hype. It didn't matter. I was happy to be here even if it cost more than I earned in a year. Fortunately, I had the inheritance from my mother to pay the bill. I considered it money well spent.

The house manager, Helena, made it clear on our first meeting she was neither maid nor cook. She was as big hearted as she was small, radiating warmth and affection for us, her charges. I lived in a second floor bedroom with two others. One was Greg, a silver-haired man in his 70s suffering from depression. He was a likeable guy who looked a lot like the actor Tom Wilkinson. As a former CEO he'd taken at least one company public and though he had money he didn't flaunt it. He'd been married and divorced with two grown kids. Having been here a month he was well settled in.

Greg was undergoing a course of electroconvulsive therapy, or ECT, for his depression. They took him away every other morning and brought him back in the afternoon, after which he was quiet for the rest of the day. Since we were both early risers we drank coffee in the gazebo. This was where he confided in a ghostly whisper he didn't think the ECT was working.

Our roommate, Brandon, was on the opposite end of our age spectrum. A tall thin black kid, Brandon couldn't be more than 20 years old. He was devastatingly handsome but I never once heard him speak during his stay with us. I was curious why but respected his privacy. It was only later someone explained that Brandon believed we could read his thoughts. Maybe that's why he found talking unnecessary.

We were not permitted to leave the residence during the first ten days of our stay. After that we could sign out with permission. There were limitations to how far we could range, or how long we could remain away, but they didn't bother me. I preferred sticking close to home.

One thing Las Alamedas was good at was providing a safe, structured environment. Every day we had something to do whether it was household chores, going to therapy, or taking a field trip. The field trips were interesting. Outings varied by day of the week and were always chaperoned. Monday was swimming, Tuesday was tennis. Weekends included a visit to a local gym or bookstore.

Since depressed people never feel like doing anything the staff incentivized us. We got four dollars for every field trip we participated in but could only spend the money on an edible treat like a candy bar. It's the most basic kind of reward system yet it worked.

Doing things for ourselves, whether it was making breakfast or participating in a field trip, was supposed to help us re-enter the world. But not everyone thrived. One woman, who'd had so much cosmetic surgery she was scary to look at, never got out of bed, took a shower, or shared a meal with us. She was the exception, though. Most times, the strategy worked.

The one field trip I loathed happened on Thursdays. That was when we food shopped at Lucky's. For some reason, the staff had decided we'd get better faster if we did all the food shopping, so the outing was mandatory. But asking eleven severely depressed people to take turns preparing the largest meal they'd ever cooked in their lives could show questionable judgment. Yes, we had the occasional calamity, somebody couldn't get out of bed, or mysteriously disappeared, but most of our meals turned out fine.

Still, buying breakfast, lunch and dinner for eleven people is a challenge even when you're sane. The staff helped by grouping the items we needed to purchase by category so we could find them more easily. Nevertheless, it was a trial.

My first Thursday at Las Alamedas I wasn't sure what was happening. The highest functioning of us crowded into the van and were driven to Lucky's where we disembarked, shopping list in hand, to invade the super-sized store.

Lucky's was the kind of place that sucked the serotonin right out of you. And that was before you encountered five miles of unfamiliar shelving. We wheeled our carts around the store on a mentally-impaired scavenger hunt searching for commodity-priced offerings. The off brand luncheon meat so grossed me out I couldn't help but feel there was a lifetime of failure in that transaction alone. This may have been my compromised thinking but Lucky's had no shortage of triggers. The fluorescent lights were dispiriting, the open space oppressive. At least half the people looked like candidates for Las Alamedas.

When we finished, we met in front of the same cash register, eleven shopping carts in a slow-moving conga line. We looked like an audition for a local production of *Cuckoo's Nest* only nobody was clapping. I would have liked to escape but where would I go? Whole Foods? I couldn't afford it.

*** 

Las Alamedas was the first place you went after being discharged from the hospital, so the staff were concerned for our safety. They kept a close eye on us, especially when dispensing medication. They also searched our rooms daily looking for contraband like weapons or drugs. I didn't mind the intrusion; they were just trying to help. It was nice to know someone cared.

There wasn't much emphasis on one-on-one therapy, though. Officially, we met with our counselor twice a week, but most of our therapy was done offsite between the hours of 10 and 3. My therapist, Janik, was a young Polish guy with a Phd and a lovely manner. Our first session was mostly Janik offering me encouragement, which I greedily

227

lapped up. However, I couldn't help but notice he was wearing a t-shirt with a Beretta logo. It was a funny fashion choice for a therapist.

At one point I told Janik I was concerned I wouldn't be able to hear what was said in my therapy sessions.

"If you only get half," he told me, "you'll be doing better than a lot of people here."

I had a hard time believing him but took it on faith.

\*\*\*

One thing about mental illness is you're usually worse off than you think. I was shell shocked after Hillcrest. My ability to get anything done was seriously compromised. When Janik suggested I begin the process of applying for health insurance I found the thought overwhelming. I did my best but didn't get very far.

People suffering from clinical depression are incredibly fragile. What you say, or how you say it, has a significant effect. The staff had been doing this work for so long they knew how to handle us. Still, I was encased in bubble wrap. It was such a dissociative feeling I couldn't connect with the world around me. Instead, I went off on tangents.

For example, I'd been unable to find the charger for my electric razor. I'd rummaged through my box at Allie's but it was nowhere to be found. My concern for its whereabouts took on legendary proportions. If I didn't find it, my world would collapse, and no replacement would do. I spent so much time worrying about it I failed to deal with more important things like health insurance.

It's strange when your brain is the enemy; when the very thing you depend on to navigate the world can no longer be trusted. It's not unusual for small things to take on a greater role when depressed. During the great de-accessioning I'd given one bookcase to Allie and kept the other for myself. But somehow she ended up with all the bookcase hardware. How was I going to hang my shelves without it? It was this kind of obsessive thinking that indicated I had a long way to go before getting better.

Treating depression is like solving a problem while someone holds your head underwater. Las Alamedas promised we'd get better but since I had no idea how this would happen I took it on faith. Allie once told me that people in her AA group said, "Fake it until you make it." I mimicked daily life, hoping it to jump start my battery. Mostly though, I was too far gone to hold a charge.

I also had a secret. We were not supposed to have a car at Las Alamedas. I didn't know this rule when admitted but I not only had a car, I'd parked it in front of the house where I could see it. Best of all, there was a box cutter in the glove compartment from my move. I was going to give Las Alamedas my best shot but if things didn't work out I could always slit my throat. It's surprising how much better I felt just knowing it was there.

# Chapter 47
# The Program

There's something therapeutic about a house full of crazy people. Despite being addicted, suicidal, or depressed we formed relationships faster than in the real world. The reason why is we weren't judgmental.

Las Alamedas was like prison to the extent that no one was "innocent." We were all here for a reason. As a result, friendships took root regardless of age, race, creed or sex. The place would have been a utopia if we weren't out of our minds.

Hanging out with people half my age turned out to be enjoyable. It had been so long since I'd talked to a 20 year old their perspective was refreshing. Rob was a 30 year old drug addict with blue-black hair and a thick beard. He was so skinny you wanted to feed him. We met under the gazebo where the smokers gathered. Practically every addict at Las Alamedas chain smoked and since Helena didn't allow smoking in the house they gravitated outside. Sooner or later, we all ended up in the gazebo.

Within minutes of meeting, Rob told me he'd been to rehab five times.

"I've also died three times," he added. "The first two were overdoses. The third was when my heart stopped."

This was only one of a dozen horror stories I heard at Las Alamedas, but Rob's were especially hair-raising. Sober, he came across as sensitive, honest and funny. I could spend hours listening to him. If I didn't know better I'd think addiction was one long, hilarious escapade.

But Rob was not alone. There were two more addicts who frequented the gazebo to smoke. One was a 25 year old kid with kinky hair named Bix. Bix told me that during a drug induced psychosis he unplugged all the electronics in his apartment to keep them from talking. He also warned me about Kelsey.

"Watch out for her," Bix said, puffing on a cigarette. "She's a drama queen."

Bix's prophecy turned out to be true but not in the way I expected. Kelsey was a 26-year-old heroin user. She wasn't bad looking if you could get past the piercings. She had three in her left cheek and a variety of tattoos snaking across her neck. She also had a nose ring and on her 26th birthday got permission for a chin piercing. I'm not sure what took her so long since that seemed the least painful one to get.

Kelsey was catnip to men and she knew it. She had the rare ability to get the chest beaters to compete for her affection. Though I'd yet to see evidence of this skill Bix's warning proved prescient. Within a month, Kelsey had three guys in the program clawing for her attention.

One thing I noticed about Kelsey was her moods swings. One day she was bubbly, the next she refused to come down from her attic bedroom. Most of the time, however, she was personable to the point of vulnerability.

Despite the drama implication, I liked Kelsey. I was old enough I could get to know her without being a player. I was also nonjudgmental. When she showed me her needle tracks I told her they looked like tiny black ants running up her arm. This made her laugh. Her stories were also mesmerizing. Who else do you know gets ready for work by snorting a line of heroin in the morning? Somehow the awfulness of Kelsey's addiction made me feel better.

\*\*\*

The daily program we attended was held on the second floor of a nondescript building near the Palo Alto train station. The program attracted more people than just us - there were also "day students" who lived in the surrounding community.

The program started at 10:00am because most mentally ill people can't get their act together before then. We were bused in by a van and spent the next six hours sitting on overstuffed sofas the texture of black licorice. Lunch was provided.

The program was designed to last thirty days during which it taught us the skills necessary for coping with our illness. Chief among these were acknowledging our feelings but not reacting to them; practicing self-compassion; learning to regulate our emotions; and reframing negative thoughts.

231

Some of these strategies were on the nursery school level. Then again, so were we. For instance, they asked us to identify how we were feeling by pointing to a chart with smiley faces. The objective was to teach us to recognize emotions. They also made us brainstorm a list of things to do when depressed. These included going for a walk, watching a movie, or wearing perfume. Many of these strategies were common sense but you'd be surprised how little common sense a depressed person has. It helped to be reminded.

One thing I noticed was that people were constantly nodding off during group. I didn't know whether it was their meds, insomnia, or boredom, but it incensed me. How could you get better if you weren't paying attention? I was so desperate I would try anything. This turned out to be the right frame of mind but not everyone shared it.

Occasionally, I saw Oona at the program. Usually, she was sitting on the smokers' bench near the back door looking thoughtful. She was living at another residence, so I didn't see her much. When I did, she looked sad. But Kelsey, who knew her, said she was doing fine. Like Rob, there was something about Oona that made you root for her. Now, if I could only root for myself.

*** 

One Sunday early in my stay I was lying in bed in my room when my phone lit up with a text from Allie.

*Can you talk?* she asked. *I'm feeling sad.*

Allie and I had traded the occasional text since I got my stuff. Contact had been sporadic since the majority of my energy was spent on getting better. Hoping to play a lover's reassuring role, I did my best to cheer her up without understanding what was making her sad. The next night she texted the explanation.

*I'm moving back east.*

The news came as a shock. Whether she had hid it out of cowardice, or to protect me, I didn't know. One thing was clear, she may not have acknowledged abandoning me at Hillcrest but moving back east without telling me was a far greater transgression. And I was trying to cheer her up!

232

Allie's announcement felt like a blow. I may have tried killing myself but it wasn't because of her. Now that she'd told me she was leaving, I felt myself sinking. The way I looked at it, I'd made considerable sacrifices to be with Allie. I'd given up my dog, my home, and my possessions, worked two jobs neither of which I could do, and never once wavered in my love for her. In the meantime, I had accepted her impulsiveness, her promiscuousness, and her anger. Surely, I deserved to be grandfathered in here somewhere.

I tried squeezing the life out of my phone but mostly I felt sad. I'd lived my life far more responsibly than Allie, yet when I became overwhelmed she took off. And still I loved her. The truth is I'd have done anything for Allie. Why then would she leave?

Breakups rarely go smoothly, especially when possessions are involved. In my case, I had to get my few remaining boxes out of her loft before she left. Yes, I'd passed my probationary period but Las Alamedas had strict rules. I could only leave for three hours, I had to stay within Palo Alto, and I was not allowed to drive my car. They would kick you out for violating these rules but I had no choice. I had to see Allie one last time.

*** 

It's hard enough having a love affair when you're sane, but losing your lover when crazy added to the noise in my head. The situation was exacerbated by my not being able to leave Las Alamedas for more than three hours. It would take me at least an hour to get to The Dutch Boy and another hour to get back and that was provided there was no traffic. Since I was worried about getting caught, I picked a Saturday when both staffing and traffic was light. As I pulled up to The Dutch Boy, Allie was waiting by the gate. I can't recall whether she helped me carry my boxes to the car but I don't think so. What I do remember is her asking for my key.

Few moments are freighted with more significance than returning a lover's key. The last time I'd seen her she insisted I keep it. Now, she wanted it back. It took only a small effort to slip it off my key ring, but it felt like the surrender at Appomattox. There was only sadness and regret.

We made love one last time; a far softer, more delicate process than the one we were used to. I saw it as a means of keeping our relationship alive, but for Allie it was just sex. Either way, my time constraints went out the window. I was kidding myself if I thought our coupling was anything more than one last dip in the pool. Still, I was hoping it would maintain our bond. After all, Allie held out the promise of reuniting once I got better. Perhaps this abandonment was only temporary.

When we finished, Allie wrapped her arms around me and murmured, "This is how it should be." But a few minutes later she made a weird, gurgling sound and sat up in bed.

"Who's going to take care of me?" she said, tears pooling in her eyes. "Am I ever going to find someone to share my life with?"

I was probably the wrong person to ask but as Allie hugged her knees I rubbed the small of her back in consolation. I was surprised she wanted to be "taken care of." Allie had always been a fierce promoter of female independence. But there was no mistaking the catch in her voice, the flood of tears.

I wasn't looking for someone before Allie and I wouldn't be looking after, so being alone wasn't a problem for me. The problem was I still loved her. Worse, I wouldn't be getting over it anytime soon. That I was in love with a woman who'd cast me aside for reasons she wouldn't explain didn't seem fair but that's the way it was.

Like it or not, Allie was leaving. I would have to get used to it.

# Chapter 48
# Russell House

After a month at Las Alamedas I was transferred to Russell House.

Russell House was much less restrictive. There were no staff on the premises though a married couple checked in on us at night. We were also responsible for buying our own food shopping, cooking, and med compliance. Independence was a welcome step forward.

My visit to Allie, which I pulled off without getting caught, was two weeks ago. Now, she was halfway across the country on her drive east while I settled in at my new residence.

Russell House was close enough to the program that I could walk every morning. I never knew where I was, partly because I didn't know Palo Alto but mostly because I wasn't thinking clearly. After a few weeks, however, I realized the program was only a block from a restaurant I'd frequented. It just goes to show how depression had scrambled my brain.

Since Russell House was only a block from railroad tracks I watched the commuter trains rush past my window every morning as I lay in bed. It felt good knowing I was no longer a member of the rat race but I felt sorry for the people on the train who still were.

The grounds around Russell House were a sanctuary. There was a sitting area in back with a table and chairs where I spent hours either reading or watching the squirrels traverse the overhead wires. It was a safe place for a troubled mind to rest.

I'd been warned about the slightly predatory woman who lived next door. I'd been told she took undue interest in the mentally ill. Though I wasn't sure what this meant the few times I talked with her I never had a problem. She was wonderfully sympathetic for a person who lived next to a house full of crazy people.

By my second week I'd nicknamed Russell House "Squalor Hall" because my four roommates, two in their teens, did not good housekeepers make. The bathroom was especially nasty. I had to take my glasses off before entering otherwise I'd see too much.

I also began watching episodes of *Law & Order* every afternoon when I got home from the program. It's a show I usually despise for being formulaic but there was something comforting about its neat, tidy endings. My life may have been in chaos but at the end of every hour I knew the criminals would be safely behind bars. Too bad life's not that easy.

Mental illness is not at all what I expected. Everything may look the same but none of it feels right. It's like an episode of the *Twilight Zone* where the protagonist wakes up in a familiar place to find everything has changed. I'd regained my sense of geography but when I walked the neighborhood many of the houses felt dark and evil. A healthy person might say I was projecting but it didn't feel that way. It was more like an invisible threat announcing itself. Every step filled me with dread.

Then there were days when I felt someone had taken the lid off a teapot exposing me inside. It was the same panicky feeling I got when I was lost driving and had to double back over ground already covered.

I wrestled with these fears every morning as I walked to the program. It meant putting into practice what they taught. I may not have been able to make these anxieties go away but acknowledging they existed helped to diminish their power. The more I challenged their existence the weaker they became.

By the end of the month my anxiety began to fade. I not only walked to the program I started exploring the neighborhood. On weekends I hiked the "Dish," four miles of paved trails owned by Stanford University. It was hard going, I had to push myself, but I could tell I was making progress.

If I had a complaint it was that Russell House was lonely. I had four housemates who, for various reasons, I didn't connect with. One I learned had been living there for two years and did nothing all day but participate in role playing games on the Internet. I missed my children who were in Japan visiting their grandmother, but I was glad they had no idea what had happened to me. To offset my loneliness, I began attending Alcoholics Anonymous meetings. I also went to a bipolar support group and Al-Anon. Though I didn't suffer from these things the meetings made me feel less lonely.

Most of the time I was too wrapped up in my problems to notice when something changed but when I lost one of my housemates it came as a surprise. The only consolation was that Rob was the replacement.

I was thrilled to have Rob at Russell House. The residence was not for drug addicts - they went to a different one with stricter regulations, but there was no room at that particular inn, so Rob joined us. The first thing we did was go to meetings together. We started with AA then added Narcotics Anonymous (NA). NA meetings were the best. The stories were more exciting, the food better, and the girls prettier. Still, there's nothing like a depression support group to improve your self-esteem. The people who attended were in such a funk they made me feel better. It's sad I still suffered from snobbery but it was a sign I was getting better.

One Friday night, Rob and I headed to a NA meeting. We'd just pulled up in front of the church when we noticed a gathering of people standing on the lawn. It felt like a party. Men and women were mingling in groups, laughing and talking. The evening felt special when I recognized the faces of people I knew. There was Greg, my former roommate, who longed for company just like me. He was talking to Bix, who was smoking a cigarette and smiling. Kelsey was also there as well as Oona, Brandon, and James. They greeted me so warmly it made me teary eyed. It was wonderful to be outside on a Friday night surrounded by my tribe. Who knew this would be the place where I belonged?

***

Around this same time a package showed up on the Russell House doorstep. No one noticed it at first, which was surprising given it was a large red Coleman cooler wrapped in silver duct tape. Our self-involvement was such that many things went unnoticed including the mail, the phone, and the deplorable state of our housekeeping. As a result, the package went unnoticed. The mentally ill are easily distracted.

Even more distracting were the relationships forming around me. When it came to Kelsey, Bix knew of what he spoke because he was the first to get involved with her. It was Bix who drove Kelsey for her chin piercing just as it was Bix who warned me Kelsey created drama. Little did I know he'd be a featured player.

But Bix was not alone. One day after walking home from the program, I found Kelsey curled up on the Russell House sofa with her feet tucked underneath the thigh of some guy she was interested in. That meant she had three young men lusting after her while I watched from the safety of my bunker.

Though Kelsey took up with Bix first, she soon targeted a tall, uncommunicative boy eight years younger. There was something off about him. I couldn't put my finger on it. He lived in the same house as Kelsey, which was where the addicts resided. One Sunday around 8:00am, which may be early for the mentally ill but late for me, there was a ruckus at our front door. A minute later I heard feet pounding up the stairs then the tall, silent kid barged into my room.

"Where's Kelsey?" he demanded, speaking in the inarticulate voice of a caveman.

I knew Kelsey was with Rob. I saw them canoodling on the sofa the night before. I was guessing they were in Rob's bed next door but I was not getting caught in the middle of a love triangle.

"No idea," I shrugged, hoping my age would give me an advantage.

After staring at me longer than felt comfortable the kid finally stomped off.

It was hard to tell what was fueling all this emotion. Was it love, hormones, or mental illness? Since love is a form of mental illness, at least among the young, I was betting it was part of the mix. In the meantime, the four-way dynamic between Kelsey, Bix, Rob and the mostly Silent Kid kept getting weirder.

What I didn't know and didn't learn until later was that Rob and Kelsey were off most nights getting high together. I was unclear what kind of drugs they were using but they were probably inject-able. I feared the worst.

I had a fatherly feeling toward Rob but within a week he was drunk every night. One evening he bummed money off me. When I told him I was worried about him he reassured me everything was okay. Then he rode into the night on his wobbly bicycle to buy a pint of vodka.

Eventually, I contacted our keepers to tell them Rob needed "a more structured environment," code for a stricter program. Meanwhile, Kelsey was kicked out of the addicts' residence and landed in Russell House. A week later, the program expelled Rob and Kelsey for substance abuse. Before she left, Kelsey bid me goodbye with a hug so strong it startled me.

When I finally noticed the cooler on the porch and read its shipping label I was surprised to see it was addressed to me. The outside world had encroached very little on my recovery but the Coleman cooler turned out to be filled with my mother's personal effects. I couldn't go near it for months.

Later that week the program held a party for Oona, who was being released. I hadn't seen her in a while but she was well put together as usual. As she thanked the staff for everything they'd done, Oona swayed slightly in an imaginary breeze. Her voice was soft but her message was sincere.

"If I can get better you can, too," she said.

When she was finished even I could hear some sniffling.

Since the majority of our residents were so depressed they found it difficult to put two sentences together I took Oona's performance as a sign of recovery. But forty-eight hours later Oona was fifty-one-fifty-ed to a hospital for trying to kill herself. Kelsey was the bearer of the bad news. It was a reminder of just how tentative our progress could be.

\*\*\*

Nice things are usually frontloaded in a relationship. Maybe that's why endings are so ugly.

Allie held out hope of reuniting but as she drove across country I felt our attachment unspooling. Everyone has their reasons for keeping a relationship going but the distance as measured by her daily odometer made it difficult for me to believe she was sincere. I employed several strategies to feel close to her. I read the same books as her book club, checked her daily progress on a map, and went to AA meetings because Allie went, but a relationship can't work if only one person carries the load.

Once Allie established herself on the other side of the country things grew strained. Given the time difference, I rose every morning at 3:00am to compose a loving text. I wanted it to be the first thing she saw when she awoke. Then I fell asleep phone in hand in case she replied.

At one point, I worked up enough courage to ask why she left. Her response was convoluted but her last sentence made sense:

*I chose me!*

Her exclamation point was so painful it felt like a shovel sunk in a mound of graveside dirt. As time went on, she responded less and less to my texts. When she did reply it was only with complaints: she was too busy, too tired, or cell reception was too poor to maintain contact. These weren't the endearments I'd hoped for.

When Allie did find time to talk she complained about the difficulties of setting up house. Her place was too small; the plumber hadn't come; her furniture didn't fit.

It was cruel to ask me for sympathy. I was recovering from a suicide attempt, my siblings wouldn't talk to me, and my girlfriend had moved across country. What did she expect?

But then Allie told me about skinny dipping in the stream behind her house and I instantly imagined her emerging naked and dripping from a pretty country creek. The thought was pure torture.

Breakups by definition don't go well. I watched as my love turned sour, curdled into anger then hardened into hate. Who can tolerate having their privileges revoked? But that's what happened. Allie tried downgrading me from lover to friend but I couldn't handle the loss in status. It was all or nothing. Halfway measures don't cut it.

Which is why I was surprised Allie didn't understand that abandoning me demanded a proportionate response. So, on August 27th, a year to the day since she first visited Woodside, I ceased all contact with Allison Katz. I not only blocked her phone and email address I deleted her from Facebook, LinkedIn and any other social media we had in common. It's not just that I didn't want to be reminded of her, I needed to "disappear her" from my life.

Two days later, Russell House declared me a free man.

# Chapter 49
# Catch and Release

Driving under the cinnabar arches of the Golden Gate Bridge was a euphoric feeling. With the Pacific glittering below, the sunroof open, and no toll booth to impede my progress I'd have blasted the radio if only I could've heard it.

A year before, if someone had told me I'd spend two months in a residential mental health facility I'd have said they were crazy. Yet here I was driving north on 101 into an uncertain future. It may have been too early to set me loose in the world but crossing that span filled me with such giddy delight I was willing to take the chance.

Before leaving Russell House I'd reached out to old friends, a couple who had once been neighbors. They invited me to stay with them and their three children until I got back on my feet. I was so grateful for their offer I took them up on it.

I still found many things difficult. Just the thought of looking for an apartment overwhelmed me but my hosts agreed to help. They didn't mind making phone calls on my behalf, or assisting me in ways I still needed until I was back on my feet. It felt good not to be judged just because I don't hear like everybody else.

Taking their dogs for their daily walk helped speed my recovery but it was picking their kids up from school and having dinner as a family that really did the trick. I was still not myself, that would take longer, but I was on my way.

After a month, I was feeling confident enough to ask my hosts how they thought I was doing. When they said I was only 40% of my former self it surprised me. What seemed like 40% to them felt like 80% to me but that's because I was indexing off a low base.

As late as October I was still stockpiling Ativan in case I had a change of heart. This was an improvement compared to death by gun or box cutter but not by much. Meanwhile, I was putting everything the program had taught me into practice. Allie once told me she needed five years to recover from alcoholism but that wouldn't work for me. I was far too impatient.

One thing that helped was to speak my negative thoughts out loud. When I did, I heard how self-destructive they were and refuted them as necessary. This meant holding conversations with myself. The car was the best place for this. It was not only private, it was where my worst thoughts cropped up. It's funny how the very thing that makes somebody "nuts," like talking to yourself, can also be therapeutic.

After six weeks my friends found an apartment for me nearby. I got my few belongings out of storage and made the move, my fourth in less than a year. It was slow going, yet I managed it. Next, I began the laborious process of applying for health insurance, disability, and a cochlear implant. It took tremendous effort (not to mention anxiety) to complete the paperwork. I also suffered from thoughts of Allie but I was determined to put her out of my mind.

Once I started feeling better I opened the red Coleman cooler that appeared at Russell House. It wasn't exactly the Covenant of the Lost Ark but there was enough of my mother's ghost inside that it spooked me. The saddest thing was a daily diary she kept near the end of her life in which she recorded the thoughts of her dementia-ridden mind. Given how much my mother prized her intellect it made for painful reading. When I saw she'd written, "John lives in California?" with a question mark I put the diary back in the cooler, sealed it up, and slipped it inside the closet, knowing she'd never want me to see this side of her.

\*\*\*

Part of recovering meant no contact with my former girlfriend. That should have been easy. She was on the east coast and I was on the west. But two months after leaving Russell House my love for Allie remained a tangible thing. I could feel its substance, its weight, its heft, its dimension. It was not a welcome feeling.

Everyone's experienced the pain of unrequited love. Time diminishes its sting but I couldn't wait. I'd already taken the first step: I'd cut off communication. Ceasing contact was a brave choice but it didn't kill my Jones for Allie. And so I commenced the time of forgetting.

To dull the heart, to willfully feel less, to numb yourself to pain, takes discipline. To help the deadening along, I took everything Allie had ever given me, anything that even remotely reminded me of her, put it in a cardboard box, and mailed it to her Hudson Valley rental with no return address. Birthday gifts, Christmas presents, paintings, letters, and photographs all went in the box.

Those things I didn't send her I got rid of. I drove a nail through the iPhone she gave me and threw the Indian moccasins I'd bought on our cross country trip in the trash. I even bought new sheets to replace the old ones, so little did I want to be reminded of what we once did on them.

By the time I'd finished nothing remained to trigger her memory. It was a painful process, especially since I did it cold turkey, but it was the right thing.

What is the speed of forgetting? How long does it take to erase someone from your memory: a month, a year, forever? Once I'd purged my house of Allie I felt a sense of safety. No longer would I be subjected to her angry outbursts, her impulsive behavior. On top of that, a communications blackout felt like a fence protecting me. There was security in knowing I'd never hear from her. There was also a sense of justice. I didn't want Allie to know how my story turned out. She didn't deserve to. Would I recover from depression? Get a cochlear implant? Publish a second book? Once she left, she forfeited any right to know.

It's amazing how motivating anger can be. Though I was not yet myself, I was determined to stand on my own two feet, particularly after what Allie and her shrink had said about me.

*Never get involved with a man who can't take care of himself.*

*He writes about those things because that's how he feels: broken and obsolete.*

How many times did I hear these things? How many times did I repeat them in my head? So many I almost believed them. Yet I'd taken care of myself in one way or another practically since I was born. And if success is measured by money as it is in this country, well, I'd made more than Allie and Ivankovich combined. So what if I didn't have any left? The point is I knew how.

When someone hurts you, really hurts you, you have two choices: you can withdraw or attack. Ceasing communication was my way of retreating but returning everything Allie had given me was a form of attack. It was my way of saying I wanted nothing more to do with her. She was a traitor in the house of love.

And then, like a fever, it passed. Slowly, through the miracle of modern pharmacology, my personality began to reassert itself. The voice in my head, once filled with self-loathing, grew dim.

I had Lexapro to thank. When I grew dissatisfied with being only 40% of my former self I insisted on being prescribed the one antidepressant I'd had success with. It may have been associated with hearing loss, but the choice wasn't difficult. Sanity trumps hearing any day.

Ironically, as Lexapro eased my depression my feelings of anger towards Allie eased too. It seemed like mourning should last longer than the month it took for the Lexapro to kick in but I was thankful for small mercies. Things were always going to be messy with Allie whether or not I lost my mind. We both did our calculations. Hers was that I remained the same lovable boy from college. Mine was that her craziness was so pronounced she wouldn't notice mine. We were both wrong.

To have a loved one forsake you is a kind of death; their memory more poison than elixir. If time heals all wounds it's only because memory dims, otherwise no one could stand it. I suppose we should be grateful.

# Afterword

A year after I finished writing this book my doorbell rang.

I can hear the doorbell just fine now. Ever since my cochlear implant eighty percent of my hearing's been restored. That's more than most people my age can say.

Imagine my surprise though, when I open the door to find Allie standing in front of me. We hadn't spoken since I'd stopped communicating, but there's no mistaking the freckles, the red hair, the impish smile. It's Allie in the flesh and she's standing on my doorstep.

Since she's caught me off guard I blurt the first thing that enters my head.

"How on earth did you find me?"

"Wasn't hard," she replies. "Ever heard of Google?"

Because she's unexpected, I don't know how to respond. I know I shouldn't be welcoming but am I angry, cold, indifferent? It takes me a while to decide.

In the meantime, we stand there staring at each other. It feels like minutes go by before anyone says anything. Since my instinct rebels against inviting her in I hold my ground and block the doorway. When it becomes clear I have nothing to say she breaks the ice by reaching into her shoulder bag, taking out a snub-nosed revolver, and pointing it at my chest.

"Why did you say those things in the book about me? You got everything wrong!"

Allie's arm wavers a bit though not enough to miss should she pull the trigger. I'd like to respond to her question but I can only see the gun.

When I tried killing myself three years ago Allie thought I might take her with me. She was wrong. Now, she's the one brandishing the weapon. That's when I realize the Geoghegans have never murdered anybody; it's the Katzs who are killers.

The longer I stare the larger Allie's gun grows. Though it's only a .38, it's big enough to do the job. Just looking down its barrel makes my mind seize up. This is a problem because I tend to defuse tense situations with a joke. Before I know it my mouth takes over.

"Do you have any idea what shooting me will do for book sales?"

Allie's answer is to bark a single, "Ha!" then she shuts her eyes before firing twice into my chest. The last thing I remember before blacking out is Allie standing over me with a triumphant look on her face.

***

OK, none of this really happened but it could have, right? You believed it - at least for a moment. The truth is endings like this only happen in fiction. Real life is messier.

In many ways Dr. Squeaky-voice was right when she said, "There are no villains here." I'm grateful Allie blasted me out of my rut. I couldn't have done it without her. That I almost died is nobody's fault but my own. If there's a villain here it's me.

Of course, having the same person break your heart twice is either careless or stupid, but all lovers are liars. We say we'll love each other forever until we don't. If that's not lying what is?

Allie's deviation from the norm was too great for me to handle. There's a difference between mistaking someone's behavior as a cry for help and failing to see they're behaving exactly as they want. Part of me will always love Allie but for my sake I can't have anything to do with her. The story we told ourselves, that we were college sweethearts reunited after forty years, was a fairy tale. The whole thing lasted a year; add the two months we dated in college and we spent less than 18 months together. It took longer than that for me to recover.

I look back now and wonder how things got so crazy. To go from whole note to half note to foot note in twelve months is embarrassing. You might say I missed the warning signs but that isn't true. I embraced them. All I can say in my defense is that love is a sort of madness. It blinds you to the point where you can't see the things you need to. Allie and I may not have been good for each other but that didn't stop me from loving her. You can call it misguided, unlucky, or an *amour fou*, but it was still love. One thing I know for sure: I get to be the horror story she tells her next boyfriend.

***

Sometimes it takes a personal disaster like losing a spouse, a child, or your hearing to reset your thinking; most of the time though our deepest wounds are self-inflicted.

Friends tell me it wasn't my fault I lost my hearing but that's too easy. When I look back I see I did a bad job taking care of myself. I thought I could live within the confines of deafness sustained by my kids and writing. That was a false premise. At the very least, I needed to accept the changes my hearing imposed. I also should have learned sign language and reached out to the Deaf community. That I didn't shows the depth of my ignorance and only exacerbated my problems. Nor should I have punished myself to the extent that I did. Thankfully, the will to live is stronger than the will to die. Said another way, life keeps its thumb on the scale.

We may be more fragile than we realize but we're also stronger than we know. We may bend, scratch, crack or scuff but rarely do we break. When we do, the Japanese have a word for the beauty of a broken object that's been fixed. They call it *kintsugi*, golden repair. It treats an object's damage as part of its history; something to be appreciated rather than thrown away. We all have our dings, dents, cracks and scratch marks but it's important to know we can be repaired. I'm living proof.

One thing that's helped is taking signing classes and engaging with the Deaf community. I realize now that the very people I once shunned, the very people I once made fun of, are the true members of my tribe. They're a lot warmer and more welcoming to me than the hearing world has been, and though I intend to live in both I am grateful for their acceptance.

Deafness is nothing to be ashamed of. It is a rich, fascinating, and culturally diverse world. Few hearing people understand this. Take it from me who once heard perfectly, it's their loss.

## Dr. Squeaky-voice

After being discharged from Russell House I texted Dr. Squeaky-voice a few more times then stopped when her answers proved unsatisfactory. Consequently, when the money dried up she vanished.

Certainly, Dr. Squeaky-voice can't be satisfied with the results of her handiwork. In retrospect, her belief that I could get better on my own could have gone either way. It might have been the shortest road to recovery or the very thing that killed me. She had no way of knowing.

And yet it's possible Dr. Squeaky-voice knew exactly what she was doing. Maybe she realized Allie and my sister planned on dumping me. Or maybe she encouraged them because she thought I was a danger. I'll never know. I'm not sure it even matters. Either way, I'm better on my own.

## My Sister

During the last day of an equestrian competition, on the last fence of the last event, either my sister or her horse misjudged the distance and both went down as one. In yet another example of how following one's bliss can be dangerous, she broke her neck, her back, her wrist, shattered her eye socket, and fractured her skull. She lay on the ground for some minutes, unresponsive and turning blue.

A Medivac was called, but was too far away to help. Instead, she endured the hour long ambulance ride to Santa Rosa hospital. When she arrived she was admitted to the ICU where she lay in a coma for nearly a week.

At first she wasn't expected to live, then not to walk. There was talk of permanent brain damage, later cognitive impairment. I didn't know what to make of this tragedy. It's too vindictive to see it as a comeuppance not to mention just plain wrong. But given what had happened between us I did not visit my sister in the hospital. Since she'd seen fit to leave me at Hillcrest, Las Alamedas, and Russell House with nary a word it seemed appropriate to return the favor. Besides, she had family to comfort her, which is more than I can say.

It took more than a year but my sister eventually recovered from the accident. She may even be riding again. I honestly don't know. Nevertheless, I couldn't help but wonder during her months of rehab whether she developed an appreciation for what it's like to become dependent on others. If she did, I never got the call.

## My Siblings

I never did hear from siblings nor do I expect to. I guess you could say our relationship found its natural level. By demonstrating that the ties that bound us were frayed beyond repair cutting each other loose was far easier. Not a happy lesson but an important one.

The doctrine of self-reliance is useful if for no other reason than to remind us that we're on our own. Most people, despite what they say, don't want to hear about your problems. Sometimes this includes family, friends, even lovers. The thimbleful of sustenance we have to offer one another simply isn't enough. This may sound extreme but Geoghegans have been exiling family members for over a century. It's practically a tradition.

## My Children

When I grew up during the 70s the conventional wisdom was that divorce was better for children than living in a house with two unhappy parents. Don't let this fool you. You spend the rest of your life cleaning up after a divorce. It not only wipes out your finances it does everlasting damage to your wife and children. I'll regret mine to my dying day.

In the meantime, Dana has stabilized. She graduated from High School (though it was touch and go at times) and even got into college. Where once she was distant she is now more affectionate. I have seen her blossom in so many encouraging ways. Whatever her problems, I hope she outgrows them or learns to deal with them better, but even if she doesn't she's still my daughter. A father's love never dims.

As for Dana's little sister, she continues to flourish. That kid is downright indestructible. Good grades, lots of friends, and every teacher's favorite. I don't know what I did to deserve her. She even took up riding which is teaching me to view horses in a whole new way. If that's not a miracle what is?

I may have started out not wanting kids but I've never regretted having them. It's funny how we sometimes make the right decision for the wrong reason. I wish I'd stop doing this but in the meantime I'll have to settle for the result. In both my kids' cases, I'm lucky.

## On Following Your Bliss

I took a vow of poverty to become a writer but given my hearing loss I'd have ended up poor anyway. Joseph Campbell's oft quoted aphorism may seem like sound advice but only if there's an addendum: "do so at your own risk." Follow your bliss is the kind of thing we tell ourselves when chasing our dreams but that doesn't make it right. We like to think there are more happy than unhappy bliss followers but until someone shows me the statistics I reserve judgment.


## My Hearing Loss

I've also decided to get a cochlear implant, thanks for asking. Since my hearing continues to decline what have I got to lose? It may not solve all my problems but what does? And thanks to Obamacare I can finally afford it.

A friend once told me my hearing loss was a gift because it forced me to lead a more authentic life. Then again he smokes a lot of pot. Still, you take wisdom where you find it. That something good can emerge from bad seems ironic, but it's one of life's compensatory gifts. I may never be the same after what happened but that's probably a good thing since I was an asshole. Learning that you can bounce back after reaching your lowest point is an important lesson. Hearing, or the absence of it, turned out to be the single greatest event to shape my adult life. As strange as it may seem, I couldn't have reached this point without it. That I was my own worst enemy goes without saying but we also make our own happy endings.

So, yes, I'm going to get a cochlear implant but I'm also going to learn how to sign. I have a whole new world to explore, the world of the Deaf. It's a rich and satisfying one and I look forward to joining the tribe. In the meantime, I have much to learn.

*** 

It would be nice to wrap up this tale with a neat little bow, but that's not how life works. I wrote this story to understand why I went crazy. Yes, there were a number of casualties when I tried killing myself, but strangely I wasn't among them.

After my last day at Russell House, I climbed into my car and headed north with the hope that this time things would be different; this time things would be better. But stories about redemption found through things like surfing or trout fishing make me suspicious. Nothing in life is as simple as redemption is portrayed. Being an adult is recognizing this.

Redemption comes in part, never in full; slowly, if at all; and always, always leaves you wanting more. Life's a struggle. You get better and try and stay that way. You rediscover joy, satisfaction, even love, but you're not redeemed. You're never redeemed.

Unlike Frank Sinatra, I can't lay claim to having done many things "my way." When I did, I often felt regret. One thing I will say though, I may have come close, but I never gave up. Given the hurdles we face that's not a bad epitaph.

As for redemption? Well, most states will give you a nickel for every bottle you return and that seems about right. After all, life is its own reward. You wouldn't want to be greedy.

# Author's Note and Acknowledgements

I wrote this book to better understand why I went crazy. Nevertheless, memoirs are only as reliable as the memory that writes them, which is to say they're inherently fallible. I've made this one as true as I can given I mishear things. A few details have been changed to protect people's privacy but everything is how I remember it. If there are mistakes they are mine alone.

Writing can be a lonely endeavor but no book is written in isolation. I'd like to thank the Mill Valley Public Library's Writers' Drop-In Group for their support especially Kate Moore for her encouragement and Barb Elwell for her laughter. I'd also like to thank Brooke Warner of Warner Coaching who read an early draft and provided invaluable commentary, as well as my friends, Jan Mock, who told me to fix the ending, and Rachel Zemach, who introduced me to the Deaf community.

Marlene Bennett deserves special mention for springing me when all seemed lost as do M.J. Landolina and W. Kurt Meinen for helping to get me back on my feet.

I also owe Ellis Amburn and my agent, Jeff Schmidt at New York Creative Management, my gratitude for making things happen. And of course, nothing would have happened if Sarah Healey hadn't agreed to edit my story, and Teddie Dahlin, the pioneering Publisher at New Haven Publishing Ltd., hadn't taken a chance on me.

Nor could I have written this memoir without the support of The SILOE Research Institute's board and staff. They believed in me from the beginning. One day, I hope to return the favor.

The Deaf community is a big tent. It contains a multitude of people with varying types of hearing loss. I'm still in the early stages of my journey but I've already learned each person embraces deafness in their own way - it's important to respect their choices. Since this book depicts the choices I made (many of them ill considered) I can't recommend my path to others. Still, I look forward to the journey. The road to deafness can be long, painful, and filled with uncertainty, but I wouldn't trade it for anything. Not only has it led to a more authentic life, it's made me a better person. For that I am grateful.

# Appendix

## Resources for the Deaf and Hard of Hearing

Below is a partial list of resources for the Deaf and Hard of Hearing in England and the United States. Please note: the list is in alphabetical order; it is not a ranking.

### England

Action on Hearing Loss (formerly the Royal National Institute for Deaf People): www.actiononhearingloss.org.uk

BID Services and the Deaf Cultural Centre: www.bid.org.uk

British Deaf Association: www.bda.org.uk

DeafAction: www.deafaction.org.uk

National Association of Deafened People: www.nadp.org.uk

National Deaf Children's Society: www.ndcs.org.uk

Royal Association for Deaf People (RAD): www.royaldeaf.org.uk

Soundz Off: www.soundzoff.org

Stagetext: www.stagetext.org

In addition to the above, there are *many* local resources for the deaf and hard of hearing including online videos teaching British Sign Language. Google for listings and details.

### United States

American Society for Deaf Children (ASDC): www.deafchildren.org

American Tinnitus Association (ATA): www.ata.org

Association of Late-Deafened Adults (ALDA): www.alda.org

Beginnings for Parents of Children Who Are Deaf or Hard of Hearing: www.ncbegin.org

Deaf and Hard of Hearing Consumer Advocacy Network (DHHCAN): www.dhhcan.org

Deafhood Foundation: www.deafhood.org.

Gallaudet University, Laurent Clerc National Deaf Education Center: www.gallaudet.edu/about/youth-programs-and-resources

Hearing Loss Association of America (HLAA): www.hearingloss.org

National Association of the Deaf (NAD): www.nad.org

National Black Deaf Advocates (NBDA): www.nbda.org

National Institute on Deafness and Other Communication Disorders (NIDCD): www.nidcd.nih.gov

Free websites that teach American Sign Language: www.aslpro.com; www.signingsavvy.com; www.lifeprint.com

In addition to the above, there are *many* federal, state, and local resources for the deaf and hard of hearing. Google for listings and details.